THE LORD'S PRAYER:

ITS SPIRIT AND ITS TEACHING.

BY

OCTAVIUS WINSLOW, D.D.

"IN THIS AGE WE BEGIN TO THINK MEANLY OF THE LORD'S PRAYER:
OH, HOW BASELY MAY THE LORD THINK OF OUR PRAYERS!"
—THOMAS FULLER.

2003
Tentmaker Publications
Stoke-on-Trent

Tentmaker Publications
121 Hartshill Road
Stoke-on-Trent
Staffs. ST4 7LU

www.tentmaker.org.uk

2003
Reprinted 2007

ISBN: 1 8990039 75 3

Originally published in 1866
LONDON:
JOHN F. SHAW & CO., 48 PATERNOSTER ROW.

PREFACE.

 HE author is indebted to an esteemed clergyman for the idea of a treatise on the *spirit* of the Lord's Prayer. He, therefore, claims to himself no credit for novelty of conception in the leading feature of his work, which he is not aware has appeared in any similar publication. This must plead his apology for adding yet another to the already numerous volumes expository of this portion of God's Word. France and Germany, England and Scotland, and more recently America, have contributed some of their most eminent writers, of varied shades of religious thought, and of marked diversity of intellectual power, who have selected this brief but comprehensive part of our Lord's Sermon on the Mount as the theme of able and useful disquisitions. Of the many expositions of the Lord's Prayer, however, whether in separate form, or, as contained in systems of divinity, there, probably, is no treatise less known, and yet of such surpassing merit, as that for which we are indebted to an American divine, yet living:—I allude to a volume from the pen of the Rev. William R. Williams, D.D., New York.* I can scarcely trust myself to refer to this masterly work, lest my admiration of its singular excellence,—its masculine thought, its varied learning, and its elegant diction, seamed as the work is throughout with a rich vein of spirituality,—should be considered as overstepping the bounds of just criticism. It is much to be regretted that Dr Williams's treatise has not been reprinted in this country;

---

* Lectures on the Lord's Prayer, by William R. Williams. Boston: Gould and Lincoln, 1851.

in default of this, however, I have ventured to enrich these pages with one or two quotations, which, though strikingly beautiful, yet, severed from their connexion, convey but an imperfect idea of the unrivalled excellence of the work in its completeness.

Opinions in the Church of God are divided on the utility of prescribed forms of prayer in general, and of the use of the Lord's Prayer in particular. The question, however, is an open one, the decision of which must be left to the conscience and the circumstances of each individual. I can myself see no serious objection to their occasional use as *aids* to a yet more unfettered outpouring of the heart, provided the sentiments are evangelical, the tone devout, and the individual using them "worships God *in the spirit.*" All prayer—as, indeed, all praise—must, necessarily, be, to a certain extent, a fixed vehicle of thought and feeling. The service of *song* in non-episcopal assemblies, is as much a prescribed form as, in the Church of England, is the service of *prayer;* and yet who will deny that both may be a *"spiritual* sacrifice acceptable to God through Jesus Christ." The argument against a form of prayer, will thus apply with equal force to a form of praise. Toplady, in his somewhat *brusquerie* style of reasoning, thus puts the case—

> "We may pray spiritually by a form, and we may pray formally and coldly without one. Suppose I was to say to a converted Dissenter, 'Sir, you do not sing the praises of God spiritually.' He would ask, 'Why not?' Was I to answer, 'Because you sing by a form. Dr Watts's Psalms and Hymns are all pre-composed; they are forms in the strictest use of the word.' The good man would reply, 'True, they are pre-composed forms, but I can sing them very spiritually for all that.' I should rejoin, 'And I can pray in the words of the Liturgy as spiritually as you can sing in the words of Dr Watts.'"

The words of the apostle, "with all prayer,"—πάσῃ προσευχῇ, "all manner of prayer,"—I think, determine the question. "All manner of prayer and supplication *in the Spirit,*" must include both extempore prayer, and prayer offered through the medium of a liturgical form. Thomas Fuller, the witty yet pious prebend of Salisbury, who flourished in the reign of Charles II., thus pithily delivers his judgment on this vexed question:—

"Set prayers are prescript forms of our own or others' composing; such are lawful for any, and needful for some to use.

"Lawful for any. Otherwise God would not have appointed the priests (presumed of themselves best able to pray) a form of blessing the people. Nor would our Saviour have set us His prayer, which (as the town-bushel is the standard both to measure corn and other bushels by) is both a prayer in itself and a pattern or platform prayer. Such as accuse set forms to be pinioning the wings of the dove, will by the next return affirm that girdles and garters, made to strengthen and adorn, are so many shackles and fetters which hurt and hinder men's free motion.

"Needful for all. Namely for such who as yet have not attained (what all should endeavour) to pray extempore by the Spirit. But as little children (to whom the plainest and evenest room at first is a labyrinth) are so ambitious of going alone, that they scorn to take the guidance of a form or bench to direct them, but will adventure by themselves, though often to the cost of a knock and a fall; so many confess their weakness in denying to confess it, who, refusing to be beholden to a set form of prayer, prefer to say nonsense rather than nothing in their extempore expressions. More modesty, and no less piety, it had been for such men to have prayed longer with set forms, that they might pray better without them. In extemporary prayer what men most admire God least regardeth, namely, the volubility of the tongue. Hence a Tertullus may equal, yea, exceed, St Paul himself, 'whose speech was but mean.' Oh, it is the heart keeping time and tune with the voice which God listeneth unto. Otherwise the nimblest tongue tires and the loudest voice grows dumb before it comes half way to heaven. 'Make it (said God to Moses) in all things like the pattern in the Mount.' Only the conformity of the words with the mind, mounted in heavenly thoughts, is acceptable to God. The gift of extemporary prayer and ready utterance may be bestowed on a reprobate, but the grace thereof (religious affection) is only given to God's servants."*

With regard to the stated employment of what is called the Lord's Prayer,—but which I would venture to term THE DISCIPLES' PRAYER, since it was a form of supplication given by the Lord to His disciples,

---

* The Wisdom of our Fathers. Selections from the Writings of Thomas Fuller. Religious Tract Society.

saying, *"After this manner, therefore, pray ye"*—I have met with no argument of sufficient weight to enforce its entire disuse. I admit, with regret, its too frequent repetition in the inimitably beautiful and comprehensive Liturgy of the English, and of the American, Episcopal Church;* yet more deeply do I deplore the superstitious attachment, the almost idolatrous homage, with which it is regarded by some Christians. But, nevertheless, as "a form of sound words" set us by Christ, and as a *résumé* of devout utterances at the Mercy-seat, ever fresh, always suitable, and never exhausted, let us believingly receive, and *prayerfully* use, at the throne of grace, this truly divine mould of heavenly thought, and exquisite model of spiritual prayer, grateful to Christ for so condescendingly, wisely, and simply teaching us *how* to pray. Above all, be it our earnest aim that, whether we pray with or without a fixed formula—and *free prayer* should be more sedulously cultivated, seeing that the Holy Ghost is promised and prepared to *"help our infirmities"*—we are found before God *"praying in the Holy Ghost,"* entwining each petition with the Name of Jesus, and bathing all in the fragrance of His atoning and intercessory merits. *"Whatsoever ye shall ask in my name, that will I do, that the Father may be glorified in the Son."*

As a lowly attempt to illustrate the *spirit* of each petition of the Lord's Prayer, prepared amid many public interruptions, and falling much below the standard he had prescribed, the author, in earnest supplication for the accompanying blessing of the Triune-God, with unfeigned diffidence lays his work at the feet of Christ's own and ONE Church, a small contribution to its sacred and devout literature. THINE, O LORD, IS THE GLORY! Amen.

BATH, *June* 1866

---

* It is an interesting and significant fact that, at the present moment, a competent committee, composed of clergymen of the Church of England and Non-Episcopal divines, are engaged upon a revision of the "Book of Common Prayer," with a view to a more general assimilation of Christian worship among the different bodies of the Church of God. Such an idea, if practically carried out, will be an immense gain to the cause of Christian union.

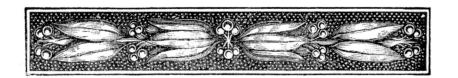

CONTENTS.

CHAPTER VII.

CHAPTER VIII.

CHAPTER IX.

CHAPTER X.

CHAPTER XI.

CHAPTER XII.

Our Father
which art in Heaven,
hallowed be thy name.
Thy kingdom come.
Thy will be done on earth as it is in Heaven.
Give us this day our daily bread.
And forgive us our debts,
as we forgive our debtors.
And lead us not into temptation,
but deliver us from evil:
for thine is the Kingdom, and the power,
and the glory, for ever.
Amen.

"Our Heavenly Father, hear
  The prayer we offer now;
Thy name be hallow'd far and near,
  To Thee all nations bow;
Thy kingdom come; Thy will
  On earth be done in love,
As saints and seraphim fulfil
  Thy perfect law above.

"Our daily bread supply,
  While by Thy word we live;
The guilt of our iniquity
  Forgive, as we forgive;
From dark temptation's power,
  From Satan's wiles defend;
Deliver in the evil hour,
  And guide us to the end!

"Thine, then, for ever be
  Glory and power divine;
The sceptre, throne, and majesty
  Of heaven and earth are Thine.
—Thus humbly taught to pray,
  By Thy beloved Son,
Through Him we come to Thee and say,
  All for His sake be done."*

_____

* James Montgomery.

CHAPTER I.

THE FILIAL SPIRIT OF THE LORDS PRAYER.

"FATHER."—MATT. vi. 9.

HEN our Lord Jesus sealed this Divinely Paternal Name upon the lips of His disciples, He was, as their Authorised Teacher, instructing them in the holy art of prayer. He alone was competent to the task. Himself the Object, as, mediatorially, the Medium of prayer, He was in every way fitted to lead them, in the spirit of filial worship, within the veil into the Holiest. In complying with their request, *"Lord, teach us to pray,"* His first lesson, obviously, was to unfold the PATERNAL relation in which God stood to them. This was a lost truth to our sinning and sinful race. In abjuring his own sonship, man had abjured the Fatherhood of God. In demanding his portion of the patrimony, and then turning his back upon his Father, he became an orphan and a fugitive upon the earth, the parental image as completely effaced from his soul, as the consciousness of his sonship was from his heart.

Such was the great truth our Lord presented to His disciples in instructing them to approach God in prayer. From no other teacher could they learn that God was their Father by adopting grace; and from no other source could they receive the Spirit whereby they should approach Him in filial love. Christ only could restore this lost truth, and supply the broken link which once united God and man in parental love and in filial worship. Thus the doctrine of the

Fatherhood of God in its relation to His Church is a doctrine of
Divine revelation. It made its advent amid the holy scenes of
Bethlehem; was uttered in sobs of woe in Gethsemane; was written
in atoning blood on Calvary; and was ratified amid the resurrection
splendours which encircled the tomb in Joseph's garden. We seek
not, in thus vindicating the Divine revelation of this doctrine, to
lessen the force of the fact that the relation of God to man as a
Father by creation was a truth recognised by the pagan world. Paul,
in his memorable address to the Athenians, quoting from one of
their Gentile poets, attests this fact. "In Him we live and move and
have our being, as certain of your own poets have said, *For we are
His offspring.*" Thus the human race may trace its ancestry to Eden,
and its origin to "the Father of spirits." But the Lord Jesus presented
the Parental relation of God in a newer light, encircled with a diviner
lustre, associated with holier obligations, and blended with a more
transcendent glory—as the covenant God and Father of His people
by electing love, most free and sovereign grace. And if, as we wander
over earth's beauties, descend its vales and climb its steeps,
expatiating amid the wonders and glories of God's creative power,
we exultingly exclaim, "My Father made them all!" what must be
the height of our admiration, what the depth of our love, as we stand
before the cross of Jesus and exclaim, "In Thee I see my Father's
image, in Thee I behold my Father's love!" We are as yet but upon
the threshold of our great subject. Let it be distinctly kept in view
that our main design in the present chapter is to unfold the *filial
spirit* of worship which the Lord's Prayer inculcates. In a formula
of devotion enjoined by Christ Himself, and as appertaining to the
new or Christian dispensation, we could reasonably expect nothing
less. Moses has retired, the legal economy is passed, the bond-
servant is freed, the shadows are gone, the vail of the temple is
rent in twain, for Christ is come, and we now enter into the Holiest,
and approach the Holy One with "Abba, Father" breathing from
our filial lips. But we have yet to learn in what way the Lord Jesus
has made known to us the Father. To the revelation of Christ we
are alone indebted for our spiritual and saving knowledge of Him
in this relation. This truth is not a dogma of Christianity, it is

Christianity itself. The gospel is an unveiling of the Divine glory, because it is a revelation of the Divine Saviour. *"For God, who commanded the light to shine out of darkness, hath shined in our hearts, to give the light of the knowledge of the glory of God in the face of Jesus Christ."* Such is the great truth which we now proceed to unfold. How does Christ reveal to us the Father?

In the first place, Christ confirms *the fact* of God's Paternity. I have remarked that we have no clear, demonstrative evidence in nature of the Fatherhood of God in its spiritual and gracious relation to His people. Creation's testimony to His eternal power and Godhead is universal and conclusive, leaving the atheist without excuse.

> "The meanest pin in nature's frame
> Marks out some letter of His name;
> Across the earth, around the sky,
> There's not a spot, or deep or high,
> Where the Creator hath not trod,
> And left the footsteps of a God."

But beyond its testimony to this truth, all nature is silent. Not one syllable does it breathe of adopting love, of pardoning grace, of reconciliation between God and man. The sun in its brightness reflects it not; the ocean in its fulness embodies it not; the wind in its majesty thunders it not; the rivulet in its music murmurs it not; the flower in its fragrance breathes it not; the rock in its fastness images it not; Creation in its endless forms of sublimity, beauty, and tenderness, fails to answer the most touching, the most momentous of all inquiries, "How may I know and approach God as my reconciled Father?" Nor this alone. While Creation was silent on a theme so vital and transcendent, human philosophy was equally mute. *"The world by wisdom knew not God."* At Athens, "the eye of all Greece," where philosophy sat enthroned in imperial splendour, issuing her lessons in authoritative tones and with matchless eloquence, they reared an altar "*to the* UNKNOWN *God.*" Truly did our Great High Priest, in His intercessory prayer, testify, *"O righteous Father, the world hath not known thee."* But what Creation could not reveal or Philosophy discover, the Lord Jesus

Christ has made known to us. How clear and emphatic His declaration, "*All things are delivered unto me of my Father: and no man knoweth who the Son is but the Father; and who the Father is but the Son, and he to whom the Son will reveal Him.*" It follows from these words that Jesus is God, and that, as the Divine Mediator, He is the Revealer of the Father. What further testimony to this great truth need we? Taking us by the hand, He gently leads us to God and bids us call Him—"Father!" This, O believer, is your filial and precious privilege! Nothing shall rob you of your birthright. You may have been a foolish and a sinful child; you may be poor and needy, little and despicable, deeming yourself unworthy to be called a son; nevertheless, the mercy-seat is your Father's meeting-place; and every atoning drop that sprinkles it, and every golden beam that bathes it, and every accent of love that breathes from it, bids and encourages your approach to God, and cry, "My Father!"

Christ was also *the personal and visible representation* of the Father. Instead of leaving us to deal with an impersonal being, an infinite abstraction, the Lord Jesus reveals to us the God, of whose glory He is the brightness, and of whose person He is the image. How explicit is the statement. "*God hath in these last days spoken unto us by His Son, . . . who being the brightness of His glory and the express image of His person,*" (Heb. i. 1-3.) "The *brightness* of His glory"—all other reflections being but shadows of God. "The *express image* of His person"—that is, of the same substance as the Father. Thus the Son is the visible image of the invisible God; so that he who by faith hath seen the Son, hath in the Son's likeness seen the Father. Has God thus been revealed to you, my reader? Have you seen Him in Jesus? Have you recognised His parental relation? Are you conscious that He is at peace with you through the atonement of His Son? Have you clasped Him in your filial affections, exclaiming, in the deep tenderness of filial love, "Thou art my Father, God!" Give your soul no rest until it rests in this truth, so divinely revealed by the Holy Ghost. "The Spirit itself beareth witness with our spirit *that we are the children of God.*"

Christ also reveals the *Parental character* of God. He might have testified to God's parental relation, leaving us in ignorance of His parental character. He might have presented to us a portrait of God's image arrayed in the infinite attributes of His being, leaving us to imagine what His will towards us was—and what the feelings of His heart. Wandering through a foreign gallery of art, I gazed with speechless wonder upon the pictures of the illustrious dead which bestud its walls—ancient masterpieces of the human pencil. But nothing could I gather from their portraits, gazing down upon me in silent grandeur, of the intellectual or moral elements which formed their living characters, or of the events which contributed to their deathless renown. But not thus with this Divine-human Portrait. We behold in the Lord Jesus a perfect unveiling of the *character* of the Father, as we recognise the express image of His person. How clearly did Christ teach this truth. *"I am in my Father, and my Father in me. From henceforth ye know Him and have seen Him. He that hath seen me hath* SEEN THE FATHER." Thus, what no angel could have made known, what no eye could have discovered, what no human heart could have conceived, what no pencil could have portrayed, and what no tongue could have described, the Lord Jesus Christ has fully made known to us—the *character* of God as a Father. Listen to His declaration once more, *"He that hath seen me* HATH SEEN THE FATHER." As though He had said, "All the glory in me which entrances you, all the beauty in me which attracts you, all the truths from me which instruct you, all the love in me which wins you, all the grace in me which sanctifies you, all the sympathy in me which soothes you, all my miracles of power and acts of mercy which command your homage, enkindle your gratitude, and inspire your praise, are the true, the perfect reflection of Him from whose bosom I descended to make Him known to you as your Father. He that hath seen me *hath seen my Father also.*" What a gentle rebuke of all our crude thoughts, dim conceptions, low views, and rebellious feelings concerning God! What injustice have we done Him! What ingratitude have we shown Him! How have we misunderstood His character, misinterpreted His dealings,

distrusted His wisdom, and misread His heart! Does Jesus, who
is the glory of all that is Divine, the perfection of all that is human,
the brightness of all that is holy, the manifestation of all that is
loving, tender, and compassionate; who is the object of my highest
adoration and the deepest love, represent the character, as He does
the person of the Father? Is the Father *all* that Christ is?
Henceforth I will no more distrust Him, misinterpret Him, or
entertain one hard thought of His conduct, or one unkind suspicion
of His love. Such be your reflection, my reader, as you stand before
this marvellous, this finished portrait of the Father. Be it your
profoundest, your constant study. Be not satisfied with an
occasional visit, with a distant view, or with a superficial
acquaintance. All that is spiritually revealed or savingly known
of the Father is embodied in the person of the Lord Jesus Christ.
Let CHRIST be your one, your chief, your constant and absorbing
study. At first His beauty may not attract you, His glory may not
dazzle you, His love may not win you. But persevere. Each
prayerful desire, each believing look, each loving visit will make
Him better known, more supremely admired, and deeply loved
who, among ten thousand loved ones, is the chief, and who, among
ten thousand lovely ones, is the altogether lovely. What the Abbè
Winklemann—one of the most classical writers on the fine arts—
so eloquently said of the *Apollo Belvedere,* when endeavouring to
deepen the admiration of those students who would become
eminent in art, I would say, with the profoundest reverence, of
the portrait of the Father as presented in the Lord Jesus Christ,
"Go and study it. And if you see no peculiar beauty to captivate
you, go again. And if still you discover nothing, go again and again
and again until you *feel* it; for be assured it is there." Precious
truth! How it elevates and enlarges my views of the Father! How
it unfolds His character, unveils His glory, and endears His
conduct. To see my Father's smile reflected in the smile of my
Saviour; to behold His glory beaming in the face of Jesus; to hear
His voice in the echoes of Christ's love; to trace His compassion,
tenderness, and sympathy in the very words and works and tears
of the Great High Priest, even when the discipline of the parental

rod is the most severe, this is heaven upon earth. What a wonderful person is the Saviour of men! Bursting forth, as a hidden sun, we behold in the glorious life and peerless character of Jesus the living portrait of that infinitely great and Divine Being whom we are invited to approach and call—"Our FATHER."

Christ also revealed *the parental heart of God.* He who from eternity dwelt in the bosom of the Father could alone make known the *love* of God. Our Lord might have revealed the mind, the thoughts, the will of the Father, leaving His *heart* still, and for ever, enshrouded with a deep and impenetrable veil. But He made His illustrious advent to our earth not so much to reveal the mind as to unveil the *heart* of God—less to expound the majesty and purpose of His will than to disclose the existence and depth of His *love.* Who but the Son of God had authority and power to utter a truth concerning the Father so great and marvellous as this—"GOD SO LOVED THE WORLD *that He gave His only-begotten Son, that whosoever believeth in Him might not perish, but have everlasting life."* How fully did the Lord Jesus here draw aside the veil and show us the heart of the Father, pulsating with a love infinite as His nature and eternal as His being. "GOD SO LOVED"—the sublimest thought, the tenderest words, the greatest fact lips ever uttered. Truly, *"Never man spake like this man."* Conducting us into the most hidden recess of the Father's bosom by the "new and living way," every step of which unfolded the eternal grace which planned it, He leads us into the very centre of God's heart, and bids us call Him *"Father."* And lest we should exclusively rest in Him the Divine gift to the exclusion of God the Divine Giver; or suppose that the Father's love was purchased and procured, and not an essential and spontaneous affection, He distinctly and emphatically declares, *"The Father HIMSELF loveth you."* How jealous was the Son of God of the Father's love to His Church. Not one ray of that love would He shade, not one stream would He divert, that He might enhance and aggrandise His own. Well did He know—for He had felt its eternal throbbings—that the love of the Father was not the effect, but was the moving cause of His sacrifice; that He died, not that His Father might love, but *because*

He *loved,* and "so *loved that He gave His only-begotten Son.*" Behold
the great truth which the Lord Jesus would teach you! He would
elevate and enlarge your thought of the Father's love, remove your
distrust, dissolve your coldness, quell your fears, and awaken in
your whole soul a responsive affection. "*The Father HIMSELF loveth
you,*"—loves you with an affection all your own; as much, as fully
yours, as if for you only, you exclusively, its deep pulsations
throbbed. It has loved you unto the death of His Son. Upon Him
He laid your sins; of Him He exacted your penalty; into His cup
He pressed all the bitterness of your death and all the ingredients
of your condemnation. Disbelieve not, distrust not, wound not His
love. Doubt the love of the mother who bore you, distrust the love
of her who wedded you, question the love of the friend enshrined
within your breast but oh, doubt not the love of your Father in
heaven, who surrendered His only and well-beloved Son unto the
death for you! There may be stages in the Christian pilgrimage in
which the existence of God's love may be obscured; afflictive
dispensations in which its tenderness may be questioned; trials
of your faith where its faithfulness may seem to fail,—nevertheless,
His heart loves you in sending all, loves you passing through all,
and will love you to the end of all the chequered events, the
changing scenes, the sunshine and the cloud, of life's pathway to
heaven.

　　Having thus revealed the parental relation and character of
God, our blessed Lord proceeds to inculcate the *filial spirit*
becoming His disciples in their approach to this their heavenly
Father. "*When ye pray, say, 'Our Father, which art in heaven.'*"
With such a Father as the Object of prayer, any spirit other than
the most filial, confiding, and loving in our approach to the mercy-
seat, would seem as dishonouring to God as unjust to ourselves.
The true spirit of a child of God in prayer is *child-like.* The proper
approach to God is *filial.* Any other than this springs from some
defective view of the parental character of God, or from a legal,
servile state of the soul. Christ illustrated in His own personal
history the same filial spirit with which He so earnestly sought to
imbue the minds of His disciples. His own Sonship was a truth

never absent from His mind. How early in His life did this appear. To the anxious inquiry of His earthly parents how striking and touching His reply, *"Wist ye not that I must be about* MY FATHER'S *business?"* From the moment when, standing in the temple surrounded by the doctors of the law, He announced His divine Sonship, to His life's last and latest hour, He maintained, through all its scenes of labour, sorrow, and suffering, the same filial love, confidence, and demeanour. How touching and instructive His words, uttered in soul-agony and tears—*"Not my will, O my* FATHER, *but thine be done."* Thus has our Lord set us an example of filial approach to the throne of grace; of child-like intercourse with God; echoing but the breathing of His own heart when He taught us to say, *"Our* FATHER, *which art in heaven."*

*"*FATHER*!" It is the language of the believing heart.* As the adoption of His people is the highest act of God's grace, so the filial response of His children to that adoption is the highest act of our faith. Could faith on its strongest pinion soar higher than the Fatherhood of God? Oh, it is a marvellous fact, a stupendous truth, that God should be our Father! Higher than this the soul cannot rise. Love then reaches its deepest yearnings. Only realise this fact, that God is your Father, and it meets every chapter of your history, every event of your life, every sentiment, feeling, and desire of your soul. All that is omnipotent in strength, all that is profound in wisdom, all that is tender in sympathy, all that is rich in infinite plenitude, is bound up in the endearing epithet—"FATHER." That Father is thine. Thou art the child of His eternity. Stupendous thought! His love to thee, His choice of thee, His purpose to adopt, His plan to redeem, sanctify, and bring thee to glory, were coeval with His being! They are eternal acts of His grace. This is not language too presumptuous, too bold, for faith. After such eternal love, such an act of mercy, such a condescension of grace, to approach God in prayer with the trembling of doubt upon the lips, with the fetters of the slave upon the soul, with distrust, suspicion, and coldness in the heart, were of the darkest hue. If God calls me His child, ingrate that I am not to respond, "My Father!" Are you a parent? Does your child doubt his relation to you as such? What would you

think of it if he did? The deep, underlying principle of all his love, reverence, and obedience is the full confidence he has in you as his parent. Have like precious faith in your heavenly Father. Let your faith be thus filial, childlike, and firm. Believe that all He does is for the best; that your highest interests are all in His hands, and in His hands are all so secure. Lock your hand in His, as your little one links its hand with yours, willing to be led, unquestioning, confiding, meekly, just where your Father leads. If God declares, "*I AM A FATHER to Israel,*" it is the deepest humility of faith to respond, "My Father, God!"

It is the language of *filial love.* How sweet the voice of love as it pronounces the name of Father! What tenderness in its tones, what significance in its language, what a world of meaning in the one title it breathes! It would seem as if every, and the deepest, spring of sensibility in the soul were unsealed the moment love breathed to heaven that Name. This is what our Father looks for in our filial approach to Him through Jesus. "*My Son, give me thine HEART.*" Himself love—essential love—paternal love—unchanging love—He asks for *love* in return. And what is the love He asks, the love which He himself inspires and accepts? It is the filial affection of the loving child. There may be love in a slave towards his owner, love in a servant towards his master; but the love of the child toward its parent distances and transcends all love. Let your love to God be filial—the expression of adoption—the sentiment of an obedient child! This will impart sweetness to your Father's commands, will expel all reserves from your disobedience, and invest your service for Him with the most perfect freedom. "*I will run the way of Thy commandments, when Thou shalt enlarge my heart.*" Filial love alone expands the heart to the utmost limit of God's commands. And when the precept, the command, the discipline are traced to the authority, and to the love, and to the hand of a Father, the filial heart bows in the most profound, cheerful, and holy acquiescence. God asks the love that casts out all slavish fear. He wants you to love Him intensely as a Parent. Securing this, He has secured your most perfect confidence, your most holy obedience, and your most unreserved surrender as a child. Look less at the depth, the great undertaking, the costly sacrifice of your love, than at its filial, obedient character. A son may be deeply conscious of his affection for his parent, while yet incapable of demonstrating as he would wish its reality and depth. You, too, may feel that you love God as your Father, obey Him as His child, and yet have no power to embody that love in worthy and brilliant expression. Still you love Him. You love Him in poverty, you love Him in sickness, you love Him in suffering, you love Him in chastening, you love Him in rebuke. And in that sleepless night, and on that bed of pain, and from that chamber of solitude and sorrow, the fragrant incense of your filial love ascends to Him in solemn prayer and praise, while you cry, "My FATHER, it is Thy hand that chastens, and it is well!"

It is the language of *the spirit of adoption in prayer.* It is in direct fellowship with God that the filial spirit of the Lord's Prayer is the most seen. True prayer is filial. It is not so much the supplication of the petitioner, as the communion of the child—a loved child in the closest, sweetest fellowship with a loving Father. *"Ye have not received the spirit of bondage again to fear; but ye have received the Spirit of adoption, whereby we cry, Abba, Father."* If ever this Divine Spirit breathes His quickening, emancipating, and enlarging grace, it is when the believing soul is in audience with God. The real test of our Divine sonship is—communion with our Heavenly Father. We may read of adoption, and speak of adoption, and desire to act from a sense of adoption; but it is at the mercy-seat, when the soul is wrapt in communion with the Invisible, that the believer fully realises the blessedness of fellowship, the closeness of communion, the solemn consciousness of soul-nearness to the Heavenly Parent. It is then no matter of doubt. We could as easily question the reality of our own existence, as doubt the fact that God was our Father. There is no engagement of the believer so self-evidencing as communion with God. The act is so unearthly, the inspiration is so divine, the emotion is so holy, the feeling so ecstatic of a soul in filial fellowship with the Infinite, that it reaches the highest elevation of assurance which it is possible to gain this side of glory. It seems but one step from that sacred height of spiritual fellowship and holy rapture, and the soul is in heaven, expatiating amid the wonders of the upper world. Cultivate a filial approach to God in prayer. Do not, yielding to a false idea, deem it humility to doubt your sonship. The profoundest lowliness is to acknowledge, and the deepest holiness is to experience, it. Draw near God as your Father, and commune with Him as His child. You may then open wide your mouth in prayer, supplication, and confession. You complain of straitness, lifelessness, and reluctance in devotion. You cannot trace the glow of love, the strength of desire, the sweetness of communion, in your approaches to the throne of grace of which others speak. May not the cause be found in the imperfect realisation of your adoption, in the faint conception you have of the Parental relation of God to you, in the little filial affection and confidence which marks your approach to the throne of grace? Remember that true prayer is nothing less than the warm, confidential intercourse of a believing child with God. Wrestle with the Holy Ghost for this inestimable blessing. Give Him no rest until, baptizing you afresh in the cloud and in the sea of His quickening grace, He imparts to you the clearer witness and seal of your divine and inalienable sonship, enabling you to exclaim with an emphasis of meaning and tone of sweetness unexperienced before—"*My* FATHER*!*"

> "Descend, immortal Dove,
> Spread Thy kind wings abroad;
> And, wrapt in flames of holy love,
> Bear all my soul to God.
>
> "Behold, my heart expands
> To catch the heavenly fire;
> It longs to feel the gentle hands,
> And groans with strong desire.
>
> "Thy love, my God, appears,
> And brings salvation down;
> My cordial through this vale of tears,
> In paradise my crown."

The filial spirit which breathes through the prayer taught His disciples by our Lord is not less exhibited *in times of trial,* than in seasons of communion. Times of parental correction are often times of blessed realisation of our adoption. The rod is sent, among other

<u>holy purposes, especially for this</u>. It awakens the slumbering affections of the soul. Then the chastened child cries out to God. The spirit of prayer, so long stagnant, is stirred up. The heart so cold and torpid is set upon seeking the Lord. The chastening is seen as belonging to a child and as coming from a Father. May this be the hallowed and happy issue of your present trial! Look at it as *parental*. Your Father's heart prepared, and His hand presents the cup. His wisdom, love, and righteousness ordained and arranged the whole. Even more than this. What is the heart of God towards you as His chastened and sorrowing child? The words of inspiration alone can supply the answer. *"Like as a FATHER pitieth his children, so the Lord PITIETH them that fear Him. For He knoweth our frame; He remembereth that we are dust."* Tender relation! touching image! A father's pity! This is our God. This is your Father. He has corrected you, but not in anger. He has brought you low, but He has not given you over unto death. He has removed some blessings, but He has not taken all. He has blown upon some flowers of your heart, but others,—perhaps lovelier and more precious—still live and bloom to delight you with their beauty, and to gladden you with their fragrance. The pleasant gourd which covered and refreshed you is withered and gone; but He who made it to grow, and then removed it, spreads over you the undying foliage of His love; and the sun shall not smite you by day, nor the moon by night, for "upon all your glory there shall be a defence."

CHAPTER II.

THE CATHOLIC SPIRIT OF THE LORD'S PRAYER

"Our Father."—Matt. vi. 6.

THE Lord Jesus having presented the *Paternal* character of God, and the consequent *filial* spirit of His children, naturally blends with it the *fraternal* relation which the children of God sustain to each other. He could not separate the Fatherhood from the Brotherhood. The existence of the one relation necessarily involved the existence of the other. If I am a child, I am a brother. In returning to God as my Heavenly Father, I do not turn my back upon my spiritual kindred. In earnestly seeking to be well assured of my adoption, I do not sink the social relation in the personal of my religion; and in putting in a humble title to a filial union with God, isolate myself in affection, sympathy, and fellowship from a fraternal union with the whole household of faith. In this light prayer is never exclusive and selfish. I am indeed privileged—and oh, how great and precious that privilege is!—to call God "My Father," but I must never forget that Jesus taught me to say, in concert with the one family, "Our Father." And that when I enter into my closet it is my privilege, as my duty, to bear before my Father, not my personal sins and sorrows only, but those also of the holy brotherhood to which, by a divine affiliation, I belong.

The unity of His Church was a truth dear to the heart of Christ. As the hour of His mysterious passion darkened, this truth dilated before His mind and occupied a more distinct and prominent place in His discourse. Foreseeing the divisions of sect and the differences of judgment and the alienation of affection which would spring up in His Church after His ascension to glory—defacing its beauty and impairing its strength—standing as beneath the shadow of His cross, He prostrates Himself at the feet of His Father, and binding the whole brotherhood around His heart, He prays, *"That they all may be* ONE, *as Thou, Father, art in me, and I in Thee, that they all may be one in us; that the world may believe that Thou hast sent me."* This sublime petition of the Great Intercessor is being partially answered *now* in every act of brotherly love, in every recognition of fraternal relation, in every lowly, loving effort to manifest and promote the visible unity of the Church. Upon all such shall light the blessing of the "peacemakers!" But the full, the perfect accomplishment of this desire of the Saviour's soul awaits the day of His second coming. Not until then will the world fully believe in His Divine Messiahship and mission, for not until then will the whole Church appear in its visible unity.

The Lord's Prayer pre-eminently breathes a CATHOLIC SPIRIT. The inspiration of the Spirit of love, taught us by Him who is the Incarnation of love, and clustering us as one family around the feet of Him who is "Love," it would he marvellous did it not teach us to love as brethren. The fraternal affection is cognate to the filial. If I love my God who begat, I must love, from the very necessity of the case, him who is begotten. If my affection for God be truly filial, my affection for the children of God will he truly fraternal. My return to God as my Father is the impulse and measure of my return to man as my brother. The prodigal in the Gospel, when he severed the tie that bound him to his father, by the same act of selfish expatriation severed the tie that bound him to his brother. "Give me the portion of goods *that falleth to me."* Thus man's revolt from God, was man's alienation from man. Hence the fell hate of nations, the strife of parties, the jealousies, the feuds, the injustice, and the wrong which have armed nation against nation, church against church, man against man, and have made this once fair and beauteous world a very aceldama. All springs from one cause—man became the enemy of God, and so became the foe of his race. But the Lord Jesus came to gather together His people of all nations and tongues around one mercy-seat, teaching them to say—"*Our Father,*" thus uniting in the one "household of faith" Jew and Gentile, male and female, bond and free—all one *in* Christ, and all one *with* each other. Let us now proceed to illustrate the *catholic spirit* of this beautiful formula.

The foundation truth is—the ONE Father of us all. I speak now only of the election of grace—the family of God. We who through grace believe, have not many, but ONE Father. "Have we not all ONE Father?" By one and the same act of predestinating grace God has adopted all His children. "*Having predestinated us unto the adoption of children by Jesus Christ to Himself, according to the good pleasure of His will, to the praise of the glory of His grace, wherein He hath made us accepted in the beloved,*" (Eph. i. 5.) Still more emphatically does the apostle state this truth in another place: "*For this cause I bow my knees unto the Father of our Lord Jesus Christ, of whom the whole family in earth and in heaven is named,*" (Eph. iii. 14.)

Magnificent truth! The whole family of God one, and as one, clustering at the feet of their one Father!—the Church on earth and the Church in heaven. How real and how near is heaven! The ties that bind some hearts to the saints above, are closer and holier than the ties that bind us to the saints below. This may be explained on the principle that we admire and love, and feel closer fellowship with, that which is perfect. Do you not feel that the saints of God who are the most holy, who in their spirit and walk the most closely resemble Jesus, attract to them your warmest love and sympathy? Thus it is that the saints now made perfect, whom once we knew, by whose side we travelled, whom we accompanied to the river and saw pass over and disappear within the veil; but who, because they are beautiful in holiness, perfected in love, resplendent with glory, seem to hold our hearts in the spell of a stronger, holier love and fellowship. Sweet thought is it, too, that nothing but the rivulet of death sunders us from their fullest and eternal communion. There is but a step between you and them. How close are they to us even now! Heaven is nearer to us than earth!—nearer than India, than China, than Australia, than the Crimea. And the more heavenly we grow, and the closer our connexion with the unseen, the *nearer* shall we feel to the *"family in heaven."* Let us endure as seeing the invisible! But to go forth in silent converse with the saints in glory, need I separate myself from the communion of the saints on earth? Assuredly not! The tie is one and the same, with this difference only, that its association with heaven, its perfect freedom from all taint of sin and from all trace of infirmity, imparts to it a tenderness and invests it with a sanctity and solemnity which no tie on earth possesses. But *prayer* is the great cement of the saints below. There is not an engagement so uniting, so healing, so hallowing as PRAYER. In this holy atmosphere nothing can live but the pure, the holy, the loving. Sectarianism vanishes, bigotry expires, coldness dissolves, wounds are healed; and the saints, clustering together around the feet of the one God and Father of all, realise their spiritual unity, exhibit their indivisible oneness, and present a spectacle of holy love such as earth, with all its boasted alliances never saw, and such as heaven, from amidst its perfect harmony, looks down to see. Oh, were there a deeper and more universal spirit of *united prayer* pervading Christ's Church, it would tide over those sectarian differences and party jealousies which so much deface its comeliness, impair its power, and shade its lustre; and flowing with the effulgence which encircles the throne of grace, she would go forth, luminous and invincible, to subdue and bless the world, *"fair as the moon, clear as the sun, and terrible as an army with banners."*

What a family-uniting truth, then, is this—*OUR Father.* The very breathing of the word seems to diminish the magnitude of those minor differences that separate the children of God; while its influence upon the heart draws forth the sweetest charity and the deepest love towards all who bow their knees with us in prayer, and say—*"Our Father!"* Again, I ask, should not the *one Fatherhood* of *"the adoption of grace"* be more distinctly recognised, and constitute a more uniting truth among the true children of God? To know that whatever partition separates, or polity divides, or forms distinguish the saints; the moment persecution is awakened, or affliction befalls the Church, all arise and give themselves to prayer; and, travelling to one mercy-seat—converging as lines to a common centre—find that, after all, they are children of one family, brethren one of another, and that into the ears of one Father all pour the breathings of their hearts. Surely this divine, sanctifying, cementing truth, attended with the anointing of the Holy Spirit, must promote more visible union among the saints of the most high God. Let us study it more closely, get it in-wrought in our hearts, realise fully our personal adoption, learn to call God "FATHER" with a less faltering tongue, then will our hearts be drawn forth with a deeper fraternal affection towards all who worship in spirit and in truth the same Father, and whom that Father recognises as His. Alas! the reason why we stand aloof from the *children* so much is, because we love the *Father* so little! Did we, under a clearer sense of our adoption of God, with a deeper conviction of the debt we owed Him for this signal bestowment of His grace, walk in closer converse with God, the things which separate us from the family of God,—the differences of ecclesiastical polity, of modes of worship, the hard speeches, the slights, the woundings, the misunderstandings which engender so much suspicion, coldness, and alienation among the saints,—would be buried and lost sight of as the rugged rocks disappear beneath the flowing tide. Love—love to the one Father—would prompt us to throw the mantle of love over the one brotherhood, veiling every feature but

"The Father's image in the children's face."

The *equality of love* with which the Father regards alike all the family, supplies another strong tie of affection in the Christian brotherhood. There may be different manifestations of God's love, but, I imagine, no *degrees*. He must regard with an equal affection all whom He has everlastingly chosen. As the ground of our election of God is love—love, like His being, without beginning—so in one heart of love, which can admit of no grades in the infinitude of its affection, is bound the one family of God. In this one family of our Father there are those who exhibit different degrees of love to God, as different shades of resemblance to His image—still they are brethren, and as such it is both our duty and our privilege to recognise and love them. Should not this truth—the equality of the Father's love to His family—place us all on equal footing as children of God? Why should we not love, even though we differ? Why should we not unite, even though we are separated? Why should we not bear each other's burdens, and sympathise with each other's trials, and aid each other's efforts, and bow together at the footstool of the same Father, even though we are labouring for Him in sundered departments of the one house? If our love to the Father is genuine, our love to the offspring of that Father will be true. Love to the one will be the measure, as the evidence, of our love to the other. Oh, for more love! Were I asked what the first great need of the Church was, I should unhesitatingly reply—love. And what the second— love. And what the third—love. I marvel not that our Lord added a *"new* commandment," as it were, to the decalogue—*"That ye love one another, even as I have loved you."* Love would veil infirmities; love would seal the law of kindness upon the lip; love would rebuke slander, reprove falsehood, and suppress every thought, feeling, and word that would dishonour the Father through the child, wound the Saviour through the disciple, grieve the Master through the servant. Realising our personal interest in God's love, and remembering that He loves alike all the children of His family, with what holy guardedness should we respect the feelings, and shield the reputation, and promote the happiness of all the sons and daughters of God! Oh, how can I look coldly upon him on whom God smiles? How dare I disown one whom Christ accepts? Where is the evidence of my own sonship if I unite not in heart and voice with my brother in saying, "OUR *Father,* who art in heaven?"—and while I breathe the filial words, feel not a brother's love glowing in my heart?

And have we not one and the same Elder Brother—the Lord Jesus Christ? What a uniting truth is this! He is *"the first-born among many brethren,"*—the Elder Brother of the Christian brotherhood. How often, and with what tenderness of tone and expressiveness of meaning, did these words fall from His lips— *"My brethren!"* And how ready He ever was to acknowledge the one Father of Himself and His brethren; thus taking His place at

the head of the family as the First-Born of the many sons whom
the Father is bringing to glory. Through the one mediation, then,
of this our Elder Brother, we all approach "OUR *Father in heaven.*"
We plead alike His personal merits; we present alike His atoning
blood; we breathe alike His endearing name; we appear before our
Father clad in the garment of the Elder Brother, in whom, and for
whose sake, the Father smiles complacently alike upon all. Here
we stand side by side on an equality with each other. No national
hate, no political creed, no ecclesiastical distinction, no social caste,
nor learning, nor rank, nor wealth should be allowed for one
moment to interpose a bar to Christian recognition, fellowship,
and service between those who, washed in the blood and robed in
the righteousness of the Elder Brother, are members of Him, "*of
whom the whole Church in heaven and earth is named.*" Christ
our Brother! how close and endearing the relation! How sweet to
travel to Him as to a brother, calling His Father our Father, His
God our God! A Brother, though divine, made flesh like unto His
brethren! A Brother, the heir of all things, and making us, His
brethren, co-heirs with Himself! A brother born for His brethren's
adversity! Contemplate Christ as such. Go to Him as such. Deal
with Him as such. At all times and in all places are you welcome.
You may go to an earthly brother in the day of your calamity, and
find, in his lack of sympathy or his inability to help, that, "*better
is a neighbour that is near than he.*" But never, never shall you go
to Jesus in adversity and not find in Him all the sympathy and
succour that you need—yea, sticking closer than a brother. You
may, too, find it harder to restore to your reconciled affection a
Christian brother whom you have offended than to win a strong
city. But if you grieve and wound this Brother, and go to His feet
and confess your sin, and sob your grief upon His bosom, you will
find Him prepared, graciously, lovingly, and fully, to be reconciled—
forgiving the offender and remembering the offence no more for
ever. Oh, let us cultivate frequent and intimate transactions with
Jesus our Elder Brother. Treat Him not as a stranger. Have
confidence in His love, trust His faithfulness, rely upon His power,
embosom yourself in His sympathy. Alas! how little we deal directly

and personally with Christ! He would have us entwine Him with our every affection, blend Him with our every thought, associate Him with every transaction, bring to Him every want, confess to Him every sin, and repose upon His heart every sorrow. Should not this truth constrain us to "love as brethren;" and to seek on all occasions to manifest the essential unity of the brotherhood before a God-hating, a Christ-rejecting world?

And does not *the same Spirit of adoption* dwell alike in all the children of God? Most assuredly, if they are indeed His children. It is by this self same Holy Spirit that each one cries, *"Abba, Father,"* when he approaches the mercy-seat. *"For through Him we both have access by one Spirit unto the Father."* He it is who seals the uniting word upon our lips—"OUR *Father,"* and so binds us all in one fraternal chain of holy brotherhood. Refusing, then, to recognise a professing disciple of Jesus as a brother because he belongs not to my sect, and kneels not at my altar, and sees not eye to eye with me in all things, I grieve the one indwelling Spirit, wound the Saviour in the house of His friends, bring barrenness into my soul, and go far to ignore my own fraternal relation to the family of God. But behold the true catholic spirit which the Lord's Prayer breathes—"OUR *Father."* And in whomsoever that spirit truly dwells, and whoso breathes that prayer from his heart, is bound, as with the solemnity of an oath, to *"love the brotherhood."* For, brethren, to kneel before the throne and say, *"OUR Father,"* and then go forth and in angry polemics, and heated strifes about questions which admit of perfect freedom of judgment, and which after all may resolve themselves into mere human opinion, and *"bite and devour one another,"* until well-nigh *"consumed one of another,"* is a spectacle which might bedew an angel's eye with tears, as in reality it clothes a demon's tongue with exultation. Yes, beloved, God *is* "OUR Father." He enshrines us all in one parental heart, accepts us all in His beloved Son, seals us all with one Spirit of adoption; cares for us all, provides for us all, protects us all, sympathises with us all alike; and who are you, and who am I, that we should denounce and despise one of these whom God OUR Father claims as His child?

And what a fraternally-uniting truth is this, that our Father is bringing us all *to one parental and eternal home.* A part of the family is already there—*"the family IN HEAVEN."* Those who once shared our earthly home, sat with us at the family board, clustered with us around the domestic hearth, and who departed in the faith of Jesus, are not lost—they are housed in the Home of the Father in heaven, and are gathered around the Lamb, basking in the sunshine of His ineffable glory. What a soothing thought is this! how sanctifying, how uniting! Bereaved one! sorrowing not as those who have no hope, raise your eyes from the shrouded remains, the sepulchred dust of the holy dead, up to the sunlight world of glory, purity, and bliss into which they have entered, and think of them only as *there!* They are not here, they are risen. They have ascended where no sin taints, nor sorrow grieves, nor unkindness wounds, nor sickness wastes, nor death separates. The sun shall not smite them by day nor the moon by night. No faithless friendships, nor lying tongue, nor throbbing brow, nor aching heart, nor weary frame affects them now. They mourn no more indwelling sin, they fence no more with ungodly men, they battle no more with the prowling tempter; they have fought the last fight, have gotten the victory, have unclasped the armour, and have exchanged the shield for the palm, and the sword for the crown—and are for ever with the Lord. What a uniting link is this in the family of God on earth! What holy love, what powerful attraction, what tender sympathy, what united prayer, what mutual comfort, should the thought of the present state of our friends in heaven inspire those who have similar bereavements, kindred sorrows, like consolations, the same hopes, and are hastening to join them on high! How closely should these things draw the holy brotherhood together! Why should we not, though of different communions, break through the fence and leap over the wall of separation, and pour out our sorrowing hearts together in mutual fellowship at the feet of OUR Father in heaven? Could these happy spirits, who have fled from the religious divisions and strifes of the Church on earth, bend from their thrones and speak, with what holy earnestness, with what glowing love, with what celestial and touching eloquence would they exclaim—"Your different forms of church polity and worship are *human,* your essential faith and heavenly hopes are *divine!* Oh, love as brethren! We *now* see the folly of our divisions, the sin of our contentions, the iniquity of our jealousies, strifes, and alienations. Here there are no different communions, no separating walls, no exclusive altars,—nothing to impair the power, or shade the lustre, or disturb the music of that love which now knits every heart in the closest fellowship, and blends every voice in the sweetest song. We are now with Christ! In the effulgence of His glory all is absorbed and annihilated that once created a cloud, or inspired a jarring note. His love so overflows our souls that we are transformed into love, we are all love, and nothing but love one toward another. All our thoughts and feelings, worship and service, so centre in Christ, that, forgetting earth's divisions and strifes, or, remembering them but to deepen our humility and heighten our song, we now feel, as we never felt before, how human, how light, how insignificant were the things which once separated,—and how divine, how real, how lasting are those which now unite us in a fellowship as holy, as close, and as eternal as the unity of the God we adore."

Let us endeavour to approximate, in some measure, to the sentiments and feelings of the glorified saints. Let us realise in some degree what that love in heaven is that constrains the most fierce polemics and the widest sectarians, who once wrote and spake and strove with each other so fiercely and so bitterly, each for his own communion, now to meet in the embrace of a love that buries all the past of earth's infirmities in its infinite depths and its eternal flow. Oh, in the light of one close view of eternity, in the experience of one moment's realisation of heaven, how unimportant and puerile the contentions as to whose *orders* are the most valid, or whose *church polity* is the most apostolic! *OUR Father,* who art in heaven! look down upon Thy one family! and so fill it with Thy love, that, casting out all selfishness, coldness, and alienation, all may meet at Thy feet, and love as brethren, and worship Thee as the one God and Father of all.

The topic discussed in this chapter belongs essentially to

practical Christianity. The unity of the Christian Church, the oneness of the family of God, is not a cold, abstract truth—it is vital, warm, sanctifying. Am I one of God's children? Do I acknowledge as my brethren—of every nation and tongue and sect—all who, through the Person, and by the Sacrifice of Jesus Christ, approach God as their Father? Then how precious and sacred to my heart should be the character, the reputation, and the happiness of my brother, thus recognised and thus loved! Would I allow the tainted tongue of slander, the cruel breath of malice, the floating rumour of falsehood to rest upon a brother or a sister bound to me by the fond tie of nature, but with a solemn and indignant protest? Would I not shield them as myself? How much nearer and dearer to me should be the *Christian* character, and the individual peace of a child of God, a brother or a sister in Christ Jesus! Refraining myself from all evil speaking and evil thinking— all that would shade His fame, impair His influence, and wound His feelings—with what wakeful jealousy and holy indignation should I rebuke the foul slanderer, silence the tongue of falsehood, and defend the character and reputation of my brother as I would the sacred and endeared name of my blessed Lord! How pointed and holy the divine precepts touching the duty of saint with saint! "*Speak not evil one of another, brethren. He that speaketh evil of his brother, and judgeth his brother, speaketh evil of the law, and judgeth the law,*" (Jas. iv. ii.) "*Love as brethren, be pitiful, be courteous: not rendering evil for evil, or railing for railing: but contrariwise blessing,*" (I Pet. iii. 8.) "*Walk in love, as Christ also hath loved us,*" (Eph. v. 2.) "*Let all bitterness, and wrath, and anger, and clamour, and evil-speaking, be put away from you, with all malice: and be ye kind one to another, forgiving one another, even as God for Christ's sake hath forgiven you.*" "*Let brotherly love continue.*" Were these divine and holy precepts more conscientiously and strictly observed, were they entwined more closely with the intercourse of saint with saint, and of the saints with the world in daily life, how much evil would be prevented, how much alienation of affection would be averted, how many Christian brethren, now sundered in intercourse and fellowship by misrepresentations, evil-speaking, and mischief-making, would be united in the sweetest communion and in the holiest service for Christ! Oh, to remember that every shaft hurled at a brother's fair fame pierces him through the heart of Jesus! *"He that toucheth you, toucheth the apple of mine eye."*

"Must I my brother keep,
    And share his pains and toil;
And weep with those that weep,
    And smile with those that smile;
And act to each a brother's part,
    And feel his sorrows in my heart?

"Must I his burden bear
    As though it were my own,
And do as I would care
    Should to myself be done;
And faithful to his interests prove,
    And as my neighbour love?

"Must I reprove his sin,
    Must I partake his grief,
And kindly enter in
    And minister relief;
The naked clothe, the hungry feed,
    And love him not in word, but deed?

"Then, Jesus, at Thy feet
    A student let me be,
And learn as it is meet
    My duty, Lord, of Thee;
For Thou didst come on mercy's plan,
    And all Thy life was love to man.

"Oh, make me as Thou art,
    Thy Spirit, Lord, bestow;
The kind and gentle heart
    That feels another's woe,
That thus I may be like my Head,
    And in my Saviour's footsteps tread."*

---

* Rev. Dr Raffles.

How uniting and hallowing is this truth in its influence upon the *family institution!* Each domestic circle, trained in the fear and love of God, morning and evening touchingly illustrates this fraternal bond in its approaches to the mercy-seat. At the feet of one heavenly Father all cluster when bending at the family altar. Whatever selfishness may have divided their interests, whatever dissensions may have disturbed their unanimity, whatever differences of judgment may for the moment have rippled the tranquil surface of domestic life, *here* all meet as one, and with one heart and with one voice uplift their prayer to God and say, "*OUR FATHER, which art in heaven.*" How touching the scene! how holy the bond! how tender, sacred, and uniting the thoughts, the sympathies, and the love which now beat responsive in each bosom, and diffuse peace and repose over each mind! Should not this truth—the one Fatherhood of our God—sanctify and endear the various ties of the domestic circle, preventing those jealousies, discords, and divided interests which too frequently invade the sanctuary and embitter the happiness of the home circle. Let this truth have its full weight in promoting family love and domestic concord; in strengthening and hallowing the parental, the filial, and the fraternal relations; and all pious families will then be centres of moral influence, healthful and far-reaching in their extent, beauteous types of the Father's house into which all the children of God will ere long be gathered. And as we approach eternity, and realise more the heavenly glory, do we not feel a closer drawing towards all who love the Lord Jesus Christ in sincerity? Standing once by the dying bed of a child of God, he stretched forth his emaciated hand, cold and clammy with the moisture of death, and, grasping mine, exclaimed, "The nearer I get to heaven, the dearer to my heart are the Lord's people of every branch of His one family." Such, too, was the testimony, a few days before his death, of an eminent professor of an American university— "The longer I live the more dearly do I prize being a Christian, and the more signally unimportant seem to me the differences by which *true* Christians are separated from each other." How sweetly these dying testimonies to the unity of the Church of Christ chime with the dying prayer of Christ Himself for His universal Church, *"That they all may be* ONE." "The last note of this divine strain breathes love and union, and sweetly closes the most fervent production of any spirit that has ever tabernacled in the flesh. Let us catch with loving ear this music of His dying voice, as it rises and swells with the ecstasy of gratitude and hope; trembles with anxiety for His 'little flock' in the midst of an angry world, and sinks away in a joyful cadence of eternal glory, love, and blessedness, in which hover images of peace and union between Himself, His disciples, and His Father in the everlasting home of heaven." Into that home we shall soon enter. And could then a blush crimson our cheek, or a tear bedew our eye, or a pang pierce our heart, how deep would be our shame, how intense our grief, how inexpressible our agony, that, in our pilgrimage to its mansions of love, we should ever have felt unkindly, have thought unkindly, have spoken unkindly, have acted unkindly towards one who, with us, bent his knees and bowed his heart at the mercy-seat, and prayed—"OUR FATHER, WHO ART IN HEAVEN."

> "Oh then the glory and the bliss,
> When all that pain'd and seem'd amiss
>   Shall melt with earth and sin away;
> When saints beneath their Saviour's eye,
> Fill'd with each other's company,
>   Shall spend in love the eternal day."*

---

* Keeble.

CHAPTER III.

THE CELESTIAL SPIRIT OF THE LORD'S PRAYER.

"Our Father, WHICH ART IN HEAVEN." MATT. vi. **9.**

HERE are three points of light in which the invocation of the Lord's Prayer may be viewed. I have already considered the first two—the *paternal* and the *filial*. It remains that we consider the third one—the *celestial.* *"Our Father, WHICH ART IN HEAVEN."* It was *to heaven,* where God is, and from whence He came, that Christ sought to uplift the hearts of His disciples. The earthward tendency of the renewed mind, even amid the solemn engagement of prayer, He, from whom no thought of the heart is concealed, perfectly knew. Who among the most spiritually-minded has not complained of the undevoutness of heart, the vagrancy of mind, the foolish imaginations, and probably sceptical thoughts which so often obtrude upon the believer when he would fain enter his closet and shut the door about him and be alone with God? At the very moment when, unclasping and uplifting the pinions of his soul, he would fain rise in faith and love and fellowship, he finds himself encompassed and assailed by a legion of mundane, atheistical, graceless thoughts and affections, which fetter the soul, stifle its aspirations, distract its meditations, and arrest its flight. What an impediment, too, to real, spiritual prayer does the believer find in the tendency of his mind to lose sight of *God's Dwelling.* True, solemnly true, God's presence is everywhere; yet, while earth is His footstool, heaven is His dwelling-place. And where He is, thither would He have the heart and mind of His supplicating child travel and repose. Hence the emphatic declaration of our Lord—"*Our Father,* WHICH ART IN HEAVEN." Let this be the truth which now engages our study.

In ascribing *locality* to God—in portraying heaven as His dwelling—we must not forget, as I have just remarked, one of the most solemn and, to the Christian mind, most sanctifying and consolatory truths, that there is not a place nor a spot in the vast universe where God is not. His presence pervades all space, engirdles the globe, brightens the bowers of heaven, darkens the caverns of hell. Who can hide himself from God? What mountain can cover, what rock conceal, what darkness veil the soul from His sight? "*Whither shall I go from Thy Spirit? or whither shall I flee from Thy presence?*" Saint of God! can you not in truth exclaim, "Lord! whither would I flee from Thy presence? Flee from Thy presence! it is my heaven below, and it is all the heaven I expect or wish for above! If I take the wings of the morning, and dwell in the uttermost parts of the sea; even there shall Thy hand lead me, and Thy right hand shall hold me." Child of God! take the divine consolation of this truth. Where can you be where Christ will not be with you? Are you anticipating a new and untried stage of life? Are you about to relinquish the ties of home, perhaps of country, for a distant clime, to be exiled amid strangers, to battle with a new position of toil, temptation, and peril? Oh, let your child-like faith now grasp this great and precious truth, which shall be for your stay, strength, and comfort in all places whither God conducts you—"EVEN THERE SHALL THY HAND LEAD ME, AND THY RIGHT HAND HOLD ME." The promise is, "*MY PRESENCE shall go with thee, and I will give thee rest.*" Go, then, beloved, leaning upon this divine staff, and it shall be well with you for time and for eternity. Other staffs, the beautiful and strong, may break; other props, the near and loved, may fail; but your covenant God in Christ will never leave nor forsake you. Go, then, where He leads you; pitch your tent in India or in China, in Australia, or in America, within that tent He will dwell, above and around it He will spread the wings of His power and love; and in all your engagements and difficulties, loneliness and want, temptations and sorrows you shall be enabled to exclaim, "Nevertheless I am CONTINUALLY WITH THEE: Thou hast holden me by my right hand. Thou shalt guide me with Thy counsel, and afterward receive me to glory. Whom have I in heaven but Thee? and there is none upon earth that I desire beside Thee."

And yet our Father has His fixed and appropriate dwelling-place. The Scriptures of truth represent heaven as His abode. At the dedication of the temple, Solomon uses this language, "*But will God indeed dwell on earth? behold, the heaven, and heaven of heavens, cannot contain Thee.*" And we have the prayer of the prophet Isaiah confirming this truth: "*Look down from HEAVEN, and behold from the habitation of Thy holiness and of Thy glory.*" And to crown these statements we have the declaration of Jehovah himself—"*HEAVEN is My throne, and earth is My footstool.*" We must suppose, then, that the highest heavens—sometimes called the "heaven of heavens," and "the third heaven"—is the place of God's dwelling. The "third heaven," into which the apostle in his rapture ascended, is a remarkable expression. The Jews were wont to speak of the lower world, the middle world, and the supreme world. The lower heaven includes the aerial world immediately over us—the clouds and the atmosphere. The central heaven embraces the firmament above it—the sun, the moon, and the stars. The supreme or third heaven is the highest of all, the supposed seat of the Divine Majesty, the region where God dwells, where Christ, seated at the right hand of the Father, conducts His intercessory work, and where the glorified saints are gathered—whose wonders Paul saw, whose music he heard, whose joy he felt but who, on returning to earth, was impressed with the seal of silence, forbidden by God to communicate what he had seen and heard and felt of the invisible world. Surely if God had permitted any intelligence to be conveyed to man of the place and condition of the departed spirits; if intercourse had been allowed between the dead and the living, we might suppose that this occasion would have demonstrated the fact. And yet the veil was not uplifted, and the silence of the apostle's lips was unbroken. Not one of the countless millions who have been received up into heaven have ever been permitted to revisit earth with communications concerning its glories. So fixed is the law, so settled the principle that has ever, on this point, regulated the Divine conduct. It would seem as if God would anticipate and confound the daring imposture of Mohammed, and of every other pseudo-prophet, and for ever demonstrate the essential difference between true and false inspiration; causing to stand out in bold relief the dignified silence of the great apostle of the Gentiles, in contrast with the contemptible puerilities of the profane prophet of Mecca. The inquiry which, doubtless, arises in many minds why Paul was forbidden to make known what he had seen in heaven, may be more speculative than profitable to pursue. My own conviction, however, is, that God would allow nothing to transpire calculated to lessen the dignity, sufficiency, and importance of His written Word in the eyes of men. A revelation other than that which, by Divine Inspiration, He had already given, would he most assuredly attended with this inevitable result. "But surely," you reply, "to have known more of heaven, more of the glories of paradise, more of what awaits the righteous, would have been useful in solving the doubts, confirming the faith, animating the hope, and soothing the trials, affliction, and sorrow of the saints on their way through much darkness and tribulation to the celestial world." Not so. Let God be the judge. If the present divine revelations of the heavenly world sometimes dazzle and confound us, how should we, in this imperfect state, be able to compass a fuller and more overpowering discovery? And if the doubt will sometimes arise, though the revelations are divine, what would be our unbelief of revelations predicated only upon the human? Enough, too, is made known of heaven to give us a clear and intelligent idea of its negative and its positive bliss. It suffices us to be assured that sin is annihilated, that tears are dried, that disease is banished, that pain is unfelt, that death is destroyed, that parting is unknown, that rest is enjoyed, and that peace, fellowship, and love reign universally and for ever. In addition to these are the positive elements of bliss. With Jesus, for ever beholding His glory. Blessed with the "glorious company of the apostles, the goodly fellowship of the prophets, the noble army of martyrs," encircled by time "spirits of just men made perfect," and reunited to all that we loved on earth and parted in death in the hope of eternal life. Is not this enough to support us in trial, to soothe us in sorrow, to animate us in duty, and to fortify us against temptation and sin? Will not this suffice to endure suffering patiently, to bear the cross cheerfully, and to mitigate the grief of parting; remembering that, *our light affliction which is but for a moment, worketh for us a far more exceeding and eternal weight of glory?*" Once more, in anticipation of the ETERNAL HEAVEN, this EVERLASTING REST, our Father would have us live a life of faith. The sight, the fulness is to come; until then we are to take God at His word, believe all that He has revealed and promised, and live and die as did the worthies of old, of whom it is written, that, *not having received the promises, but having seen them afar off, and were persuaded of them, and embraced them, confessed that they were strangers and pilgrims on the earth.*" Soon heaven will be entirely revealed and fully known. Ere the sun, which ascended upon us in rosy beams in the morning, shall set in a flood of gold and purple at night, we may fall asleep in Jesus, and wake up amidst heaven's unclouded and eternal splendour. Ecstatic thought! entrancing prospect! Absent from flesh, for ever with the Lord! What! shall I soon see Jesus? Will the great, the solemn, the glorious mystery which so long absorbed my affections, awakened my desires, engaged my earnest thoughts, and occupied my dearest study, be all explained? Will the grand secret be soon revealed? Oh, for the pinions of the dove, that I might fly into His presence, fall at His feet, wake my harp to His praise, and repose in that ineffable bosom on which I have so often sobbed my griefs, and which once sobbed and bled for me.

> "Why should I shrink at pain or woe,
>   Or feel at death dismay?
> I've Canaan's goodly land in view,
>   And realms of endless day.
>
> "Apostles, martyrs, prophets there
>   Around my Saviour stand;
> And soon my friends in Christ beloved
>   Will join the glorious band.

> "Jerusalem! my happy home!
> My soul still pants for thee;
> When shall my labour have an end
> In joy, and peace, and thee!"

How appropriate, then, the third or the supreme heaven as the
DWELLING-PLACE OF JEHOVAH. Let me briefly illustrate this thought.

Heaven is a glorious place—the *place of glory*. The glory of God,
indeed, is everywhere. There is no place in the universe unreached,
no spot unillumined by its splendour. The constellations reflect it,
the earth exhibits it, man illustrates it. *"The earth is full of His
glory."* But heaven is especially the place of glory, because it is God's
dwelling. The palace of the Sovereign of earth and heaven should
be worthy of the Divine Majesty that occupies it. But what heaven
can circumscribe God? What palace can, in its magnificence and
dimensions, be commensurate with the glory and greatness of the
eternal, the uncreated One? How profound was this conviction and
how reverential the feeling in the mind of Solomon at the dedication
of the temple he built for God *"Will God in very deed dwell on the
earth? behold, the heaven and heaven of heavens cannot contain
Thee; how much less this house that I have builded Thee?"* Where,
then, on earth shall we travel for the temple worthy of the Deity?
Shall we repair to the Gothic cathedral, to the ancient abbey, to the
costly sanctuary reared by human hands? Most true, all who
worship God within these sacred structures "in spirit and in truth"
shall find Him there, shall feel His presence, hear His word, and
receive His blessing. But God has a more befitting, a more sacred,
and a more Divine temple upon earth than this—it is the heart of
the humble and the soul of the contrite. His own words can alone
convey this marvellous truth. Had He not spoken it, who would have
believed it? and because He has spoken it, who will dare deny it?
*"Thus saith the Lord, The heaven is my throne and the earth is my
footstool. Where is the house that ye build unto me, and where is the
place of my rest? For all these things hath my hand made, and all
these things have been, saith the Lord; but to this man will I look,
even to him that is poor and of a contrite spirit, and who trembleth
at my word."* A truth more marvellous, words more precious, an

assurance more comforting, cannot be found in God's revelation. While heaven, the third heaven, the heaven of heavens, cannot contain Him, He finds a home and rears a temple for Himself within the heart of a poor sinner, who, lying in the dust, penitent, contrite, humble, confesses and deplores his sins. Is *your* heart this temple, my reader? Is *mine?* Vital and solemn question! Its answer, as in the sight of the Searcher of hearts, decides our conversion, sets to rest the fact of our being the temple of God through the Spirit. And is it so that, with Job you exclaim, "*I have heard of Thee with the hearing of the ear: but now mine eye seeth Thee. Wherefore I abhor myself, and repent in dust and ashes?*" Is it so that, with David you exclaim, "*I acknowledge my transgressions: and my sin is ever before me. Against Thee, Thee only, have I sinned, and done this evil in Thy sight?*" Is it so that, with the publican you smite upon your breast and exclaim, "*God be merciful to me a sinner?*" Oh, divine and blessed evidence, that "*the high and the holy One who inhabiteth eternity, whose name is Holy,*" also dwells within the compass of your heart, and finds there His loved and sacred and eternal dwelling. Thus fragrant to God is the "*sacrifice of a broken and a contrite heart,*" thus precious is the humble and the penitent mind ; thus glorious in His eye is the temple of the soul draped and shrouded with the emblems of holy, spiritual mourning, lamentation, and woe for sin. Lord! make my heart Thy home—my body Thy temple!

Our Father dwells in heaven, too, because it is A HOLY PLACE. "Thus saith the high and lofty One that inhabiteth eternity, whose name is Holy, I dwell in the high and *holy place.*" Essential Holiness can alone dwell in a holy atmosphere. Sin can never enter the abode of God. In the heaven of heavens, where Jehovah dwells, iniquity has no existence, there in nowise enters anything that defileth. Every thought, and word, and feeling, and aspiration there is in harmony with divine and infinite purity. Is not this the chief perfection, the strong attraction of heaven to you, beloved, that there you will be sinless as Christ is sinless, holy as God is holy? What is this fond anticipation of your heart, but an offshoot of that divine and holy nature into which you are begotten of God? A stronger evidence of your conversion does not exist than this hunger and thirst of your soul after *holiness,* this longing desire, this joyous expectation of perfect freedom from the taint and thraldom of sin. There is nothing in the flesh in sympathy with Divine purity; for, *"in me, that is, in my flesh, dwelleth no good thing."* If, then, you find, amid much that is contradictory, much that would contravene the validity of such a state, a real, earnest, though often feeble and fluctuating desire after conformity to God's holiness, a true loathing of sin, a sincere and prayerful resistance of its promptings and its power, you may, with all assurance, write yourself an humble child of God, a true disciple of the Lord Jesus Christ. The breathing after sanctification *is* sanctification. The thirst for holiness *is* holiness, just as the vital heaving of the lungs is life. Oh, may the Holy Ghost increase this desire, strengthen this breathing of the new nature within us! May we be content with nothing short of an intense and supreme panting of the soul after God! There is the very element of heaven—heaven in its first fruits, its early dawn, its pledge—in the real earnest, though often thwarted effort, of the renewed soul after the holiness that is perfect in heaven. This state of mind may be attended, yea, even be produced, by deeper discoveries of the depravity and corruption within; you may appear to yourself to be more unholy, to be at a further remove from sanctification than ever; nevertheless, hold fast your confidence, for the Holy Ghost is employing this deeper ploughing for your deeper sanctification, for your more matured meetness for the holiness of glory. Yes; heaven, with all its favoured blessings, its sweet attractions, its sparkling glories, its treasured ties inviting us to its pleasant coast, would be no heaven to a saint of God were he doomed still to wear the chains of corruption, still to trail along its starry pavement and through its sylvan borders, this wretched "body of sin and of death." But, oh, entrancing thought! the moment my spirit rends the last fetter, and crosses the threshold of glory, it floats in an atmosphere genial with its heavenly nature, breathes the air of its native clime, and is as complete in holiness—the state oft sighed, and wept, and prayed for—as God is complete. Let this assurance nerve your arm in the conflict with sin, let this prospect animate you in your strivings after sanctification, and let the end of all God's corrective discipline reconcile you to the cup your Father gave you, even to make you *a partaker of His holiness!*

Our Father dwells in heaven, *as the abode of perfect happiness.* God is perfectly happy because He is perfectly holy. The two states are inseparable; holiness and happiness are correlative terms, they are cognate truths. Sanctification is the essential element of peace, joy, and assurance. God—I speak it reverentially—can only restore fallen man to happiness by restoring him to holiness. Sin and happiness are more antagonistic and irreconcilable, in the experience of the believer, than any elements in nature of opposite qualities. By some ingenious process of science, the alchemist may so change the properties of opposite elements, as to effect either amalgamation or fusion; but God, infinite as is His nature, vast and exhaustless as are His resources, possesses no secret by which He can unite and harmonise, in the salvation of man, sin and holiness; no moral process by which He can make the sinner happy, peaceful, hopeful, and still leave him the vassal of Satan and the slave of concupiscence. Christ came to destroy the works of the devil, both in the world and in the soul of man. God's plan, therefore, in the restoration of man to happiness, is not to reconcile the two opposite and antagonistic forces of sin and holiness, but to dethrone and destroy sin, and upon its ruins rear the fabric of righteousness, the temple of the Holy Ghost, to the eternal praise of the glory of His grace. This He does in the conversion of the soul, by which the children of adoption become partakers of the Divine nature, and, through the sanctification of the Spirit, and the hallowed discipline of affliction, more and more partakers of their Father's image.

But God is happy. He would have remained so, infinitely, independently, supremely happy, had He never created an intelligent being to whom He would display, and with whom He would share it. He might have remained in His own solitary grandeur, ineffably, supremely happy, in the eternal contemplation of His own glory, dwelling in light, which no man hath seen or can see. And even after His creation of intelligent beings, He might have hurled every angel from heaven, and have swept every creature from the earth, and not a drop had diminished the fulness, nor a cloud had shaded the lustre of His own essential felicity. It is true that the redemption of His Church has made such a revelation of Himself as will command the admiration, homage, and love of countless millions of intelligent beings throughout eternity; but, since it was God's happiness to save man—and infinity cannot be either lessened or augmented—the salvation of the Church has not made God more happy than He was from everlasting. To this happiness our Father who is in heaven admits His children. Having given them Himself to be their Father, He intends that they shall share the happiness of which He is the infinite ocean and the illimitable supply. What a provision He has made for our participation of this happiness through Christ! He is the sole medium, the divinely-appointed channel. *"There is one Mediator between God and man, the man Christ Jesus."* All the outflow of God's love, all the distillings of His compassion, all the sunbeams of His happiness, come to us through Jesus. And, oh, what a happiness to know Jesus, to possess Jesus, to stand in Jesus, to commune with Jesus, and to possess the blessed hope of coming with Jesus in the clouds of heaven when He shall appear in His glory! Is not *this* happiness? You may pass through deep trial; be the subject of constant suffering; eat the bread and drink the water of affliction; feel lonely, desolate, and forlorn; nevertheless, if Christ is yours, your Saviour, your Friend, your Brother, your Portion, and you are looking forward to the prospect of being with, and of enjoying Him for ever, no bird within its cage can sing more sweetly than your imprisoned heart its note of happiness, its psalm of praise. Possessing Christ as your portion, with His boundless, pure, inexhaustible resources, changeless love, deep, tender compassion, as all your own, you may boldly challenge every foe, and confidently confront every difficulty and trial in the language of the patriarch, *"When He giveth quietness, who then can make trouble?"*

Heaven, then, as the home of the Father, defines the home, final and eternal, of the family. Home! what marvellous magic is in that word! Home! what talismanic power does that thought possess! Home! around what spot do our holiest associations, our fondest memories cluster? To what shrine do our warmest affections travel—across oceans, and mountains, and deserts, and continents—is it not the home and the hearth of our childhood? Home! it is the circle of the purest affections, the focus of quintessential happiness, the hive in which the sweetest sweets of life are found. It is youth's temple, manhood's shrine, the sanctuary of age, the archive of the past, and the ark of the future. The human heart has many dwelling-places, but only *one* home. No exile can efface its memories, no distance can dissever its ties; no prosperity can eclipse its lustre, no crime, no shame, no suffering, can tear its portraits from the picture-gallery of the soul. Perhaps the most true and touching illustration of this feeling is, when we are for the first time, and it may be for ever, leaving home. We were never so sensible of our home attachment as at that moment. The simplest object, the most trifling association, enchains us to the spot:—

> "We do not know how much we love,
>   Until we come to leave;
> An aged tree, a common flower,
>   Are things o'er which we grieve.
> We linger while we turn away,
>   We cling while we depart;
> And memories, unmasked till then,
>   Come crowding round the heart.
> Let what will lure us on our way,
> Farewell's a bitter word to say."

"I know of no passage in classical literature," says an eloquent writer, "more beautiful or affecting than that where Xenophon, in his 'Anabasis,' describes the effect produced on the remnant of the ten thousand Greeks, when, after passing through dangers without number, they at length ascended a sacred mountain, and from its peak and summit caught sight of the sea. Dashing their bucklers with a hymn of joy, they rushed tumultuously forward. Some wept with the fulness of their delicious pleasure, others laughed, and more fell on their knees and blessed that broad ocean. Across its blue waters, like floating sea-birds, the memorials of their happy homes came and fanned their weary souls. All the perils they had encountered, all the companions they had lost, all the miseries they had endured, were in an instant forgotten, and nought was with them but the gentle phantoms of past and future joys. O home, magical spell, all-powerful home! how strong must have been thy influences when thy faintest memory could cause these hungered heroes of a thousand fights to weep like tearful women! 'With the cooling freshness of a desert fountain, with the sweet fragrance of a flower found in winter, you came across the great waters to these wandering men, and beneath the peaceful shadow of your wings their souls found rest!" Graphic and glowing as is this picture of the magic influence of home upon the returning exile, it pales before the believer's eye as he catches, from some Pisgah height, a view of the New Jerusalem, the happy home where he is for ever to dwell—its walls of jasper, its gates of pearl, its sunlight dome, its golden streets, its crystal waters, its tree of life, its central throne, the Lamb seated thereon, its countless multitude of holy, happy beings, all united in adoration of the Lamb that was slain. And when the soul has actually crossed the flood, and planted its foot, weary and sore, upon the golden sands, what its ecstasy, what its transport to find itself in heaven at last! Heaven was the starting-point of our race, and heaven will be the final home of its ransomed portion. The exquisite story of the younger brother who exchanged his home for exile, poverty, and want; but who, in penitence and faith, with confession and supplication, returned to its sacred shelter and met a father's welcome, is the true position of redeemed humanity. The sinner saved by grace, the wanderer restored by love, retraces his steps back to God, and home to the heaven from whence he originally departed. Heaven is the family home of all the children of God. It is the Father's home. Thither, day by day, hour by hour, the Father is bringing His sons and daughters—the adoption of grace. He Himself is there, and where should the children be but with the Father? Not *one* of that redeemed family shall be absent from the domestic circle. The white-haired parent, whose sun had run a long and holy course and then set in a flood of golden light—is *there!* The youth of manliness and beauty, the flower and hope of the family, whose

sun went down while it was yet day—is *there!* The child of prattle
and of song, the sunbeam and the cherub of the house, whose
brightness and music death has in a moment darkened and
hushed—is *there!* The infant of a day, just opening its languid eyes
upon the world of sin, then closing them, as if saddened by the
scene it beheld—is *there!* Yes, enriched and domesticated by the
countless number of the family who have departed in the faith of
Jesus, heaven is daily growing more winning and endeared to
faith's far-seeing eye as the Father's house. And is not our record
on high? "*Rather rejoice*," said Christ to His disciples when they
reported to Him the subjection of demons to their power—"*rather
rejoice that your names are written in heaven.*" Oh, what a signal
and precious mercy to have a name written in heaven! Better,
infinitely better, to have it enrolled there than emblazoned on the
page of historic fame, engraved in brass, sculptured in marble, or
set in diamonds upon a mother's heart! But all the names of the
family of God are written in the Lamb's Book of Life, and written
there from the foundation of the world. *Rejoice* in this! You ask,
"How may I know it?" The Lord has not left you without evidence.
Is the name of Jesus engraved upon your heart? Has the Holy
Spirit shown to you in measure its evil, brought you to see its
darkness, its vileness, and its treachery? Has the discovery led to
a renunciation of your own righteousness, to an abandonment of
all hope based upon the law, to a believing, simple, loving
acceptance of the Lord Jesus? Have you been led by the Spirit as
a poor, empty sinner to the blood and righteousness of the
Redeemer, looking only to Jesus, trusting only in Jesus, clinging
only to Jesus as the limpet clings to the rock, as the shipwrecked
mariner clings to the plank, as the dying man clings to the last
hope of life? Are you combating with sin, hating the garment
spotted by the flesh, striving after and, in some degree, attaining
unto holiness? Then, be ye assured that your name is written in
heaven. If the Spirit of Christ has written the name of Christ, and
pencilled the image of Christ, however faintly traced and dimly
seen, upon your softened, believing, loving heart, doubt not the
fact that your name is enrolled in glory on the pages of that volume

in which divine love wrote it from eternity, and from which Christ our Captain will pronounce it when the great muster-roll is read in the last great day. Oh, mercy of mercies, to have a name written in heaven! Lord! write Thine own precious name upon my heart, and I will sing aloud of Thy righteousness all the day long.

Heaven, too, is the residence of the Elder Brother, and must therefore be the final home of all His brethren. How often, and with what emphasis of meaning, did Jesus associate Himself with His brethren in glory. *"That where I am, there ye may be also." "Father, I will that they also whom Thou hast given me be with me where I am, that they might behold my glory." "With Christ,"—"present with the Lord,"—"for ever with the Lord,"* were modes of expression by which Jesus and the sacred writers instructed and comforted the saints in the prospect of their departure. The return of Christ to heaven, His entrance within the veil, was as the Representative of His Church, as the First Born of His brethren. When He had found the *"pearl of great price,"*—His Church,—for the discovery and rescue of which He purchased the *"field"*—in this sense, and in this sense only, becoming the Saviour of the world—He returned in triumph to heaven, claiming and possessing it as the just reward of His sufferings, and as the fittest cabinet of the ransomed and priceless jewel. From Christ his Elder Brother not one of the brethren—the meanest and unworthiest—shall be separated. The family would be broken, the home circle would be incomplete, were a place vacant at the banquet which shall celebrate the return of every wanderer home to God. Oh, the rejoicing, oh, the merriment when all shall safely arrive at heaven! What blissful reunions, what joyful recognitions, what fond greetings, what mutual congratulations, what entrancing music will resound through the bowers, and reverberate through the high arches of heaven, when the whole family on earth and in heaven shall meet in glory! Is not this prospect worth living for, worth dying for? Is it not worth the struggle with sin, the battle with the world, the endurance of suffering, the light affliction, the cross, the moral, even the physical martyrdom which the gospel of Jesus involves? Yes! Christ our Elder Brother took the veritable nature of His brethren, wore it in poverty, suffering, and humiliation on earth; and then bore it to heaven as the first-fruits of that redeemed nature to be gathered home by the angel reapers at His coming. How did Joseph's soul yearn to have his brethren with him in Egypt, that they might see his greatness and be nourished at his side! Listen to the language of Joseph's spiritual Prototype. *"Father, I will that they also whom Thou hast given me be with me where I am, that they might BEHOLD MY GLORY."* What yearning of soul is here! what breathing of love! what power of will! *That* petition shall be answered! Until then how incessantly and intently is the Elder Brother occupied in our behalf. Every moment, every thought, every affection is engaged upon, and entwined with, our present and future well-being. For us Christ is praying, for us He is governing, for us He is waiting, and with us He is sympathising until His brethren are complete, and the last and least—the Benjamin of the family—is brought home to see His greatness, to share His glory, and to celebrate His praise. Who, with any true, experimental knowledge of Him, would not love with the intensest affection of his heart, serve with every power of his ransomed being, make any sacrifice, and die, if need be, a martyr's death for *such* a Brother? Are we wearing *His* nature, as He still wears *ours?* Are we growing more divine, as He is changelessly human? Are we not ashamed of Him, as He is not ashamed of us? Are we living a Christ-imitating, a Christ-exalting life, even as He once lived a man-abased, yet a man-saving life?

I can only further remark, that the expression, *"Our Father, which art in heaven,"* clearly describes heaven to be *the only befitting abode of the saints in glory.* Earth is not the proper realm for the holy ones. This world is indeed a school for the culture of our Christian graces, and a sphere for the exercise of Christian service, but here we have no abiding place. The moment a sinner is by grace transformed into a child of God he becomes a stranger here, an alien and a pilgrim. Heaven, henceforth, is the goal, the aspiration, the home of his spirit. God has provided and garnished a heavenly abode for the heavenly mind, a pure dwelling for the "pure in heart," a beauteous world for the beautiful in holiness. For this He is daily preparing you. All His providential dealings, and gracious operations; all your mental and spiritual exercises—

every tempest, every furnace, every temptation—God is employing to *prepare* you for the *prepared* place. Accept every stroke of His rod, every discipline of His hand, as bent on this mission of love. Blend every trial, every affliction, every rebuke of your Father with a sweet, sunny thought of heaven. *Suffering* and *glory* are united in golden links in the history of the saints. St Peter speaks of himself as a "witness of the SUFFERINGS of Christ, and *also a partaker of the* GLORY *which shall be revealed.*" And again, "*If we* SUFFER *with Him, we shall also* REIGN *with Him.*" Look, then, beyond the dark waters and the leaden skies which lie between you and the holy, peaceful coasts of glory; and let faith's eye often peer within the door opened in heaven, and behold the place where your weary spirit, erelong, will fold its drooping wing, smooth its ruffled plumage, lie down and rest upon the ineffable bosom of your glorified Lord. Thither they have arrived, and there they repose, who have out-sped us in the race, have reached the goal, and anticipate our coming. We mourn them not as lost, but as saved; not as far-sundered from us, but as nearer now than ever; not as wearing the sin-tainted and disfigured robe of the flesh, clasped with the girdle of suffering; but as clad with the holy, beautiful vestments of the Father's house, the glory-robe of heaven, all encircling and worshipping the Lamb that was slain.

> "Thus heaven is gathering, one by one, in its capacious breast,
> All that is pure and permanent, the beautiful and blest;
> The family is scatter'd yet, though of one home and heart,
> Part militant, in earthly gloom, in heavenly glory part.
> But who can speak the rapture when the circle is complete,
> And all the children, sunder'd now, before their Father meet?
> One fold, one Shepherd, one employ, one everlasting home:
> 'Lo, I come quickly.' Even so, amen, Lord Jesus, come!"*

This view of the celestial spirit of the Lord's Prayer is suggestive of many practical lessons. We are instructed in the first place to *look up* in prayer. The proper attitude of the mind in approaching God is a heaven-bent attitude. The whole soul should be in the

---

* Bickersteth.

ascent. When we draw near to our heavenly Father we must remember that, *He is in heaven.* Earth with its cares and ties, its sins and sorrows, must be left below. For the time being we professedly have exchanged, in our mental and spiritual flight, the terrestrial for the celestial—the communion of the saints who are on earth, for the higher communion of our Father who is in heaven. How consonant with this the experience of the psalmist! *"My voice shalt thou hear in the morning, O Lord; in the morning will I direct my prayer unto thee, and will LOOK UP."* Alas! how little is there in our experience of this *looking up* to God in trial, in trouble, in sin. We look *down*, we look to the right hand and to the left, and there is none to help, none to deliver, and we despond and despair. It is just because our eyes are earthward and not heavenward, manward and not Godward. What a tendency, too, is there to look within ourselves, and not from ourselves, through Jesus, up to our Father who is in heaven! We look at the darkness, at the vileness, at the barrenness, at the deadness of our hearts— absorbed in the profound contemplation of our own poverty, vileness, and unworthiness—rather than up to the loving, gracious, forgiving, paternal heart of God. But our whole Christian course must be a *looking up.* The more we look to God, and the less to our own selves and to man, the holier and the happier shall we be. The memorable intercessory prayer of our Great High Priest when on earth is thus introduced, *"And Jesus LIFTED UP his eyes unto heaven, and said, Father."* Such, too, has been the attitude of the Lord's people in all ages. *"Mine eyes,"* says David, *"are ever toward the Lord."* Thus, too, prayed Jehoshaphat, *"O our God, wilt thou not judge them? for we have no might against this great company that cometh against us; neither know we what to do: BUT OUR EYES ARE UPON THEE."* Then again the psalmist, *"Unto Thee lift I up mine eyes, O Thou that dwellest in the heavens. Behold, as the eyes of servants look into the hand of their masters, and as the eye of a maiden into the hand of her mistress, so our eyes wait upon the Lord our God until that he have mercy upon us."* Look up, then, tried believer! Look up, then, tempted saint! Look up, then, suffering child! Your help cometh whence your trouble came—*from above.* Affliction springeth not out of the ground, but is a Heaven-sent discipline; and from hence cometh the divine strength that will sustain, and the grace that will sanctify, and the love that will soothe. Oh, look up! Look up to Jesus, your Elder Brother, now appearing in the presence of God for you. Look up to the sun shining behind the clouds, to the rock towering above the billows; to Jesus, the Author, the Sustainer, the Finisher, and who, holding out the diadem, waits to be the Crowner, of your faith.

Another lesson we are taught by the celestial spirit of the Lord's Prayer is, *to seek heavenly blessings.* Our Father *is in heaven.* Naught but *heavenly* blessings should satisfy our desires. Earth's choicest are poor; its sweetest unsatisfying; its loveliest fading; its fondest passing away. If born again, God has given you a spiritual nature, which will be content only with spiritual things. The nutriment which nourishes the divine nature must be divine; the good which satisfies the heavenly nature must be heavenly. Our Father is in heaven, where our heart's treasure is, and from heaven our dearest blessings flow. *"If ye then be risen with Christ, seek those things* WHICH ARE ABOVE, *where Christ sitteth at the right hand of God."* Oh, let us be earnest after *heavenly* blessings! Deeply do we need them! The wants of the soul are infinitely greater, more important and imperious, than those of the body. Yet, how we pamper and gratify the one, and how we starve and neglect the other. How eager our pursuit of the earthly!—how languid our desires for the heavenly!—as though the body, so soon to return to its original element, were of greater moment than the soul, which never ceases to exist. Great is our need of heavenly blessings. We need more love to God, more conformity to Christ, more of the anointing of the Spirit; a fuller assurance of our conversion, and a higher enjoyment of a present salvation. We need more personal, heart-religion; more spiritual life; a walking in closer fellowship with the unseen and the eternal; and a more filial and confidential converse with God. Since, then, our Father is in heaven, prepared to send down from above every good and perfect gift; and since Christ, our Elder Brother, is at His right hand, prepared to endorse every petition, and to urge every request, let us *look up* through the blood of Christ, and importune God for that grace, and strength, and help, which will promote our heavenliness, and fit us all the more perfectly for heaven itself.

What, my reader, is the real state of your soul? What is your hope for the future? Which the destiny that awaits you—heaven or hell? In the one or the other you must spend your eternity. Nothing will be admitted into heaven but the heavenly, the holy, the pure. None enter its holy gate but those who have washed in the Lamb's blood, and are robed in the vestment of His righteousness. None enter there but those who love God, and have union with Christ, and are the temples of the Holy Ghost. Oh, decide the question now! Heaven and Hell begin upon earth. So real is their commencement, so unmistakable their evidence, every individual may arrive at a moral certainty as to which of the two he is speeding his way. Think of the joys of heaven, of the sorrows of hell! Think of the eternal glory, of the endless woe! Happy with Christ and the saints for ever, or for ever the companion and the associate of demons and the damned! Ground the weapons of your enmity against God, repent and believe in Jesus, and henceforth you will become a child of the HEAVENLY PARENT; your conversation in heaven; shedding around you the reflected purity and lustre of that world of holiness and glory in which the Father dwells, and into which, ere long, will be gathered and assembled, in domesticated union and eternal fellowship, the one family of God.

Children of the kingdom! repose, amid the weariness of your pilgrimage, upon the slopes of glory. Soon heaven will be reached— soon its golden spires, and sunlight dome, and towering turrets will burst upon your view—soon the portal will appear, and the pearl gate will expand upon its golden hinges to admit you to an innumerable company of angels, and to the spirits of just men made perfect, and to Jesus the Mediator, and to God the Judge of all. Your path through death's lone valley will be all light, shining with increasing effulgence unto the perfect day. It was a strangely-beautiful remark of a child, when asked how his little sister, who had lately died, went up to heaven, replied, "She put her foot *upon the sun,* and went up." Thus will ascend to glory every child of the light. Perhaps the spirit, in its celestial flight, will make the sun in the natural firmament a stepping-stone, from which it will spring into higher regions of glory. But, beyond all doubt, it will stand upon, and be clothed with, the divine "Sun of Righteousness," borne upon whose wings, and radiant with whose lustre, it will float away into the world of light and song, of bliss and immortality—and so shall it be for ever with the Lord!

> "What is a scene of glory? I would say,
> A Christian standing on the verge of heaven,
> One foot on earth, *another on the sun,*
> Standing sublime on Pisgah's lofty mount,
> Spreading his wings, and ready for his flight;
> Leaving earth's dim and shadowy things behind,
> Catching already on his heaven-bound soul
> The beams of that bright land to which he goes.
> Done with the world, its sorrows, and its cares,
> Its empty joys, and vain delusive hopes.
> Done with the world, its sufferings, and its sins,
> Its follies, and its frailties, and its fears.
> Done with the world, and entering upon heaven,
> With all its bright realities unseen
> By mortal eye, full opening to the gaze
> Of faith, so soon to be matured in sight.

> "The sight of Jesus bursting on the eye,
> The songs of angels floating on his ear;
> The palm of victory, the spotless robe,
> The crown of glory, and the golden harp,
> Unfolding to the eyes, that close on earth
> To open on the glorious things of heaven.
> Around him waving the celestial wings
> Of the angelic band, that waits to bear
> His parting spirit to its heavenly home.
> This is a scene of glory, in whose light
> The brightest scenes of earth grow dim and fade;
> The beams of this world's glory cease to shine,
> E'en as the morning sun puts out the stars."*

---

* Tough.

CHAPTER IV.

THE REVERENTIAL SPIRIT OF
THE LORD'S PRAYER.

"HALLOWED be Thy Name. "—MATT. vi. 9.

ATERNAL as the Name of God is, it yet is HOLY. Instructing us in the most intimate and confiding intercourse possible for man to hold with God—the intercourse of a *child*—our Lord yet sought to invest it with the profoundest reverence of the saint. In teaching us that God was our Father, He would also remind us that, *"holy and reverend is His name."* That, while our access to Him may be filial and trustful, it must also be holy and reverential—HALLOWING the name we address as FATHER. Who could teach us this truth as Christ taught it? He only could read the awful syllables of that divine name. It was *essentially* in Him. He had come from heaven with robes from which flowed the lustre of *holiness*. Back to the confines of that heaven He would lead us, by teaching us that it was the metropolis of our Father, and the great centre of purity. He knew how God's name was hallowed there. With what solemn strains it breathed from the harps of glorified saints! and with what trembling awe it dwelt upon the lips of Seraphim and Cherubim, as they cry, *"HOLY, HOLY, HOLY is the Lord of hosts!"* He had come down to make it as hallowed on earth as in heaven. Disarming our sinful mind of its natural dread of God, by teaching us to approach Him as our Father; and lest, through the depravity which taints and deforms all our holy things, there should arise a feeling or sentiment derogatory of the divine honour, our Lord touches as with a living ember from the altar of heaven's worship the lips of His disciples, and bids them say, "HALLOWED be Thy name." Thus did He unite in the act of prayer, *reverence* and *love:* reverence disarming love of undue familiarity, and love divesting reverence of servile awe. *"HALLOWED be Thy name."*

This petition may be considered as taking precedence in the Lord's Prayer, as it most properly should; since all other things must resolve themselves into the manifestation of the *divine glory.* The disciples are thus taught to pray that Jehovah's name might be hallowed. In other words, that His name might be *glorified.* It was worthy of the Great Teacher who had come to reveal His Father's glory, to place in the foreground of the blessings petitioned by the Church, *the glorifying of God,* as the first and the last great end we were to seek. As all things, all beings, and all events spring from the glory of God, so all terminate in His glory. It is a solemn truth that, saved or lost, all intelligent beings were made for God, and all shall result in the hallowing of His great and august name.

The Name of God is a word of awful and significant import. It is nothing less than God Himself. It is frequently employed to signify His being, sometimes His authority, and at other times His word and worship; but always resolves itself in God Himself. The grand view here presented of God is, His HOLINESS. Whatever perfections compose His name, those perfections are holy, and are to be hallowed and held in reverence by all His creatures. We are not, therefore, surprised to find with what solemnity of manner and emphasis of language God has revealed and guarded the sanctity of His name. *"Speak unto Aaron and to his sons, that they profane not* MY HOLY NAME *in those things which they hallow unto me, saith the Lord,"* (Lev. xxii. 2.) What an impressive illustration of the holiness of God is this! Here we are taught, that so holy is the Name of God—so holy is God Himself—that even in the very act, and at the very moment, of hallowing, we may unwittingly profane it! This the children of Israel might do by eating, while ceremoniously unclean, the offerings which the priests had sanctified. And the priests themselves, who bore the vessels of the sanctuary and presented the offerings of the people, might be ceremoniously unclean, and so defile, by their unhallowed touch, the vessel and the sacrifice. So truly and solemnly has Jehovah declared, "I will be SANCTIFIED in them that come nigh me, and before all the people I will be GLORIFIED." Is there no danger of our falling into a like sin? May we not wave before God a censer flaming with "strange fire," or present a sacrifice which our unwashed hands have tainted and marred? May we not offer to Him "*the blind, and the lame, and the diseased?*"—the dregs and drivellings of our talents, our property, and our time—offerings we should shrink from presenting to man,—*unholy* sacrifices presented to the holy, and *dead* sacrifices to the living Lord God? (Ponder seriously Mal. i. 7, 8.) How pertinent and impressive the charge addressed by God to the ministers of Christ's gospel, and to all employed in His service, "*Be ye* CLEAN *that bear the vessels of the Lord!*" Who can listen to these words of deep, solemn import— remembering the imperfections that have traced, the iniquities that have tainted, and the failures that have attended much that we have done for the Lord; the errors of judgment, the duplicity of heart, the self-seeking and man-pleasing; the languor of love, the luke-warmness of zeal, the admixture of unbelief; the unholy motive and idolatrous end which have attached to all our professedly holy doings; how little we have been influenced by love to Christ and actuated by glory to God,—who, I ask, can review all this, and not place his mouth in the dust in the solemn consciousness of having polluted and profaned God's holy name? What a heart-searching consideration this for both ministers and people! In engagements most holy, in services most spiritual, in communion most close, in offerings most costly, what need of vigilance, and self-examination, and prayer, lest we profane rather than hallow, insult rather than honour the Name of the Most High God! And when all is done,—when, from the holy altar of our God we retire to the solemn sanctuary of our chamber,—what need have we to prostrate ourselves before Him in confession, and repair to the blood-sprinkling of that great and merciful High Priest who has made an Atonement for His people, as well for their holy as for their unholy things! How strongly is this truth shadowed forth in the type of Aaron and the children of Israel. Speaking of the plate of pure gold put upon the forefront of Aaron's mitre, upon which was engraved "HOLINESS TO THE LORD," this was the divine instruction, *"And it shall be upon Aaron's forehead, that Aaron may bear* THE INIQUITY OF THE HOLY THINGS, *which the children of Israel shall hallow in all their holy gifts; and it shall be always upon his forehead, that they may be accepted before the Lord,"* (Exod. xxviii. 38.) Solemnly instructive truth! The Lord Jesus Christ, our true Aaron, has in His own person made atonement for the *"iniquity of the holy things"* of His saints; and now in glory, upon that head once crowned with thorns, that

"Head so full of bruises,"

is still worn the mitre which insures the purification from all taint, and the divine acceptance of our persons and offerings as *holy* sacrifices unto the most holy Lord God.

It is a most instructive view of the subject of this chapter to mark the profound sanctity in which God regards His own name—which is nothing less than a holy regard of Himself. He is said to *be jealous* of it. "Thus saith the Lord God, I will be *jealous for my holy name,"* (Ezek. xxxix. 25.) Jealous of its divinity, jealous of its sanctity, jealous of its honour. Jealousy in the fallen creature is an infirmity and a sin; but jealousy in the holy Lord God is a divine and holy perfection. Think of this, you who despise that name, you who forget it, you who refuse to acknowledge it, you who lightly regard and profanely use it—remember that God is jealous of its honour, and will by no means clear the guilty who trample it beneath their unhallowed feet. "*I, the Lord thy God, am a* JEALOUS GOD." See, too, the motive-power with God which His great name supplies. "Thus saith the Lord God, I do not this for your sake, O house of Israel, *but for mine holy name's sake."* For the credit, for the glory of His holy name He does it. What will He not do for His name's sake? From what difficulty will He not deliver you, from what temptation save you, from what want rescue you, and what good thing withhold if we but plead in believing prayer the honour, the glory of His great and holy name? See how Joshua pleaded it—"And what wilt Thou do *with Thy great name?*" Such, too, is the power belonging to the name of JESUS! Most imperfectly are we acquainted with its preciousness on earth, its prevalence in heaven. What suppliant will not the Father accept, what supplication will He not grant, presented in the name of Christ? What sinner will He not receive, and what sin will He not pardon, for the sake of that name which is above every name, the incense of which fills heaven with its fragrance? Jesus saith, "Whatsoever ye shall ask the Father in *my name,* He will give it you." How divinely and touchingly, too, has God associated His name with the lowliest grace in the soul. *"Thus saith the lofty One that inhabiteth eternity, WHOSE NAME IS HOLY, I dwell in the high and holy place, with him also that is of a contrite and humble spirit."* Never did a soul shelter itself beneath the awful name of God with a warrant more divine, or with a welcome more cordial, than he who approaches it in a penitent, contrite, and humble spirit. Never was its holy and solemn shield thrown around a sinner so completely and so lovingly as him. O Lord! withhold what gifts, refuse what blessing, or take away what good Thou mayest, grant me graciously the contrite and humble spirit, overshadowed by the love, the sanctity, and the power of Thy paternal name!

And see how God notices the hallowing of His name by His people. Speaking of Levi, God says, *"My covenant was with him of life and peace; and I gave them to him for the fear wherewith he feared Me, and was afraid before MY NAME,"* (Mal. ii. 5.) Who that understands in any degree the solemn import, and realises the divine holiness of God's name, will not fear and reverence it? But is this hallowing of God's name a sentiment deep and practical even among some who would startle at the charge of profaning it? Are we not often betrayed into the use of it thoughtlessly, irreverently, and needlessly? And may not in our ordinary, and even our religious phraseology sometimes be traced a degree of profanity, unintentional and unsuspected by ourselves, yet not the less chargeable with the sin of taking God's name in vain? What exclamations of surprise more common to many individuals than these: —"God bless me!"— "My God!"—"Good God!"—"Good gracious!"—"A Godsend!"—"God knows!"—"Good heavens!"—a phraseology irreverent and undevout, infringing closely upon the third command of the divine decalogue, *"Thou shalt not take the NAME of the Lord thy God IN VAIN; for the Lord will not hold him guiltless that taketh His name in vain."* And will not this remark apply with equal appropriateness and force to the heedless and flippant manner in which the National Anthem of England is frequently quoted and sung? Do we not too frequently forget that this patriotic and spirit-stirring composition, unsurpassed for its sublimity and pathos, is a solemn PRAYER addressed to Heaven? that it is a nation's invocation to the Most High God, on behalf of its earthly sovereign, blended with that dread Name which breathes in trembling awe from the lips of Seraphim and Cherubim? With what profound reverence, then, should it be ever quoted, and with what devout feeling should it be ever sung! When referring to it in ordinary conversation, would it not be more reverential to quote it as the "National Anthem," rather than be betrayed into a flippant and irreverent mention of that Divine Being with whose great name the prayer is associated? That subject's heart is the most loving and loyal to an earthly sovereign which enshrines the profoundest sentiment of affection and reverence for the Divine. From his heart of hearts will every true Christian in the realm send up to heaven his devout and fervent prayer in its widest compass of meaning, *"God SAVE the Queen!"* Examples of the solemn reverence in which God's name has been held by individuals and nations are not wanting. It is recorded of Locke, the great logician, that he never used the name of God without uncovering his head. And it is well known to those who have travelled in Turkey, that a Muslim will never tread upon a piece of paper lest perchance the Divine Name should be imprinted upon it. A diviner philosophy than Locke's, and a purer faith than the Mohammedan's, teaches us reverentially to fear and devoutly to use the name of God Most High.

Under this head, the reverence for which I plead, constrains me to place all species of *levity on the solemn subject of religion.*

Nothing more quickly or truly indicates an irreverent and undevout mind than this. The individual that can provoke a smile, or indulge in an *esprit,* or shape a witticism at the expense of what is divine and sacred, is undevout indeed. He that can treat wantonly any religious subject, who can speak lightly of prayer, turn the Bible into a jest-book, and interlard secular conversation with religious phraseology or Scripture language in sport, may well pause in heart-searching thought, ere he breathe to Heaven the solemn petition—*"Hallowed be Thy name."* Will the great God hold such an irreverent and profane mind guiltless?

Let me proceed to show in what way God has Himself hallowed His own name. From the earliest revelation of His will, God has been intent upon this great matter—the vindication of the holiness and supremacy of His great name. His entire work of creation has been to make His name—which is Himself—known and renowned in the earth. All nature testifies to its existence, illustrates its power, and reflects its glory. Bold unblushing atheist! thou art rebuked and confounded by the heavens above thee and by the earth beneath thee. Creation, in its countless wonders and beauties, witnesses for its Maker and hymns His praise; whilst thou, His intelligent and deathless creature, in the depravity of thy heart dost boldly declare, *"There is no God!"* or, in the deeper depravity of thy life exclaimest, *"No* God for me!" How wilt thou tremble in the last dread day! As these heavens are rolled up in a scroll, and the elements melt with fervent heat, and the earth passes away, they will do homage to the power and the fiat of their Creator; whilst thou wilt stand at His dread bar convicted, sentenced, and condemned for the crime of having sought to efface His being, His name, His glory from the universe. Believer in Christ! read the name of God in the works and wonders of creation! Thy Father in heaven made them all, thy Redeemer moulded them all, the sanctifying Spirit quickened them all, and all testify to the power and wisdom and goodness of Him who permits you in filial love to call Him—"Father!"

God has hallowed His name *in His revealed Word.* I have already fortified this statement by quotations from inspired truth.

It has been shown with what distinctness of revelation and solemnity of manner God has unveiled and guarded the holiness and greatness of His name. *"Thou hast magnified Thy Word above all Thy name."* That is, God has put a greater glory upon His Word because that Word is a clearer revelation of Himself, than He has upon any other manifestation of His name. Creation confounds atheism; but revelation, a clearer manifestation of God, resolves conjecture into certainty, and doubt into assurance. So that the revealed Word of God is a greater magnifying of His name than any other illustration of its divinity. This, clearly, is the meaning of the passage, *"Thou hast magnified Thy Word above all Thy name"*—*i. e.,* above every other manifestation of Thy name. To deny, then, the truth of the Bible, to throw suspicion upon its integrity, or to tamper in any degree, or with any part of revealed truth, is an act of profanity against Jehovah, the guilt of which is only paralleled by its punishment. The Bible is true, or it is not true it is wholly inspired, or it is not at all inspired. "It is the Bible, or it is no Bible."* To suppose that God, all whose works are finished and complete, would communicate an imperfect revelation of His mind and will to man; that He would construct and preserve, through all ages of the world and through all the changes of time, a book partly divine and partly human, partly apocryphal and partly gospel, in which falsehood and truth were closely and strangely intermixed, is to suppose that the only work He has left imperfect is His master-work of all—that which was intended to be the most complete and finished revelation of Himself; and thus to weaken all our convictions of God's perfection, and to falsify all our belief of His goodness. The modern assaults of scepticism upon the Bible have called forth a host of able and ardent defenders of its truth. I am, however, not a little apprehensive that even in the defence of the Bible some of its honest and zealous champions may not have started theories of inspiration as perplexing to the minds of the unlearned friends of the Bible, as involving unguarded and undesigned concessions to its foes. But, setting aside these various

---

* Dr Chalmers.

hypotheses—what inspiration is, and what it is not—how far the plenary, the dynamical, the human element extends—the humble believer will take his stand upon the divine averment, which no reasoning has yet been able to overthrow, that, "*ALL SCRIPTURE is given by INSPIRATION OF GOD;*" that, "*holy men of old spoke as they were moved by the Holy Ghost;*" and thus he will receive the Bible as divine, as the truth of God, as the whole truth of God, and as nothing but the truth of God. This may be thought a short and easy method of disposing of the whole question, but we believe it to be a perfectly logical and safe one. There is no *via media* with regard to inspiration. It admits of no compromise, allows of no classification, submits to no analysis. The Bible is wholly divine, or it is not divine at all. It is not enough to say that it *contains* the word of God; *it is* the Word of God. To affirm that this part is inspired, and that the other is not; to teach that this book or chapter or verse is of man, and the rest is of God, is a solemn, a perilous trifling with that Book which Jehovah has exalted above all His name. If God smote the men of Bethshemesh, fifty thousand three score and ten, because that, with profane eye, they peered into the ark, think you that He will hold him guiltless who denies the truth, impugns the integrity, or tampers with the sanctity of the divine ark of His revealed Word?

But even, where the truth of the Bible is fully received, may there not exist on some occasions a tendency to deal lightly with God's Word, closely approximating a profane handling of its contents? In this light must be regarded all flippant quotations of Scripture, all attempts to perpetrate a pun, or to give utterance to jest or witticism, at the expense of the dignity and sanctity of God's holy Volume. Not such was David's spirit. His language was, "*My heart STANDETH IN AWE of Thy word.*" Princes were banded against him, but he heeded not their persecutions nor stood in awe of their power. But he had a high regard, and holy reverence, and a devout affection for God's Word. He stood in awe of it,—in awe of its divinity, of its revelations, of its holiness, of Him whose word it was! How low must be the spiritual state of that religious professor, how irreverent the mind, how earthly the heart, that can deal lightly with the Bible, that can treat it as a common book, as the record of men, and not, as it is in truth, the Word of God !* What says the Divine Author of the Scriptures? *"To that man will I look, even unto him who is of a humble and a contrite spirit, and who* TREMBLETH AT MY WORD.*"* It is a distinctive mark of the truly regenerate mind that it stands in awe of God's Word. "I would advise you all that come to the reading or hearing of this book, which is the Word of God, the most precious jewel and most holy relic that remaineth upon earth, that ye bring with you the fear of God, and that ye do it with all due reverence, and use your knowledge thereof, not to vain-glory of frivolous disputation, but to the honour of God, increase of virtue, and edification both of yourselves and others."† Oh that the Word of God may be increasingly precious to our souls! All other writings in comparison are diluted and insipid, and fail to meet our case. The knowledge of sin sweetens it, the season of affliction explains it, the time of adversity endears it, the voice of the rod enforces it, the mercy, loving-kindness, and faithfulness of the Lord confirm our faith in its truth, while the assaults of its foes and the treachery of its friends but make it all the more precious to our hearts. *"How sweet are thy words unto my taste! yea, sweeter than honey to my mouth!"* *"Thy word is very pure, therefore thy servant loveth it."*

> "Lord, I have made Thy word my choice,
>   My lasting heritage;
> These shall my warmest powers rejoice,
>   My warmest thoughts engage.

---

* *"Jest not with the two-edged sword of God's Word.* Will nothing please thee to wash thy hands in but the font? or to drink healths in but the church-chalice? And know that the whole art is learned at the first admission, and profane jests come without calling. . . . Dangerous it is to wit-wanton it with the majesty of God. Wherefore, if without thine intention, and against thy will, by chance-meddling, thou hittest Scripture in thy ordinary discourses, yet fly to the city of refuge, and pray God to forgive thee."—THOMAS FULLER.

† Cranmer.

"I'll read the histories of Thy love,
　　And keep Thy laws in sight,
While through Thy promises I roam
　　With ever fresh delight.

"'Tis a broad land of wealth unknown,
　　Where springs of life arise
Seeds of immortal bliss are sown,
　　And hidden glory lies.

"The best relief that mourners have,
　　It makes our sorrows blest;
Our fairest hopes beyond the grave,
　　And our eternal rest."

But nowhere has God so hallowed His great and holy Name as *in the Lord Jesus Christ.* In the words addressed by Jehovah to the children of Israel, in reference to the Angel who guided their journeyings, there is a remarkable shadowing forth of this truth. Thus we read—*"Behold, I send an Angel before thee, to keep thee in the way, and to bring thee into the place which I have prepared. Beware of Him, and obey His voice, provoke Him not; for He will not pardon your transgressions: for My name is in Him,"* (Exod. xxiii. 20, 21.) Of whom does God here speak, but of the Lord Jesus Christ, the uncreated Angel—the Angel of God's presence, who was with the Israelites at the receiving of the law in Mount Sinai— who saved and redeemed them, and carried them all the days of old, and against whom they rebelled, and whom they tempted in the wilderness. That this Angel was no less a being than Christ, is manifest. He alone, as God, possessed the prerogative of pardoning sin, the exercise or the withholding of which this Angel possessed. It would be absurd to say that He would not pardon, were not the power held in His hands of exercising this divine prerogative. Thus, then, this Angel whom the Israelites were to follow and obey, was none other than Christ. Now, God's Name was in Christ—His divine Name—His paternal Name—His pardoning Name—His gracious Name—His Name of "Love." It is in the light of this truth we understand the words of our intercessory High Priest's memorable prayer when on earth, *"I have manifested* THY NAME *unto the men whom Thou gavest Me out of the world. I have declared unto them* THY NAME." Nowhere has God made His Name so conspicuous, glorious, and precious as *in Jesus.* It is true, I breathe its fragrance in the scented air, see its beauty in the vernal landscape, adore its wisdom in the heavens above me; but I am conscious of its power, and taste its love, and behold its glory alone in Christ I *behold* it in nature, but I *feel* it in Jesus. It is only by faith in Jesus I properly read the Name of God. The works of creation, multiform and beautiful, are but the syllables of God's Name—His Name abbreviated. But in the person and work of the Lord Jesus, His Name is written in full, and with His own hand—JEHOVAH JESUS. Our Lord's whole life was a continuous sanctifying of His Father's Name. Everywhere, and in every act, He acknowledged its divinity, upheld its authority, vindicated its sanctity, magnified and illustrated its greatness. God's Name was in Him; and the solemn consciousness of being the sacred depository of so great, holy, and awful a treasure, invested with the beauty and perfumed with the fragrance of holiness, every thought, word, and act of His life. His obedience to God's holy law, His zeal for His Father's honour, His jealousy of His Father's glory, His full redemption of the Church, entrusted to His hands by God, was a living comment on the petition He daily taught, *"Hallowed be Thy Name."* Reader, beware of Him, and obey Him, for God's great and holy Name is in Him! You approach not a mere creature, you deal not with a finite being in your transactions with the Lord Jesus Christ. Beware of Him! It is not a human Name you profane, it is not a created being you deny, it is not a subordinate authority you denounce, when you deny His Deity, reject His Atonement, and trample His truth and claims to your love, faith and obedience, in the dust. You tear the robe of dignity from an infinite being; you pluck the crown of royalty from a kingly brow; you trample in the dust the sacrificial work of a Divine Redeemer. Oh, beware of His anger, beware of His power, lest, at last, you be numbered among those who will hide themselves in the dens and in the rocks of the mountains, and exclaim, *"Fall on us and hide us from the face of Him that sitteth on the throne, and from the wrath of the Lamb, for the great day of His wrath is come, and who shall be able to stand?"* But you who are hidden in this Rock need not dread that day; <u>for the Name of Jehovah Jesus will then be your strong tower, into which you shall run and be safe.</u> *Upon* the Rock, and *within* the Rock, you need not fear that it will fall upon you and grind you to powder. You have contemplated God's great Name as it flashed in the lightning and reverberated in the thunder of Mount Sinai, and you have been petrified with fear. Approach Mount Calvary, and read God's Name, written in crimson letters upon the cross, and you will dissolve into love. Believe in Christ, and the *"peace of God, which passeth all understanding,"* will diffuse its divine serenity through your soul. You are not come unto the mount that burneth with fire, nor unto blackness, and darkness, and tempest; but you are come to JESUS, the Mediator of the new covenant, and to the blood of sprinkling, and grace will hide you there while His judgments pass you by.

<u>God hallows His Name in His dealings with His saints.</u> In some <u>of those dealings clouds and darkness may veil the brightness and tenderness of His name.</u> "Verily, thou art a God that hidest thyself." Nevertheless, profoundly dark and inexplicably mysterious as His way often is with His people, His gracious Name of "Father," remains unchanged and unchangeable. His very Name is a pledge of covenant faithfulness, *"The Lord will not forsake His people, for His great NAME'S sake."* <u>He might find ample reason to justify His abandonment of them in their own inconstancy and unfaithfulness, rebellions and backslidings; but because of His own name He will never cast them off.</u> That name binds Him to the fulfilment of every covenant promise, to the protection of His Church in all her history; to His presence with His people in all their sufferings, trials and wants. So great, so holy, so sacred to Jesus is it, that for His honour and glory He will never leave nor forsake His people. <u>Plead this truth in believing prayer when His providences appear to contravene His promises; when He hides Himself, and you cannot perceive Him; when His frowns veil His smiles; when the waters come in upon your soul, and you cry, *"Lord! save, I perish."*</u> Then

The Lord's Prayer 73

cling to this divine, this potent name; for its holiness, its faithfulness, its honour, pledge Him never to forsake you. *"The* NAME *of the Lord is a strong tower; the righteous runneth into it, and is safe."* Speak we of God's dealings in the forgiveness of His people's sin? Again, His Name is hallowed: *"I, even I, am He that blotteth out thy transgressions for mine own sake,"* (Isa. xliii. 23.) In other words, for His Name's sake, which stands for His whole being. Thus may the saints, burdened with guilt, stricken with sorrow for sin, approach God with holy boldness, suing out their renewed forgiveness, since, not for their sakes, but for His own sake—for His great Name's sake—God will blot out their sins, and will remember their transgressions no more. Speak we of the dreary path the children of the light often tread? Still is God's Name hallowed by their trust in it. *"Who is among you that feareth the Lord, that obeyeth the voice of his servant, that walketh in darkness, and hath no light? let him trust in the* NAME *of the Lord, and stay upon his God."* What a strong staff to lean upon—what a sure lamp to trust to in one's dreary way, is the Name of Jehovah! expressive of every divine perfection, and filling the soul with ineffable delight.

But the question now occurs, How is God's name to be hallowed? Before, however, we supply the answer, let there be a deep and solemn conviction of the fact, that our Father's great and holy Name is everywhere dishonoured. The sin of *profanity* is one of the great social evils of society. The irreverent and undevout use of God's dread Name confronts us everywhere, and on all occasions. It may truly be said that, *"because of* SWEARING *the land mourneth."* What place is entirely exempt from the existence and guilt of this sin? In the *pulpit,* occupied by the prophet who prophesies lies in God's Name—His *Name is profaned.* In the *sanctuary,* where heartless prayer, and vain repetitions, and ritualistic forms take the place of pure, spiritual, and holy worship—*God's Name is profaned.* By the *press,* in much of the popular literature of the day—the story, the narrative, the song—*God's Name is profaned.* On the boards of the theatre, in the orchestra of the opera, in the "tuneful quire" of the sacred oratorio, in which divine worship is mimicked, and the dread Name of the Divine Object of worship is undevoutly, and even defiantly used—*God's Name is profaned.* In the *witness box,* where stands the man who calls the God of truth and justice to sanction his deception and perjury—*God's Name is profaned.* In the desecration of His holy day—the Sunday newspaper, the Sabbath-train, the selling and the buying, the casting of accounts, the writing of letters, the making of calls, the forsaking of God's sanctuary, and lightly regarding the ministry of His word—*God's Name is profaned.* In view of these wilful and flagrant breaches of His law, may not God, in truth, exclaim— "My NAME continually, every day, is BLASPHEMED!" How should the children of God sigh and cry for this great sin! But we turn to a brighter view of the subject:—

How may the children of God honour and hallow their Father's Name?

That we cannot make it more holy is obvious; and yet we may *hallow* it. First, by a deepening sense of its holiness. We cannot grow in a knowledge of God without growing in a conviction of His holiness. And it is no light attainment in our spiritual training for heaven. Superficial views of the divine holiness irresistibly lead to superficial views of sin. What an exceeding sinful thing does sin appear when placed in the searching light of God's infinite holiness! *"Thou hast set our iniquities before Thee, our secret sins in the light of Thy countenance,"* (Ps. xc. 8.) "The light of Thy countenance!" Terrible mirror! seen through this divine medium, how real, how dark those hidden sins of the heart appear, of which no being but God is cognisant! Faithful glass! reflected from its divine lens—the infinitely holy perfections of Jehovah—we startle at that, the sin of which we had not seen, the very existence of which we had not suspected. And but for the cleansing of Christ's blood, and the shelter of His arms, whither could we fly? Thus we hallow our Father's Name by a growing sight of its infinite purity, and by a deepening hatred and abhorrence of our sin. This deep conviction of its holiness will constrain us to guard its sanctity with the most jealous vigilance. How fearful and widespread is the sin of profanity! Do not multitudes, many professing and calling themselves Christians, *"blaspheme that worthy Name by which ye are called?"* Are we duly affected by this fact? Do we stand up in vindication of God's honour? With what filial affection and wakeful jealousy a loving, dutiful child will shield the honour of his father, and vindicate the purity of his mother's name—that name bequeathed to them in death an unsullied and precious legacy. Could such a child listen, but with burning indignation, and with almost murderous resentment, to the slander and the insult which envy and revenge, falsely and maliciously, should cast upon a memory so sacred and so dear? And shall the name of an inferior and erring parent be more sacredly reverenced and vigilantly guarded than the worthy Name by which we are called— the Name of our Father in heaven? Let us see that we be ever faithful to God, loyal to Christ, by vindicating our Father's honour, by meekly yet firmly rebuking the swearer and checking the profane. Remind them that God will not regard as venial lapses the unhallowed intermixture with our conversation and our literature His Name in that day when He shall arraign the world He once made and will then judge. Ye profane! ye guard with the most jealous and sleepless care the integrity and the honour of your own sinful, paltry name, while in your story and your jest, your falsehood and your frivolous talk, ye profane and dishonour the dread Name of the Father in heaven—the holy Lord God Almighty. How shall ye escape the damnation of hell?

(2) We may hallow God's Name *by bringing it into the daily exercise of faith*. It is our Father's Name, carved in the humanity of His Son. In the daily walk and battle of faith, we are to make constant use of it. The knowledge of it is to deepen our reverence, inspire our love, encourage our trust, comfort our hearts, and embolden our supplications at the throne of grace. We are constantly, and in everything, with godly fear and filial confidence, to deal with the Name of our Father in heaven. *"They that know Thy Name will put their trust in Thee." "Do Thou for me, O God, for Thy Name's sake." "For Thy Name's sake, pardon mine iniquity, for it is great." "Quicken me, O Lord, for Thy Name's sake." "Unite my heart to fear Thy Name." "For Thy Name's sake, lead me and guide me." "I*

have remembered Thy Name in the night." *"Bring my soul out of prison, that I might praise Thy Name." "Thy Name [Jesus] is as ointment poured forth."* Thus do the children of God hallow their Father's Name by running into it, pleading it, casting themselves upon it in all times of trial and difficulty and need. By pureness, by faith, by love unfeigned, ever remembering that God's divine and holy Name is in us, we are to move amid the darkness and the taint of the world as a living, flaming censer, shedding around us the light, and wafting above us the sweet odour, of our sanctity—so hallowing God's great Name.

(3) *By a meek, submissive spirit, under the discipline of our Father's correcting hand,* we hallow His Name. So long as there is any collision of our will with His; so long as we cherish the secret feeling of rebellion and hostility to His dealings, we cease to sanctify it. I believe that the highest honouring of God's Name, on the part of the children of His adopting grace and love is, in saying from the heart, *"Thy will, not mine, be done."* Suffering child of God! afflicted saint of the Most High! in what a favourable position are you now placed for magnifying and hallowing your Father's great Name! Oh, what lustre the meek and humble, quiet and silent yielding of your spirit to Him may shed upon its paternal holiness! How may you glorify God in these fires! How may you magnify Christ's Name before the world, endear it to the saints, and glorify it in the eyes of angels, by meekly bowing your head in the storm, exclaiming, *"The cup which my Father hath given me, shall I not drink it?"*

And, most surely we hallow it *by a full, implicit, believing trust in the Name, and person, and work of Jesus.* There can be no proper hallowing of God's Name, while there is any slighting of the Lord Jesus Christ. The Father will have us honour the Son, most beloved of His heart, *even as* we honour Him. *"He that honoureth not the Son, honoureth not the Father, who hath sent Him."* We cannot entertain too exalted views of the Lord Jesus. Our great danger is, the reverse of this. In honouring the Son, we hallow the Name of the Father. To Jesus we are to repair, as to the great Depositary of the Father's fulness—divine and mediatorial. *"In Him dwelt all the fulness of the godhead bodily"*—Essentially. *"It pleased the Father that in Him all fulness should dwell"*— Mediatorially. Now, we glorify God by living a life of faith upon this supply, by drawing largely from this fulness, by heavy drafts upon this infinite sufficiency of merit and grace and strength and love. <u>Every sin you take to Christ's blood—every corruption you take to His grace—every want you take to His supply—every sorrow you take to His heart—every burden you hang upon His arm—you impart a deeper emphasis to this sublime petition, *"Hallowed be Thy Name."*</u> How endeared to our heart should the Saviour be, since the Father's Name is revealed and glorified through Him, and by us in Him! We must ever keep in mind the grand central truth of the Bible, that Christ is the great Revealer of God. All other religion but this is sentimental and unsaving. It is not seeing the glory of God in the panorama of nature that will save, but seeing the *"glory of God in the face of Jesus Christ."* It is not even seeing God *through* Christ, but it is seeing God IN Christ, *"God manifest in the flesh."* By creation, I know that there is a God; but in the God-man, the man Christ Jesus, I see what God is—how holy, how gracious, how merciful, how compassionate, how loving! How near does this bring God to us, and us to God, and by a medium that links Him in sympathy with all that I am as human; while it unites me in grace and glory with all that He is as Divine! We see what the life of the believer should be—a daily magnifying the Name of the Lord Jesus; for in doing we hallow the Name of our Father in heaven. It is a solemn thought that the Name of Christ is in every child of God. Our character is more sacred, our position more responsible, our dignity more exalted than the angels' in heaven. We are temples of God, through Christ and by the Spirit. How closely entwined, then, should the Lord Jesus be with our every thought, and feeling, and act! How should we hallow His illustrious and precious Name, by conformity to His precepts, obedience to His commandments, consecration to His service. <u>Christ should be associated with all we are, with all we have, and with all we do. For us to live should be Christ</u>. The oneness of Christ and the believer admits of no divided interests. Christ has taken us into union with His person, identifying us with all the blessings of His grace, and with all the glories of His kingdom. We should, therefore, be jealous and watchful lest any object, or creature, or self-seeking, should insinuate itself between Christ and our unreserved dedication. If Christ maintains intact this undivided supremacy in our souls, all other objects will subordinate themselves to Him, and He will be all in all. Our talents, our property, our rank, our time, our whole being, will be the spontaneous offering of love laid at His feet; and the *"name of' our Lord Jesus Christ will be glorified in us, and we in Him,"* and so God's great Name will be hallowed. Nor will it terminate here. There awaits every disciple and confessor of Christ, the reward of grace. At the glorious appearing of our Lord, the imperfect service we did for His cause—the little suffering we endured for His Name—the short period we bore His cross, will brighten into a crown of life, and deepen into a sea of joy, and bloom into a paradise of glory, and expand into an eternity of bliss. *"Unto you that fear My Name shall the Sun of righteousness arise with healing in His wings."*

It is a truth as inevitably certain as it is overwhelmingly solemn, that God's great Name will be hallowed by all beings, either in mercy or in vengeance. It must be so! Not the shadow of a shade will rest upon the divine glory of that dread, that holy Name. The love it expresses, the holiness it contains, the justice it embodies, the power it wields, will be displayed either in the salvation or in the condemnation of every being of the human race. It will be glorified in its mercy or in its justice by every saint in paradise, and by every sinner in tophet. The voluptuous Dives, sitting in state and feasting on his good things; and the ulcerated Lazarus, pining in want at his gate, fed with the crumbs that fell from his table, will wake the echoes of that Name through eternity—the one in groans of despair piercing the dark regions of hell, the other in anthems of praise, floating in sweetest music over the sunlight plains of heaven. Justice or Mercy must be the doom, and will be the theme of all. What, my reader, will *yours* be? Deem it not difficult to decide. Emigrants to a foreign land know to what port they are bound. The voyagers to eternity may know, to a moral certainty, whither they are going. Heaven and Hell commence on earth. Are you among those who do not hallow God's Name?

Responding to this petition, it may be, in the heartless devotions of each Sabbath, do you yet, in the transactions of daily life, regard it with indifference, or in social intercourse breathe it with profanity? Think you that that tongue which has taken His great and holy Name in vain; that those lips which impurity has defiled, and oaths have blistered, can unite in the holy music of heaven? Impossible! There remains but one doom for the profane—he goes "to his own place!" Decide scripturally, decide solemnly, decide now. Heaven or Hell await the issue!

CHAPTER V.

THE PROPHETICAL SPIRIT OF
THE LORD'S PRAYER.

"Thy kingdom come."—MATT. vi. 10.

T is the remark of an eminent Christian and accomplished scholar,* that such is the simplicity and fulness of the Lord's Prayer, it suits alike the lips of childhood in the first lispings of devotion, as the tongue of the matured saint in his most rapt worship. The petition to which the present chapter directs our thoughts strikingly illustrates this observation of the German divine. *Thy kingdom come!* Truly here are shallows for the lamb, and depths for the elephant. In regarding this petition as expressing the prophetical spirit of the Lord's Prayer, let it not be supposed that a full exposition of the words in all their bearings will come within the scope of our immediate design. All that we can present is a 'gentle crush' of this rich cluster gathered from the fruitful vine beneath whose shade we sit, distilling into the reader's cup a portion only of the sweet wine of the kingdom which it contains. Prophecy takes a wide range of inquiry, since it includes all revealed truth—truth illustrated in the past history of the Church, and truth to be illustrated in its future; events fulfilled, and events yet to be accomplished. And as our chief design in this work is the spiritual edification of the believing Church of God, we

---

* Stier.

shall keep this object as closely as possible in view in our brief opening up of these words—"THY KINGDOM COME."

"I am a great King, saith the Lord of hosts." His empire is commensurate with His greatness. The mind fails to grasp the extent of His sovereignty. We must contract our views of God himself ere we can circumscribe His government. Were it like earth's monarchies, limited and measurable, we might expect to find God less strict and vigilant in His administrations, less imperial in His sovereignty, and less severe and inexorable in His laws. But His empire, like His being, is illimitable. Stretching from world to world, beyond all known or imaginable limits; wielding His sceptre over countless myriads of intelligent, responsible, and immortal beings, all subject to the same laws, all held by the same moral obligations, all accountable to the same absolute and almighty Sovereign, who does not see the grandeur and feel the force of Jehovah's declaration, "I am a GREAT KING, saith the Lord of hosts!" Let us contemplate the several parts of His empire.

The *kingdom of nature* is His. Every particle of matter owns Him its Maker, and yields obedience to Him its Sovereign. The sun, the moon, the stars, the earth, the water, the wind are His subjects, doing His will, and obeying His commands. All are the servants of our Father in heaven. And since the believer is at peace with God through Christ, all God's works are at peace with him. With what lustre will this truth beam forth in the millennial age of the Church! The present economy of the Christian must ever expose him to the consequences of the fall. The pestilence rising from a distant shore, the simoom sweeping across the desert, the storm lashing the ocean, the lightning scathing, the earthquake entombing, the blight and the mildew destroying, must frequently be destructive agents employed by God in gathering His righteous ones to Himself. But when the New Heaven and the New Earth shall have come—sin annihilated, the curse repealed, death abolished, and all its messengers destroyed,—God will reconcile all things to Himself and all things will be reconciled to man. The enemies of man will cease, because man himself will cease to be the enemy of God. For this millennial age the earnest expectation of the creature waiteth, for this the sons of God sigh, and for this the souls beneath the altar cry, "How long, O Lord, holy and true?"

The *kingdom of providence* is His. The world is not, as some would have us believe, a fatherless world. To suppose that God would create a planet like this, people it with intelligent and responsible beings, and then leave it without a government—which would be if left to its own—contradicts all our cherished ideas of His wisdom, and goodness, and power. No world, when the annals of all worlds shall be unfolded, will present a history like this. The creation of man in the Divine likeness, his fall in Adam, his redemption by Christ, the bringing to heaven *"a people afore prepared unto glory,"* will be the wonder, the study, and the praise of saints and angels through eternity, and will contribute a revenue of glory to Jehovah endless as His being. Over this world, thus occupying so distinguished and marvellous a place in the history of the universe, God reigns. All empires exist by His will, or fall at His command. All accomplish His purpose and execute His behest. *"His kingdom ruleth over all."* The atheism of the unrenewed mind would banish God from the government of His own empire, and reduce the world to a state of helpless orphanage. Little do the wise and the prudent of this world consider that what they vauntingly term "the laws of nature," and "the course of nature," is but one continuous administration of an infinitely wise and an all-beneficent Providence. If we heard a musical instrument of countless strings pouring forth the most exquisite harmony, should we not infer that some skilful hand had swept them? Or, if we saw an army on the battle-field moving in the most perfect order and achieving the most heroic exploits, should we not infer that it was under the supreme control of one masterly mind? Or, if we saw a building spring from the base into an edifice the most beautiful and symmetrical, should we not acknowledge the hand of an architect? Or, if we saw a richly-laden vessel from an opposite hemisphere conducted accurately and safely across the ocean into port, should we not infer that its course was guided by some skilful commander? Thou atheist! the world around, above, beneath thee is that instrument, that army, that vessel, that building, and God's sceptre is swayed over all—for *"of Him, and through Him, and to Him are all things: to whom be glory for ever. Amen."*

But this is only a general view of God's kingdom of providence. There is a particular and a personal view most precious to the believing mind. *"The Lord reigneth." "He sitteth in the throne judging right."* Amidst the darkness which often enshrouds, the pain which attends, and the sad reverses which follow the providential dealings of our heavenly Father, is any fact more peculiarly assuring and consolitary than this—that God is on the throne judging right? There may be perplexity, there may be humiliation, there may be straitness and even want, nevertheless God is in all, and over all, guiding all the events of our individual history, small and great, for time and for eternity, not according to our mind, but according to His own. Come and rest beneath the shadow of His wing. All your history is arranged, anticipated, and provided for in the covenant of grace. Every affliction, every sorrow, every temptation, every want, every event is there, all inscribed upon one page; upon the opposite is written every support, every soothing, every supply, every deliverance; for though your house be not as you desire, yet God has made with you, through Jesus the Mediator, a covenant ordered in all things and sure. This is your salvation and your desire. It may please your heavenly Father to keep you low, to allow you but little or nothing in hand; nevertheless we can want nothing that shall be for our real good. And what is for our good must be left to His wisdom to determine, to His faithfulness to provide, and to His love to bestow.

> "Eternal God! we look to Thee,
> To Thee for help we fly;
> Thine eye alone our hearts can see,
> Thy hand alone supply.
>
> "From path to path we roam for rest,
> But all our march is vain;
> We seek for life among the dead,
> For joy where sorrows reign.
>
> "Alas! by passion's force subdued,
> Too oft, with stubborn will,
> We blindly shun the hidden good,
> And choose the specious ill.

> "Not what we wish, but what we want,
>   Oh, let Thy grace supply,
> The good, unask'd, in mercy grant,
>   The ill, though ask'd, deny."

In close relation to the kingdom of providence, is God's higher *kingdom of grace*. God's kingdom is but one. Nature directs us to providence, and providence leads us to grace, and grace conducts us to glory, and glory is the end and consummation of the whole. The coming of the Son of God in flesh, was the advent of a new dispensation, the creation of a new sovereignty, and the enthronement of a new King in the Church of God. *"The law came by Moses, but grace and truth came by Jesus Christ."* Thus, partially interpreted, the kingdom of God is *already* come. No wider view of this kingdom can contravene this fact. Indeed, Christ's kingdom of glory, which is to come, is but the expansion and completion of Christ's kingdom of grace, which is now. Christ's kingdom, in the reign of His glory, is the development of a germ, the perfection of an embryo, now existing. The kingdom of Christ branches into two distinct affiliated parts— the kingdom of grace within the soul, and the kingdom of grace, or the Church of God, in the world. With regard to the first, our Lord distinctly said, *"The kingdom of God is within you."* True religion is the religion of the heart. It consists not in meats and in drinks, but in righteousness, peace, and joy in the Holy Ghost. It is the life of God in the soul of man. This is conversion. It is the advent into the heart of Christ's kingdom of grace, dethroning and ejecting Satan the usurper, and henceforth bringing the whole soul into subjection to the sceptre of Jesus. *"The king's daughter is all glorious WITHIN."* *"Grace reigns through righteousness unto eternal life."* A divine Sovereign, a spiritual kingdom, and a gracious sceptre, henceforth subjugates the whole man to its rule, bringing the will, the mind, the affections, into obedience to Christ. What a glorious kingdom is this! What a marvellous being is the believer! He is a king's son, he has a kingdom within him, and is himself a king. How solemn and sanctifying this truth! Could we always live in the realisation of it, what manner of persons should we be in all godly conversation! Two declarations would then never be absent from the mind—they would mould and tint every action of life—*"Christ in you, the hope of glory;" "Know ye not that ye are the temple of God, and that the Spirit of God dwelleth in you?"* Such is the religion of Jesus, such the religion of the Bible, and such the religion of all that are Christ's, apart from which none can be saved. The religion of the highest philosophy, the religion of the purest ethics, the religion of the strictest ritualism, the religion of the most gorgeous worship, can never be a substitute for the kingdom of Christ's grace within the soul. Has this kingdom *come* to us? Have we passed from death unto life? Are we born again? Have we Christ in us, the hope of glory? These are vital questions which must be fairly met, and honestly and scripturally answered, as in view of eternity. The history of Christ's kingdom of grace in the soul, will form one of the most marvellous volumes read in the light of eternity. The fact will then be unveiled, that there was more of God, more of His power, and wisdom, and holiness exhibited in the soul of a sinner saved by grace, and brought home to glory, than would have been exhibited in the creation of ten thousand worlds like this. This world will be destroyed. *"Passing away,"* is even now inscribed upon it all, and all will be dissolved. *"The heavens shall pass away with a great noise, and the elements shall melt with fervent heat; the earth also, and the works that are therein, shall be burnt up;"* but the kingdom of grace in the soul of man will be as lasting and as glorious as the eternity of God. Its present spiritual history is changeful and chequered. It must necessarily be so, since the grace of God dwells amidst a mass of original, unmitigated, and irreconcilable evil. Conceive of a tropical plant of exquisite nature and delicate form placed amid the Polar regions! What but an incessant exercise of supernatural power could preserve its vitality, clothe it with blossom, keep it in perpetual bloom and deathless fragrance? Such is the grace of God in the believer—a holy and beauteous plant of paradise, brought from a foreign clime and inserted in an unkindly soil, and yet living, blooming, and flowering—delighting the eye with its beauty, and perfuming the air with its sweetness, to the praise of the glory of His grace, by whose perpetual power it lives. The two natures of the regenerate—his own nature and the divine, the old Adam and the new—are in direct and irreconcilable hostility the one to the other. Light and shade, though they may exist in the landscape and harmonise on the canvas, cannot possibly amalgamate without totally neutralising and destroying each other. Thus nature and grace, dwelling for a time in the same renewed heart, may so mingle and blend as to baffle the skill of the most acute analysis. How difficult, nay, how impossible often, to decide accurately upon a state of grace, a case of conversion! The only comfortable and satisfactory conclusion to which we can arrive is this—*"All that the Father giveth Me shall come to Me."* *"The foundation of God standeth sure, having this seal, The Lord knoweth them that are His." "I give unto them eternal life; and they shall never perish, neither shall any man pluck them out of My hand."* This train of thought may account to the Christian for the fluctuations of spiritual feeling, the constant warfare through which he passes, the sunshine and cloud, joy and sorrow, hope and despondency, victory and defeat which constantly alternate in his daily religious life. Nevertheless, we are safe. So long as Christ is upon the throne of our heart, and the Holy Ghost is within the temple of our soul, we are divinely assured that neither the one nor the other will ever abandon the believer—not the heart of evil within, nor the gates of hell without, shall ever prevail to rob God of a child, or the Saviour of a jewel. Let this truth cheer your heart, encourage your soul, lift up the hands that hang down, and strengthen the knees that are feeble in grace, ye saints of God. Not one throb of spiritual life shall die, not a spark of divine love shall go out, not a grain of precious faith shall perish, not an atom of divine grace shall be destroyed, not one ransomed by Christ shall fail to come to the heavenly Zion, "with songs and everlasting joy upon their heads; they shall obtain joy and gladness, and sorrow and sighing shall flee away."

In connexion with the foregoing truth, what significance and impressiveness are found in the petition taught us by Christ, *"Thy kingdom come!"* Did He not contemplate, in this petition, the coming of His kingdom of grace with greater power, manifestation, and faith in the souls of His people? Most assuredly! Who of us feels not the need of more vital religion, of more spiritual quickening, of a larger degree of divine life in the soul? How small a measure of spirituality we have! How little real godliness! How limited our knowledge of Christ! How low our thoughts of God! How slow our progress towards heaven! Oh that this kingdom might come with more divine power in the soul, with more of the quickening energy of the Holy Ghost in our hearts! Cease not to breathe this prayer and urge this request with Christ, until His kingdom within us shall be completed. His work is perfect. He will perfect that which concerneth us. Having begun a good work in the soul, He will complete it. It shall never tauntingly be said of the Divine Architect, that He began to build, and was not able to finish. The plant shall flower in heaven. The living water shall spring into everlasting life. The building shall be crowned with the topstone amidst shoutings of "Grace, grace unto it!" The minor shall reach his majority, the heir his inheritance, the exile his home, and the embryo child the full-grown man in Christ. This spiritual, hidden kingdom in the soul of the regenerate, shall merge into the kingdom of glory, as the bud bursts into the perfect flower, as the key-note swells into the full harmony, as the twilight-dawn melts into the effulgence of meridian day. Lord! so carry on, deepen, and complete Thy work of grace in my heart, and to Thee shall be ceaseless praise!

The second branch of this inquiry is, *The kingdom of Christ in the world*. How early we read of this kingdom. *"In those days came John the Baptist preaching in the wilderness of Judœa, and saying, Repent ye, for the* KINGDOM *of heaven is at hand,"* (Matt. iii. 1, 2.) Similar to this is the language of our Lord Himself:—*"Now after that John was cast into prison, Jesus came into Galilee, preaching the gospel of the* KINGDOM *of God,"* (Matt. i. 14.) Such, too, is the meaning of the various similitudes employed by our Lord in the parable. *"The kingdom of heaven is like unto a grain of mustard seed which a man took and sowed in his garden;"* is *"like unto a treasure hidden in a field;"* is *"like unto a merchantman seeking goodly pearls;"* is *"like unto a net that is cast into the sea."* This kingdom, or Christian Church includes all nations, and tongues, and peoples. Breaking down the middle wall of partition between Jew and Gentile, bond and free; obliterating all national and ecclesiastical distinctions, it embraces, as its subjects, the whole election of grace, and extends its immunities and its privileges to all the regenerate children of God, found in what nation, or clime, or church they may. While yet upon the threshold of our subject, this may be the proper place to refer to the authority which our Lord gave to Peter, under what is figuratively termed the "keys of the kingdom." His words are these:—*"I will give unto thee the* KEYS *of the* KINGDOM OF HEAVEN: *and whatsoever thou shalt bind on earth shall be bound in heaven; and whatsoever thou shalt loose on earth shall be loosed in heaven,"* (Matt. xvi. 19.) The meaning of this often-quoted and much-abused passage is obvious. The wonder is, that it should ever have been disputed. And had it not been employed to favour the most daring usurpation of ecclesiastical authority and power ever conceived, the simple interpretation of the passage would never have been questioned. Not until the Papal supremacy was set up, of which "mystery of iniquity" these words are made to supply the great pillar, did men ever dispute their meaning.

The words of our Lord are clearly figurative, yet embodying an important truth; and the explanation must be sought in the use of the same phraseology in other parts of the sacred writings. For example, it was said by God of Eliakim, an eminent type of the Lord Jesus, *"The* KEY *of the house of David will I lay upon his shoulder; so he shall open, and none shall shut; and he shall shut, and none shall open,"* (Isa. xxii. 23.) We also read of the Pharisees, that they withheld *"the* KEY *of knowledge."* In precisely this same sense, our Lord employed this figure in His memorable words addressed to St Peter: *"I will give unto you the* KEYS *of the kingdom of heaven,"*—i.e., As the preacher of my gospel to both Jew and Gentile, unto whom now I send you, I give unto you authority, power, and skill to *"open the door of faith"* to both; to admit both into the Christian Church, and to unlock and open to both alike the truths, the ordinances, and the privileges of the Christian dispensation. To this the apostle Peter, on a subsequent occasion, thus alludes:—*"Peter rose up, and said, Men and brethren, ye know how that, a good while ago, God made choice among us that the Gentiles, by my mouth, should hear the word of the gospel, and believe,"* (Acts xv. 7.) Now that these *"keys"* belonged not exclusively to Peter, but were equally conferred upon the other apostles,—thus giving no ground for the notion of supremacy on the part of Peter, or authority over the rest of the apostles,—is clear from the fact, that this power, thus primarily conferred upon this apostle, was afterwards conferred upon *all* the apostles,—to whom our Lord addressed precisely the same words—*"Verily I say unto you, Whatsoever YE shall bind on earth shall be bound in heaven; and whatsoever YE shall loose on earth shall be loosed in heaven,"* (Matt. xviii. 18.) Such then, in a few words, were the "keys" entrusted to St Peter; and such is the slender basis upon which this monstrous fiction of the Papal Supremacy rests! Peter, with the whole college of apostles then, and with the whole body of Christian ministers now, had authority from the great Head of the Church, the only King in Zion, to open the glorious truths and mysteries of the gospel; to admit converts into the Christian Church; to pronounce God's free mercy, pardon, and forgiveness to all who should truly repent and believe in Jesus Christ. Pendant from the girdle of every ambassador of Christ are these "keys." Great is our office, and solemn our responsibility! Our commission is to *unlock* the treasury of God's Word, and reveal *the unsearchable riches of Christ.* We are to explain the Word, expound, and enforce the will of God as therein revealed. Adding nothing to, and taking away nothing from, the words of this divine Book, but, as *"ministers of Christ and stewards of the mysteries of God,"* we are, *"by manifestation of TRUTH, to commend ourselves to every man's conscience, as in the sight of God,"* proving ourselves *"workmen that needeth not to be ashamed, rightly dividing the word of truth."* Woe unto us if we use this trust deceitfully; or, if mistaking our calling, we run where the Lord hath not sent, and preach what the Lord hath not commanded, "prophesying lies" in His Name! Woe unto us if we preach not the gospel of the kingdom! Woe unto us if we employ these "keys" as instruments of priestly assumption, lordly power, or ministerial oppression over God's heritage, rather than as ourselves ensamples of love, meekness, and lowliness to the flock. But, with these "keys" in our hands, or, in less figurative words, with the office entrusted to us by the great Head of the Church, what a sublime mission, what a holy work is ours! By virtue of our high and solemn function, as ministers of the Lord Jesus, we apply the key to the divine treasury of Christ's gospel, push back the bolt of the lock, and throw wide the gate of the kingdom of His grace, so filled with all the treasures of divine love, for the admission of poor, lost sinners, sensible of their poverty and need, and coming to Christ and to the fulness and freeness of His grace just as they are, with the assurance, drawn from His Word, and reiterated again and again by us, that, *"Whoever will may drink of the water of life freely; that, him that cometh unto Christ He will in no wise cast out."* Woe unto us if sinners are misled through our ignorance, or are lost through our infidelity! The blood of souls upon him who has failed to save both himself and those that hear him, is deep and indelible; and its testimony, in the judgment of the last day, terrible and damning. Woe unto us if we preach any other way of salvation than only and exclusively through Christ! If, through wilful blindness, or the perversity of our own hearts, we substitute in our pulpit instructions human sacramentalism for spiritual regeneration; heartless ritualism for spiritual worship; creature merit for the obedience, sufferings, and death of Christ. How should the apostolic anathema ring in our ears as we stand in our pulpits—*"Though we, or an angel from heaven preach any other gospel unto you than that which we have preached unto you, let him be* ACCURSED." Soon we shall be called to surrender the "keys" to Him in whose Name we have employed them. We must give an account of our stewardship. If, by an act of self-delegated authority, we have usurped the power of these keys; if we have told "dreams," and "prophesied lies" in the Name of the Lord; and if, blind ourselves, we have led souls blindfolded into eternity, He who has "the keys of hell and of death" will destroy both us and our works in everlasting destruction. Oh that, as good stewards of the mysteries of the kingdom, as humble, holy, faithful ministers of Christ, we may yield up the "keys" of our ministerial authority and office with joy, and not with grief, receiving at the Master's hands the grateful plaudit—*"Well done, good and faithful servant, thou hast been faithful over a few things, I will make thee ruler over many things; enter thou into the joy of thy Lord."*

The kingdom of Christ is essentially *spiritual*. It is *in* the world—its light and salt and witness—but it is not *of* the world. It recognises not the worldling as its subject, and it asks not the recognition of the world as its ally. *"My kingdom is not of this world,"* was the solemn declaration of its great King. The Church of God is not from hence, it is from above. Its nature is spiritual, its laws are heavenly, its spirit is benign. It conquers by no weapon but truth, by no force but love, and reigns over no subjects but those whom Christ's grace has made willing in the day of His power. This Church embraces all of every nation, tongue, and people who love God, who trust in Christ, and whose lives are sanctified by the graces and adorned with the fruits of the Spirit. It is *one* and indivisible. It has different provinces, but one Kingdom; different overseers, but one King; different administrations, but one Lawgiver. Find its subjects where we may, men and women born of the Spirit, all speak the language, claim the immunities, obey the laws, and love the Sovereign of this one Kingdom of grace in the earth. O let us praise and adore His electing love and sovereign mercy, *"who hath delivered us from the power of darkness, and hath translated us into the kingdom of His dear Son."* As the subjects of such a Sovereign, is it unreasonable that we should be expected to *"walk worthy of God, who hath called us into His kingdom and glory?"*

And now, for the wider, holier manifestation of this kingdom, Christ taught us to send up from earth the petition to heaven—*"Thy kingdom come."* What! has this prayer no *present* significance, no *immediate* answer? Is it future and millennial only, having no reference whatever to the present obligation, consecrated efforts, and believing prayers of the Church of God? Surely our Lord when, in the days of His flesh, standing as within the vestibule of His Church, with the cross yet in view, and giving utterance to the first sermon He ever preached, never designed that this prayer should receive an *exclusive* application to the final triumph of His kingdom in the earth at His second and personal coming. What were the terms of the great commission confided to His apostles on the eve of His return to glory? *"Go ye into all the world, and preach the gospel to every creature."* Then, and upon that spot—they—the representatives of the Church in all future ages—were to commence their commission and unfold their great charter, declaring that, *"whosoever believeth and is baptized shall be saved."* Is it, then, without intelligence, without a heart, without an object we pray morning, noon, and night, *"Thy kingdom come?"* Do we not with sincerity ask that the *"word of the Lord might have free course, run and be glorified?"* that, the *"gospel of the kingdom might be preached in all the world for a witness unto all nations?"* that, by this divinely-appointed instrumentality God might *"take out of the Gentiles a people for His Name?"* Seeing, then, that *the Church of God* is the great moral chandelier which the Sun of Righteousness has appointed for illumining the world—*"ye are the light of the world"*— and, seeing that *this truth* is the great instrument of the Spirit for the regeneration of the souls of men—*"being born again, not of corruptible seed, but of incorruptible, by the word of God"*—it becomes us *practically* as well as spiritually and believingly to pray, *"Thy kingdom come."* No more enlarged and prophetical interpretation of these words—which I admit they are capable of, and to which distinct reference will presently be made,—can release us from the solemn obligation and holy privilege of aiding by our endeavours the spread of the gospel and the enlargement of the Church of Christ throughout the world. How closely are the precept and the promise thus entwined, *"He shall live and to Him shall be given of the gold of Sheba; prayer also shall be made for Him continually; and daily shall He be praised."*

In this connexion let me once more recall the reader's attention to a passage already quoted. *"And this gospel of the kingdom shall be preached in all the world for a* WITNESS *unto all nations; and then shall the end come,"* (Matt. xxiv. 14.) This duty and this promise are as yet unrepealed and unredeemed. It stands upon the face of God's Word, challenging the labours, and the prayers, and the faith of God's Church. The terms are simple and explicit. The "end" spoken of is the Lord's Second Coming; and the precursor of this "end" is, not the universal *reception*, but the universal *proclamation* of the gospel—"for a WITNESS unto all nations." The publication of these "glad tidings," the promulgation of Christianity, is here placed before us, not as holding out the idea of universal reception and belief, but simply as the grand preliminary to the advent of the millennium. The gospel is destined ultimately to triumph, Christianity universally to prevail, but not in the present dispensation nor by the agency of present means. A general conversion of the nations previous to the Second Coming of the Lord must not be anticipated even by those noble agencies— the Bible and the Missionary Societies—which are at once the indispensable instrumentalities of the Church, the glory of the age, and the conservators of the world. We say that these societies are *indispensable*. They are truly so in the present age. Not one Bible would we withhold, not one missionary would we withdraw, not one sovereign would we refuse. Nay, we most earnestly implore in their behalf *increased* sympathy, support, and prayer. *They* are the instruments by which the gospel is to he preached *"as a WITNESS unto all nations."* They are the agencies by which the Church is to fulfil her great commission to *"preach the gospel to every creature."* In arguing, therefore—as I most honestly and strenuously do— that Bible and Missionary Societies are not to regenerate the world, I yet maintain that they occupy a most important and sublime part in preparing the way for the coming of the Lord, inasmuch as but for these engines the gospel could not be preached in all the world for a witness; and but for these labourers, the Church herself would be spiritually paralysed in all her borders. "Those who have considered that Christianity is to advance to unbounded dominion without fresh interference on the part of its Founder, and that the moral condition of our globe is to be gradually ameliorated, until, independent of any new manifestation of Christ, the lion shall lie down with the lamb—such persons, we say, may naturally regard the Bible and Missionary Societies as engines through which shall be accomplished the result, that all shall know God from the least to the greatest: but if it be a consequence on the coming of Christ that idolatry is to be abolished, and every falsehood extirpated, the Redeemer himself appearing, according to the description of the Apocalypse, to 'destroy those which destroy the earth,' it must follow, that, to entertain the opinion just mentioned, is to substitute the powers of our societies for that visible making bare of the arm of Omnipotence which prophecy associates with the Redeemer's Second Advent."*

But, as I have remarked, this petition admits of a *prophetical* or *Millennial* interpretation and fulfilment. The Lord Jesus has *a kingdom of glory,* the coming of which will be contemporaneous with the *"glorious appearing of the great God our Saviour Jesus Christ."* It may, perhaps, be remarked of many Christians, that they have been so deeply absorbed in the contemplation of the *sufferings* of Christ as to overlook the GLORY that is to follow. Our Lord himself gently rebuked this exclusiveness in the two disciples with whom He journeyed to Emmaus. *"Ought not Christ to have suffered these things, and to enter into His glory?"* We read that *"the Son of man shall sit upon the THRONE OF HIS GLORY."* And again, that *"He shall be great, and shall be called the Son of the Highest, and the Lord God shall give Him the throne of His father David."* And what throne is this but the throne of glory, which, as the *"root* of David," that is, David's Lord, He is destined to occupy when He shall appear in His glory.

Previous, however, to this glorious Epiphany of our Lord, a time of GREAT TRIBULATION, a period of the most intense, unexampled trouble will take place, of which the terrible siege of Jerusalem, so closely interwoven in its narrative with the prediction of the event, was a singular type. *"There shall be GREAT TRIBULATION, such as was not since the beginning of the world to this time, no, nor ever shall be. And except those days should be shortened, there should no flesh be saved; but for the elect's sake those days shall be*

---

* Melville.

shortened," (Matt. xxiv. 21, 22.) Our Lord forewarns us that *"as a snare it shall come on the whole earth;"* and then commands His disciples, *"Watch ye therefore and pray always, that they may be accounted worthy to escape all these things that shall come to pass, and to stand before the Son of man."* In this coming fearful tribulation the Lord's people will assuredly be kept in perfect safety, and out of it they shall ultimately be delivered. To them the words of the angel to John must primarily refer, *"These are they who have come out of great tribulation."*—(τῆς θλίψεως,) THE tribulation—the *great* tribulation. The central head of this unheard of, unparalleled tribulation will, doubtless, be THE ANTICHRIST, long foretold, then developed, ripened, and fully matured, *"who will be exalted above all that is God, or that is worshipped."* The saints of the Most High, *"whom he shall wear out,"* will be the objects of his fiery persecution; but the Lord of saints will not forsake them in suffering, nor *"condemn them when they are judged."* His grace will be sufficient for them, and they will be enabled to *"love not their lives unto the death."*

And while the souls of those that were slain for the word of God, and for the testimony which they held, are crying from under the altar, *"How long, O Lord, holy and true, dost Thou not judge and avenge our blood on them that dwell on the earth,"* the Son of God will appear in the clouds of heaven, to confront the great enemy and avenge His own elect who cry day and night unto Him. *"And then shall that Wicked be revealed, whom the Lord shall consume with the spirit of His mouth, and shall destroy with the brightness of His coming,"* (2 Thess. ii. 8.)

The condition of the earth at the time of the Lord's coming will be remarkable. The Jews will still retain their distinctive feature as a scattered people—some in their own land, and others, partly in captivity, dwelling among the nations of the earth. These, however, will all be restored to their own land, chiefly in unbelief; and then will be fulfilled the beautiful prediction of Zechariah, *"I will pour upon the house of David, and upon the inhabitants of Jerusalem, the Spirit of grace and of supplications: and they shall look upon me whom they have pierced, and they shall mourn."* Then shall they fly to the *"Fountain opened to the house of David and to the inhabitants of Jerusalem for sin and uncleanness"*—that Fountain their ancestors opened, and which Christ in His love will have kept open until now—and they will wash in it and be clean, and be no more *"an astonishment, a proverb, and a byword among all nations."* Then will come to pass the magnificent prophecy of Israel's glory,—*"In that day shall the branch of the Lord be beautiful and glorious, and the fruit of the earth shall be excellent and comely for them that are escaped of Israel. And it shall come to pass, that he that is left in Zion, and he that remaineth in Jerusalem, shall be called holy, even every one that is written among the living in Jerusalem: when the Lord shall have washed away the filth of the daughters of Zion, and shall have purged the blood of Jerusalem from the midst thereof by the spirit of judgment, and by the spirit of burning. And the Lord will create upon every dwelling-place of Mount Zion, and upon her assemblies, a cloud and smoke by day, and the shining of a flaming fire by night: for upon all the glory shall be a defence. And there shall be a tabernacle for a shadow in the daytime from the heat, and for a place of refuge, and for a covert from storm and from rain,"* (Isa. iv. 2-6.) The Gentiles, still nominally Christian, will be found, some among the "wheat"—that is, Christ's true disciples; others among the "tares"— that is, acknowledging the name of Christ, but in profession only. The ten nations of the Roman world will be in alliance with ANTICHRIST; with him preparing for the great *"battle of Armageddon,"* in the valley of Jehosophat, against Jerusalem. While many *"still afar off"* will be wrapped in the profound darkness of heathenism, not having heard of Jehovah, but to whom *"shall be declared His glory and fame among the Gentiles,"* (Isa. lxvi. 19.)

But the great, the grand event which will cluster around it, as their centre, all others, and upon which all eyes will then be *fixed,* will be the personal and glorious APPEARING of the Son of Man in the clouds of heaven. *"Immediately after the TRIBULATION of these days shall the sun be darkened, and the moon shall not give her light, and the stars shall fall from heaven, and the powers of the heavens shall be shaken. And then shall appear the sign of the*

Son of man in heaven: and then shall all the tribes of the earth mourn, and they shall see the Son of man coming in the clouds of heaven with power and great glory. And He shall send His angels with a great sound of a trumpet, and they shall gather together His elect from the four winds, from one end of heaven to the other." Then will transpire the FIRST RESURRECTION of the dead in Christ, and the TRANSLATION of the living found upon the earth at His appearing. *"The dead in Christ shall rise first: then we which are alive and remain shall be caught up together with them in the clouds, to meet the Lord in the air."* Satan will be bound a thousand years, during which Christ will remain over the earth, now blessed beyond all description with peace and happiness, during which vast numbers will be converted and saved. At the end of the thousand years Satan will he loosed for a season, and a large portion of the race will again assume an attitude of rebellion against Jehovah. And then cometh the end! The second resurrection—or the resurrection of the unjust—will take place, the judgment will be set, the books will be opened, and the ungodly will be judged, sentenced, and condemned to just and eternal punishment. This final act of the great drama past, the world will then be destroyed, *"in the which the heavens shall pass away with a great noise, and the elements shall melt with fervent heat, the earth also and the works that are therein shall be burned up,"* and from its ashes will spring the long predicted *"new earth and the new heavens,"* upon which will descend *"the holy city, new Jerusalem, coming down from God out of heaven, prepared as a bride adorned for her husband."* Let the reader study the magnificent picture of the New Jerusalem, pencilled by a diviner hand than John's, until his heart bounds to be there. *"And I John saw the holy city, new Jerusalem, coming down from God out of heaven, prepared as a bride adorned for her husband. And I heard a great voice out of heaven, saying, Behold, the tabernacle of God is with men, and He will dwell with them, and they shall be His people, and God Himself shall be with them, and be their God. And God shall wipe away all tears from their eyes; and there shall be no more death, neither sorrow, nor crying, neither shall there be any more pain: for the former things are passed away,"* (Rev. xxi. 1-4.) Such is the magnificent scene which the New Earth, the eternal dwelling-place of Christ and the Church, will present. The saints will now have reached the acme of glory, the consummation of all their hopes. Soon and for ever will this be realised! Soon and for ever it will burst in all its wonder upon the Church. The Church will then have exchanged her burden of prayer for her anthem of praise, and the universal and triumphant shout will be heard, *"The mystery of God is finished!* His kingdom is come!" Yet a little while, and He that shall come will come. The events that will usher in His advent and kingdom are even now dawning. The signs in the moral and political heavens are numerous, significant, and portentous. The time is short. The coming of the Lord draweth nigh. Rise from the bed of slumber and of sloth, and labour and endure for Christ. Confess nobly His name, vindicate earnestly His truth, bear holily His cross, far and wide spread His fame, and let it be your meat and your drink both to do and to suffer His will. The kingdom is coming, the triumph is hastening, the diadem is sparkling, and all the minstrelsy of heaven are preparing for the grand, the Hallelujah Chorus—"THE KINGDOMS OF THIS WORLD ABE BECOME THE KINGDOMS OF OUR LORD AND OF HIS CHRIST, AND HE SHALL REIGN FOR EVER AND EVER." Amen. Even so, come, Lord Jesus. Come quickly.

> "Thine is the kingdom! O Father of love;
>   Thou who in majesty reignest above,
>   Thou whom archangels and seraphs adore,
>   Blessed Jehovah! thrice bless'd evermore.
>
> "Oh! let Thy kingdom on earth now descend,
>   O'er us let Thy love's golden sceptre extend,
>   Be all earth's foes and iniquities slain,
>   Take on Thyself Thy great power, and reign.
>
> "Father! Thy kingdom on earth may we see.
>   Power for ever belongeth to Thee!
>   Thine is the power! oh, matchless in might,
>   Author of goodness and Fountain of light!

"Look on the spirits held captive by sin;
  Bring to Thy fold the lost wanderers in;
  Strengthen Thine Israel, by conflict oppress'd;
  Grant us Thy victory! hasten our rest!

"Our perilous way through life's wilderness guide,
  And bear us unharmed through Death's swelling tide,
  Then, when enrolled in Thy glory we stand,
  Bathed in the light of Immanuel's Land,

"Saviour! our song in Thy kingdom shall be,
  'Glory for ever belongeth to Thee!'
  Thine is the glory! all honour is Thine,
  All praise and all power, Thou Saviour Divine!

"Weak, empty, and sinful we nothing can bring,
  Ever needing Thy strength to Thy footstool to cling:
  Yet mighty Jehovah, Thee, Thee would we praise,
  To Thee we our grateful hosannas would raise.

"The crowns Thou hast given we lay at Thy feet,
  And the songs of the bless'd even now we repeat:
  Their high-sounding anthem for ever shall be,
  'Praise, glory, and honour belong unto Thee!'

"O Lord, Thou hast promised! Thy word shall not fail,
  We long the bright day of Thy glory to hail;
  Thy kingdom *shall* come with unlimited sway,
  Thy word shall earth's princes and monarchs obey,

"Till the chorus triumphant o'er earth shall resound,
  The mighty usurper in darkness be bound:
  When all earthly thrones and dominions shall fall,
  And Jesus exalted he Lord over all.
  Saviour! Thy sceptre extended *shall* be,
  For the power and the glory belong unto Thee."

CHAPTER VI.

THE SUBMISSIVE SPIRIT OF
THE LORD'S PRAYER.

"THY WILL be done on earth as it is done in heaven."
—MATT. vi. 10.

HIS remarkable petition in the Lord's Prayer admits of a twofold application. In its first and more limited view, it may be regarded as expressing the meek submission of the child of God under the trying discipline of his heavenly Father. In its second and more comprehensive view, it supplies a key to the preceding petition, with which it stands closely linked, and explains to us what is meant by the coming of God's kingdom—even His will done on earth as it is done in heaven. *"Thy kingdom come, Thy will be done on earth even as it is done in heaven."* I propose in the present chapter to present *both* of these views of the prayer.

Whose will is this? *"Thy will"*—the will of God. The will in man is the determining faculty of the soul. All his thoughts, words, and actions—all that he resolves, undertakes, and executes—is a volition, or act of the will. There is no higher natural law of the man. In God this is infinitely and pre-eminently so. The Divine will is the supreme moving law of the universe. We speak, and properly so, of the 'laws of nature.' As Montesquieu in his masterly work on the Spirit of Laws has remarked, "All beings have their laws; the Deity His laws, the material world its laws, the intelligences superior to man their laws, the beasts their laws, man his laws." But this idea of the universality and plurality of law resolves itself into the existence of ONE all-governing, all-commanding supreme law. What are the laws of nature but the law of God? Hooker has judiciously remarked, "Of law, no less can be said than that her seat is the bosom of God, her voice the harmony of the world; all things in heaven and earth do her homage, the very least as feeling her care, the greatest as not exempted from her power; both angels and men and creatures, of what condition soever, though each in different spheres and manner, yet all with uniform consent admiring her as the mother of their peace and joy."* What does the teaching of this memorable passage resolve itself into but the sublime truth that law, which is the great bond of the universe, finds its origin in the bosom of God, in the existence and exercise of that one divine and supreme Will whose volitions go forth from their great centre in every possible direction, like rays from the sun, embracing, harmonising, and controlling every form and modification of being, whether intelligent or unintelligent. Even nations not favoured with the light of revelation have maintained the doctrine of a Supreme Power, which, if forgotten in prosperity, they have ever sought to propitiate in the day of sorrow. A vague, indistinct, though not less real idea has penetrated the savage mind that a Deity is ever present regarding the virtuous as objects of favour and the vicious as objects of displeasure.†

But to the mind enlightened by the revelation of God's Word, conjecture gives place to certainty; and the believing heart is upheld and solaced with the thought that God is on the throne of the universe, ordering all things, all events, and all beings *"after the counsel of His own will;"* that, while His paternal eye superintends the minutest actions and events pertaining to

---

* Hooker's Ecclesiastical Polity, book i.

† A striking reference to this will occur to the classical reader in Livy, lib. iii. cap. 56.

ourselves, His all-ruling Will embraces the countless varieties of existence—

"And fills, and bounds, connects and equals all!"

Let us look at God's will in two or three of its essential properties.

It is *universal*—in other words, it is supreme in its dominion. There can of necessity be but one all—ruling, all—controlling will in the universe. That will is God's. Be it His *secret* will—which is the rule of His own conduct; or, His *revealed* will—which is the rule of ours; be it His *approving* will—which we should ever consult; or His *permitting* will—to which we should ever bow, His will is the universal law of the universe, extending its sovereign sceptre over all worlds, all beings, and all events. How consolatory and assuring this truth to the Christian mind! To know that the world is under the government of law, that that law is the supreme Will of God, and that the mediatorial office of the Lord Jesus Christ clothes Him with *"power over all flesh."* In view of this truth, the believing mind can look calmly, confidently, even hopefully upon the conflict of thought and the agitation of feeling, the opposition of error and the threatening of persecution amidst whose troubled waters the Ark of God is tossing. Satan may plot, error may boast, the heathen may rage, and the people imagine a vain thing; the kings of the earth may set themselves, and the rulers take counsel together against the Lord and against His anointed, saying, let us break their bonds asunder; nevertheless He that sitteth in the heavens reigns supremely, and will make all potentates and all events subservient to the advancement and final triumph of His kingdom.

God's will is *holy*. The will of an essentially holy Being, it must of necessity be so. It can will nothing that is not in perfect harmony with its own nature. I need scarcely, therefore, remark that God cannot be the author of sin—if a conception so monstrous could even find a moment's lodgement in the reader's mind. God's will is holy in all its volitions, holy in all its rule, holy in all its results. Whatever God wills, must terminate in the display and vindication of His holiness. The *righteousness* of the Divine government is the brightest crown-jewel in the diadem of God. There must, necessarily, be events in His administration, the result either of His permitting or of His approving will, which, at the time, may seem to contravene the rectitude of His rule. But the moment the believing mind can repose upon the truth of God's holiness, that moment its perplexities are at rest; and although all is enshrined in mystery, and the events terminate in results which seem adverse to his best interests and God's glory, he can exclaim, *"But Thou art* HOLY, *O Thou that inhabiteth the praises of Israel."* Beloved, the day may come when this view of the holiness of the Divine will shall rise before you with all the freshness of a newly revealed truth. The cup trembling in your hand—the knife raised to slay the beloved Isaac—a view of the perfect *righteousness* of the Divine will at that moment may be just the truth which will strengthen your heart and nerve your arm to drink the cup, and to make the sacrifice God bids you, in meek submission to His will.

Equally *wise* is the will of God. If the rectitude of God's government cannot be honestly impeached, equally unimpeachable is its wisdom. The apparent discrepancy, the alleged contradictions in the administration of God's providential government—the events in the history of the world and of the Church, and in our own individual life—which apparently contravene the notion of a directing Power of infinite forethought and knowledge, and which clash painfully with our idea of an All-wise Hand guiding the movements of the vast and complicated machine—touch not, in the slightest degree, the perfect wisdom which superintends it all. Could we see an event as God sees it, from the end to the beginning, what to us seemed an entangled skein would prove a perfect network; and what appeared a strange commingling of colours would prove a beautiful mosaic; and what fell upon our ear as the most discordant sounds would swell into the most exquisite harmonies—so perfect are the ways of God with the children of men. Contemplate in this light your present position. The event is mysterious and stunning, the calamity dark and crushing. You walk round and round it in search of some clue that will unravel the mystery, of some ray that will relieve the gloom, of one drop of sweet that will mitigate the bitter. But this is *nature*. Now let *grace* step in and do its work. Let faith grapple with this providence, and its whole character is changed. Faith is a marvellously transforming principle. It presents every object through a different medium, and places it in a different light. It transmutes the basest metal into the purest gold, extracts the sweetest honey from the bitterest flower, finds food in the eater, pencils with silver light and fringes with golden rays the darkest cloud; impoverishes to enrich, and exhausts to replenish. Let faith have its perfect work, lacking nothing, in the present dealing of God with you. You must now look, not at the providence, but at the *promise* of God. Nor must you deal exclusively with the promise of God, but with *the God* of the promise. The promises derive all their value and preciousness from the veracity, the immutability, and the power of God to make them good. Has God said it, and will He not perform? You have to do with God, with His all-sufficiency. The inquiry of unbelief is, *"How shall Jacob arise, for he is small?"* The answer of faith is, "He shall arise, because God is *great*." We look too little at the immensity, the all sufficiency, the infinity of God. The more faith deals with the power of God, the more powerful will it become. It grows into the greatness of its Object. Dealing with the great God, itself becomes great, just as the intellectual faculty expands to the dimensions of the science it grasps, and as the taste becomes moulded and elevated to the standard of art it studies. He that would attain to true greatness in any department must study the highest and the purest model. No individual will ever rise in science or in art, in poetry or eloquence, superior to the standard he has chosen. But where is there a realm in which real greatness finds its fullest development and growth as the religion of Jesus? Religion expands the mind, refines the feelings, elevates the taste, cultivates the faculties and powers of the soul as nothing else does or can do. The reason is obvious. The subjects of thought and feeling are divine and holy, infinitely great and pure. The soul rises to the vastness of its theme. Never had Bacon or Newton reached the height of intellectual greatness and fame which they attained, had the one limited the range of his faculties to the study of philosophy, and the other to the study of science. The contemplation and study of *religion* moulded their greatness and stamped their immortality. Would we, then, be mighty in the principle, and great in the achievements of faith, it must have direct, and even frequent, transactions with God. In proportion to our acquaintance with God will be the intimacy of our dealings with Him. The walk with God of many is so remote, their confidence in Him so feeble, their fellowship with Him so unfilial, their love to Him so superficial, because they know Him so slightly, are acquainted with Him so imperfectly, and deal with Him so seldom in the minor events, the little trials, wants and cares of every day life. "ACQUAINT *now thyself with Him, and be at peace.*"

The will of God is *supreme.* Be it His secret will, or be it His *revealed* will, its supremacy is acknowledged. In heaven, in earth, in hell; in all places, over all beings, and in all events, the sceptre of the Divine will stretches its illimitable and supreme sovereignty. It is the paramount law of the universe. Every other will is subordinate to, and is controlled by, the will of Jehovah. Let those think of this and tremble who, erecting their little sovereignties, and setting up their puny wills in defiance of, and in opposition to, the supreme sovereignty of the universe, are seeking to be a law to themselves. The spectacle which you present to the eye of sinless intelligence is as appalling as your sin is monstrous. It was the opposition of man's will to God's which plunged the world in rebellion, crime, and woe. The insane and unequal conflict has been raging ever since, is raging now, keeping this world in a state of continued treason and rebellion against the government of Jehovah, and will continue so to keep it, until God's will is done on earth as it is done in heaven. The position, then, in which this statement places the unrenewed will is that of direct collision with God. This is in perfect concurrence with God's Word, "*The carnal mind is enmity against God, for it is not subject to the law of God, neither indeed can be.*" Similar to this are the words of the same apostle: "*You hath He quickened, who were dead in trespasses and sins; wherein in time past ye walked according to the course of this world. . . . fulfilling the desires of the flesh and of the mind,*" (margin: the *lusts* of the flesh.) And what a solemn picture is that, *"led captive by Satan at his will!"* Awful thought! Captive to Satan's will! Here, then, are three wills which the unconverted obey: their own will, the will of the flesh, and the will of Satan: bound by this threefold cord, they are led captive. But, on your part, let the personal conflict cease. Cease to oppose God's will, speaking to you in His word, striving with you by His Spirit, and dealing with you in His providence, lest, haply, you be found to fight against Him to your total and eternal discomfiture. Seek, oh seek importunately, the aid of the Spirit to bend the iron sinew of your will in deep submission, patience, and love at His feet—made willing, in the day of His power, to yield a loving obedience, an unreserved surrender to the Lord to be His servant, His child for ever. Oh, blissful moment when the conflict ceases, when the armistice is proclaimed, and peace transpires between God and your soul! *"O Lord, though Thou wast angry with me, Thine anger is turned away, and Thou comfortest me."*

But, if the supremacy of God's will is a terror to those who are living in rebellion against its rule, how replete with assurance and comfort it is to those who have 'kissed the Son,' and are in a state of peace with God through Him? Amidst the upheavings of the State, and the conflicts of the Church, how soothing to think that God sitteth upon the throne, judging right! The believer can look calmly, confidently, hopefully upon the stormy waters, with the firm persuasion that Christ controls them, and that all shall be overruled to the best interests of His people. While Christ reigns, let the earth tremble and the saints rejoice. Infidelity may increase and blaspheme; the man of sin may speak proud things, and vaunt itself; Christian love may wane, and Protestant zeal may flag; foes within the Church may confederate with foes without; there may be treachery in the camp, and treason in the invading hosts; nevertheless, Jesus is ruling in the Church and over the world; the government of both is upon His shoulder, and the keys of hell and of death are in His girdle; He that sitteth in the heavens will laugh, the Lord shall have in derision all the abettors of infidelity and popery—Herod and Pilate made friends, and united their forces to the overthrow of Jesus and His truth. It is a most consolatory assurance to the saints of God that our Lord's mediatorial supremacy includes *"power over all flesh, that He might give eternal life to as many as the Father hath given Him."*

There are three things contained in this petition that God's will might be done. The disciple is taught thus to ask that the will of God might be done on earth in the fulfilment of duty,—in the endurance of trial,—and in the universal prevalence of holiness.

With regard to the first, there can be no real walking in God's precepts while the will is irreconciled to God through Christ. Evangelical obedience is a willing obedience, the will brought under the supernatural and loving constraint of the Spirit. If we are not doing the will of God by holy walking in His precepts, there is a fatal collision of our will with the Divine will. Enmity must be dislodged from our will, thus disarming it of its hostility to God, ere we can either spiritually understand or become "doers of the word." How distinctly our Lord puts this truth:—*"My doctrine is not mine, but His that sent me. If any man will* DO HIS WILL, *he shall know of the doctrine whether it be of God, or whether I speak of myself."* Harmony, therefore, of will is essential to spiritual light. We are in the true position to understand revealed truth when we are walking in holy obedience to God. Just as we see more perfectly the properties and beauties of natural objects standing in the sunlight, so the truth, the harmony, and the beauty of the gospel of Christ are only distinctly discerned as the heart is right with God. Sin beclouds the understanding, holiness enlightens it; sin warps the affections, holiness expands them; sin deadens the conscience, holiness quickens it. A man of mere speculative, rational knowledge, who theoretically receives, but practically denies, the holiness of the truth; who is not a humble, sincere believer in the Lord Jesus Christ—to believe fully in whom is the will of God—cannot know, experimentally and spiritually, whether God's word is divine. But he who does God's will, who leans not to his own understanding, but is taught of the Holy Spirit, he shall know, by the truth effectually working in him, whether it is of God or of man. Let all who are in search of divine truth examine themselves, and ascertain whether they are *doing* God's will; whether they have believed the record God has given concerning His Son; whether they have accepted Christ as God's unspeakable gift of love; whether they have *"submitted themselves unto the righteousness of God."* So long as the Lord Jesus is not received, loved, and honoured, even as the Father, the mind is not in a position to know of the doctrine, to pursue the inquiry, *"What is truth?"* The truth is Christ—*"I am the truth,"*—and he who has got hold of Christ holds in his hand the golden key at whose touch the whole arcana of truth will fly open. Thus, he who lives upon Christ as his sanctification, stands complete in all the will of God.

God's will is likewise done on earth—in *the believer's patient endurance of trial.* Submission to God is the spirit inculcated by the Lord's Prayer. In the Christian life there is as much the *enduring,* as the doing, of God's will; the *passive,* as the active obedience of the believing mind to the will of God. Perhaps, more of the Lord's people are schooled in the discipline of the will to the *passive* than to the *active* part of the Christian life—in suffering than in doing. In active service for the Lord there may be a greater indulgence of our will than we have any suspicion of. The sphere may be pleasant, the work agreeable, the success cheering, the applause flattering, and so our own imperfectly sanctified will is gratified. But the *passive* school of God places the believer in a different position, and brings his will under a different discipline. Suffering is not desirable, nor affliction pleasant, nor sorrow welcome; so that when God is pleased to send either, there is necessarily a more direct and powerful subjugation of the will of the believer to the will of God. This may, perhaps, explain the reason why more Christians graduate for heaven *in the school of adversity* than any other. This, too, invests with light that apparently dark and inexplicable part in our Lord's personal history—His learning in suffering. Was He not perfect, apart from sorrow? Was He not complete, irrespective of suffering? The apostle shall reply. "Though He were a Son, yet LEARNED He OBEDIENCE by *the things which He suffered."* "It became Him for whom are all things, and by whom are all things, in bringing many sons unto glory, *to make the Captain of their salvation perfect through suffering.*" Link, then, two truths in Christ's personal experience—suffering, and the learning the lesson of obedience—and He is presented to your study in two of the most consolatory and instructive points of His history. He was a pupil in the school of suffering. There was not a moment in His career which was not a moment of graduated suffering, since, from the moment He touched earth's horizon commenced His work of suretyship. If it was in the school of affliction He was to learn, then His learning commenced at the manger of Bethlehem. He was to work out the profoundest problem in the moral government of the universe—the harmony of God's attributes in the pardon of man's sin. It was the problem of His life. All was new to Him. The difficulties of redemption, the evil of sin, the bitterness of the cross, the lesson of obedience, the tremendousness of suffering, the discipline of will, were the parts of His mediatorial work in which He was to be perfected, and perfected only in the path of suffering. I speak of His humanity now. And if the humanity of the Son of God were, in the strictest sense, our own humanity, in all but its sinfulness, then we must believe that, like ours, it was progressive—as progressive in its intellectual and moral, as in its corporeal powers. To this law it was inevitably and *unquestionably* subjected. *"And Jesus increased in wisdom and stature, and in favour with God and man."* As God, He was essentially holy, and there could not be any addition to His holiness. But as man—unless we suppose that His humanity was dissimilar to our own, which would be to loosen the great foundation-stone of our faith, and overthrow His Atonement—He grew in holiness; that is, His holiness, perfect in itself, developed and increased with His years, investing His life with a deepening sanctity and a growing lustre, until it culminated at the cross. Jesus, then, was a learner. *"He LEARNED obedience."* And the great lesson He learned, daily, hourly learned, was the doing and the enduring of His Father's will. As His sufferings advanced, the magnitude of the task dilated before His view. With the darkening of the storm the lesson grew more difficult. Just as the faggots, piled around the Christian martyr, become more and more ignited, and the devouring flames leap higher and higher, and enfold closer and closer the suffering victim, the lesson of endurance, fortitude, and meek submission becomes more difficult, more painful—so was it with our blessed Lord. While suffering taught Him how much He was to endure, it also taught Him how difficult it was to endure. And it was not until He had passed through the severest ordeal that He completely learnt the lesson of submission to the will of God. Bethlehem prepared Him for Gethsemane, and Gethsemane prepared Him for Calvary. It was in the garden that the most fearful struggle was endured, the agonising conflict was passed, and the victory was achieved. *"Thy will be done,"* uttered in sobs of grief, swelled into the pæan of triumph shouted from the cross, "IT IS FINISHED!"

In this same school of suffering *our will* is chastened and sanctified. All His saints are thus taught of God. Of Aaron it is said, *"And Aaron held his peace."* Listen to Eli: *"It is the Lord; let Him do what seemeth Him good."* Listen to Job: *"Shall we receive good at the hand of the Lord, and not evil?" "The Lord gave, and the Lord hath taken away, blessed be the name of the Lord."* And in this school God is, perhaps, now disciplining yours. In no other could the holy lesson be learnt; in no other position could the surrender be made.

> "He who knew what human hearts would prove,
> How slow to learn the dictates of His love;
> Called for a cloud to darken all their years,
> And said, Go spend them in the vale of tears."*

But this lesson of surrendered will to God, is not learnt in one or two trials. As it is the holiest, so it is the hardest lesson in our heavenly education. The child, in process of weaning, is not more fretful and resistant than the believer often in process of divorce from himself. To surrender the dearest, to relinquish the sweetest, to forego the pleasantest for God, is a heavenly ascent of the soul, steep, rugged, and painful. But, weary and footsore, the panting pilgrim at length reaches the summit, bathed in the divinest

---

* Cowper.

sunlight, and falling prostrate at the feet of His Heavenly Father, exclaims, "NOT AS I WILL, BUT AS THOU WILT." Be not discouraged, child of God, if your progress is slow in reaching this high, Christian attainment. Your blessed Lord Himself did not fully attain to it until He had *thrice* prayed. We often overlook the *duality* of trial in God's chastening of our will. A single affliction seldom accomplishes its mission. The arrival of one is frequently the herald of another yet more heavy and sad. But this is our comfort that, *"all things* WORK TOGETHER *for* GOOD *to them that love God;"* and your present *plurality* of trial is among the all things of God's everlasting covenant of grace. Think not that He will forsake you. It is the discipline of a Father's love, and will He not *"stay His rough wind in the day of His east wind?"* *"Happy is the man whom God correcteth: therefore despise not the chastening of the Almighty; for He maketh sore and bindeth up. He woundeth, and His hands make whole. He shall deliver thee in six troubles; yea, in seven there shall no evil touch thee."* May you not, then, be *happy?* If God is for you— and you are pavilioned within His perfections—who or what can hurt you? Though an host of foes or of trials should encamp against you, yet in this may your faith repose, that, the Triune Jehovah, Israel's God, encircles you as a wall of fire. Oh, what a God is He with whom the believer has to do! You have to do with the God of the Bible, the God of Christ, the God of Abraham, Isaac, and Jacob—the God of redemption, the covenant God of a chosen, loved, and redeemed people. How faintly we deal with God as He really is! We rob Him of His infinity, and think of Him as finite. We divest Him of His divine perfections, and clothe Him with human. We think Him such an one as ourselves. Oh to rise to the greatness of God—the greatness of His power, the vastness of His love, the infinitude of His resources! We limit the Holy One of Israel, we doubt the ability, the willingness, the grace of Christ to save us; we think the Spirit of the Lord straitened; and thus, bringing Jehovah down to our poor measurement instead of rising to His immeasurable greatness, we are dwarfs where we should be giants in grace; we cleave to the dust when we should soar to the sun; we carry our own burdens and nurse our own sorrows, when we should transfer them all in faith to Him who loves us. Uplift, then, your song, though it rises from the valley and echoes through a strange land.

"Is God for me? I fear not, though all against me rise;
When I call on Christ my Saviour, the host of evil flies;
My Friend, the Lord Almighty, and He who loves me, God,
What enemy shall harm me, though coming as a flood?
I know it, I believe it, I say it fearlessly,
That God, the highest, mightiest, for ever loveth me;
At all times, in all places, He standeth at my side,
He rules the battle fury, the tempest, and the tide.

"A Rock that stands for ever, is Christ my righteousness,
And there I stand unfearing in everlasting bliss;
No earthly thing is needful to this my life from heaven,
And nought of love is worthy, save that which Christ has given;
Christ, all my praise and glory, my light most sweet and fair,
The ship wherein He saileth is scathless everywhere.
In Him I dare be joyful, as a hero in the war;
The judgment of the sinner affrighteth me no more.

"There is no condemnation, there is no hell for me,
The torment and the fire my eye shall never see;
For me there is no sentence, for me death has no sting,
Because the Lord, who loves me, shall shield me with His wing.
Above my soul's dark waters His Spirit hovers still,
He guards me from all sorrows, from terror, and from ill;
In me He works, and blesses the life-seed He hath sown,
From Him I learn the 'Abba,' that prayer of faith alone.

"And if in lonely places, a fearful child I shrink,
He prays the prayers within me I cannot ask or think—
The deep unspoken language, known only to that love,
Who fathoms the heart's mystery from the throne of light above.
His Spirit to my spirit sweet words of comfort saith,
How God the weak one strengthens who leans on Him in faith,
How He hath built a city of love, and light, and song,
Where the eye at last beholdeth what the heart hath loved so long.

"And there is mine inheritance, my kingly palace, home;
The leaf may fall and perish, not less the spring will come;

Like wind and rain of winter, our earthly sighs and tears,
Till the golden summer dawneth of the endless year of years.
The world may pass and perish, Thou, God, wilt not remove,
No hatred of all devils can part me from Thy love;
No hungering nor thirsting, no poverty nor care,
No wrath of mighty princes can reach my shelter there.

"No angel and no heaven, no throne, nor power, nor might;
No love, no tribulation, no danger, fear, nor fight;
No height, no depth, no creature that has been or can be,
Can drive me from Thy bosom, can sever me from Thee.
My heart in joy upleapeth, grief cannot linger there,
She singeth high in glory amidst the sunshine fair:
The sun that shines upon me is JESUS and His love,
The fountain of my singing is deep in heaven above."*

One experience of this remarkable petition yet remains to be
considered. "Thy will be done on earth *as it is done in heaven.*"
The question arises, "How is God's will done in heaven?" We briefly
reply—God's will is done in heaven *harmoniously.* There lives not
a being in heaven whose will is not in the sweetest accord with
the will of God. The will of God is done in heaven by all celestial
intelligences, *because it is His will.* This is the loftiest motive that
can sway a created mind—no motive lower than this should sway
ours. The conviction that we are doing or suffering God's will
should be enough to annihilate every objection and silence every
murmur. Again: the will of God is done in heaven *cheerfully.* "Bless
ye the Lord, ye His angels that excel in strength, *hearkening to
the voice of His word.*" They *hearken* that they might *do.* Such
should be our obedience—a cordial, cheerful doing and enduring;
as the apostle expresses it, "Doing the will of God *from the heart.*"
How touchingly did our Lord illustrate this cheerful obedience to
God! "I *delight* to do Thy will, O my God." And, in another place,
"I seek not mine own will, *but the will of Him that sent me.*" So let
our submission to God be—a cheerful, happy submission. God's
will is done in heaven *promptly.* There is not a moment's pause of

* Paul Gerhardt.

sullen hesitation or questioning delay. Every angel poised upon his white pinion, every seraph with his hand upon his golden harp, every glorified spirit with the well-prepared anthem upon the lip, stands *ready* to obey God's command. So let His will be done by us—without reasoning or demur, without attempting to penetrate the mystery or define the end. It may demand the costliest sacrifice, impose the heaviest cross, involve the severest self-denial—nevertheless, would we imitate on earth the will of God as done in heaven? then let us not ask the reason why, but promptly and cheerfully obey, satisfied that it is the holy, wise, and righteous will of our heavenly Father.

The BLESSINGS that flow from perfect acquiescence with the will of God are innumerable. It secures our *happiness*. The great secret of all quietness and contentedness of mind under all circumstances, is in the absorption of our own will in God's. The moment there arises in the breast the least hostility to what God does, or enjoins, there is unhappiness. The harp is unstrung, and harshness and discord is the result. There is *safety,* too, in acquiescence. Never is the child of God so safe as when doing and suffering the will of God. Danger and destruction lie in the path of self-will. As much should we deprecate its rule and shrink from asserting its pre-eminence, as we would the insane standing upon the brink of an Alpine precipice, with the ice and the snow melting and crumbling beneath our feet. But, oh, the perfect safety in doing and enduring God's will! mysterious, painful, humbling though it be. There is *heavenly* blessing, too, in the soul that does God's will. In proportion to our assimilation to the perfection of God's will as done in heaven, is our approach to the happiness of heaven itself. We sit as in the heavenlies while harmony exists between God's mind and ours. No position of the soul brings us into such close and holy relation to God as when our will sweetly dissolves into His. The soul, with all its present and eternal interests, is now confidently and cheerfully surrendered to Him. No dread of rocks, and of shoals, and of a lee shore in the homeward voyage. Our Father pilots the barque, and perfect confidence garrisons the SOUL. With a divine hand upon the helm, love expanding the sails, and hope sitting serenely upon the prow, the heaven-bound vessel careers her pathway through sunlight and through storm; and so He bringeth us to our desired heaven. One word shall sum up all that we would further say upon this part of the subject—the cheerful doing and the patient suffering of our Father's will resolves itself into *perfect satisfaction* with all that He does. It is the daily lesson of life, the secret of our growth in grace, the essence of our personal holiness. *"This is the will of God, even your sanctification." "And be ye transformed by the renewing of your mind, that ye may prove what is that good and acceptable will of God."*

"THY WILL BE DONE!" This is the most solemn prayer it is possible for man to breathe. Unconverted reader, are you aware what this petition involves? Are you prepared for the answer? God's will is that you should be *holy*—are you ready to give up your pride, your avarice, your lusts, your worldliness, your secret sins? God's will is that *uprightness* and *integrity* should mark all our doings—are you willing to have your ledger examined, your accounts scrutinised, your bills taxed, and your commercial transactions placed in the light of day? God's will is, that we should *love* Him with a simple, single, and supreme affection—are you willing that He should enter the garden of your soul, and gather this lily, and pluck that rose, and mow down that daisy, and break the stem of that beautiful and stately plant, that henceforth He might possess your heart? God's will is that you should *believe* in and *accept* His beloved Son as your only Saviour, your righteousness, redemption, and hope—are you willing to cast overboard your self-righteousness, to part with your religion of duties, and rites, and forms, and receive Christ as a poor, empty sinner, trusting only in His blood and righteousness? No! perhaps you are not prepared for any part of this sacrifice! And yet, morning and evening, you pray, *"Thy will be done!"* Oh, it is the most solemn, fearful prayer lips ever uttered! When next you breathe it, add yet another: "Lord, renew me by Thy Spirit, strengthen, sanctify me by Thy grace, that in doing and in suffering I may stand complete in all Thy holy will."

The universality of God's will done on earth, will be the universality of the reign of holiness. The millennial age of the world, which is to be ushered in by the Coming of the Lord in person, and with great glory, will be the dawn of an era of righteousness, peace, and happiness, such as creation has not witnessed since its primeval state. In that day, when *"the Lord's feet shall stand upon the mount of Olives which is before Jerusalem,"* when *"the Lord shall be King over all the earth, . . . and His name one," "in that day shall there be upon the bells of the horses, HOLINESS UNTO THE LORD; and the pots in the Lord's house shall be like the bowls before the altar. Yea, every pot in Jerusalem and in Judah shall be holiness unto the Lord of hosts: and all they that sacrifice shall come and take of them, and seethe therein: and in that day there shall be no more the Canaanite in the house of the* Lord *of hosts,"* (Zech. xiv. 20, 21.) Then will the prayer—for centuries the burden of the Church—be fulfilled, and in the new earth and the new heaven, in which righteousness supremely reigns, God's will shall be done. O my Father, God!

> "Let Thy will, not mine, be done;
> Let my will and Thine be one."

CHAPTER VII.

THE DEPENDENT SPIRIT OF
THE LORD'S PRAYER.

"Give us this day our DAILY BREAD."-MATT, vi, 11.

 CREATED being must, of necessity, be a *dependent* being. The constitution of his nature involves this as its condition, There is but One who is independent, because there is but One who is self-existent. God owes His being to no other and higher power than Himself. He stands alone—alone the eternal, self-existent, independent Jehovah. Of no other intelligence can this be said. There is not an angel in heaven who is not as much dependent upon God for every breath he draws, as the insect sporting its momentary existence in the sunbeam. The fall of man has presented an impressive illustration of this truth. Dependent upon God in his pristine state of holiness, he is infinitely more so since bankrupt of all original righteousness and strength. His condition of utter feebleness and reliance upon a power other and infinitely above his own, finds no parallel in the history of creation. Not an intelligence expatiating amid the glories of the upper world, not a tribe cleaving the blue vault of heaven, or traversing the deep paths of the sea, or roaming the wide circuit of the earth, hangs upon God for its existence and sustenance in a condition so feeble, helpless, and dependent, as the fallen creature man. But the *regenerate* man alone feels and recognises this truth. He alone is conscious of this fact. He has been taught by the Spirit that he is *"without strength,"* and that when he was without strength, Christ died for him. Man is self-destroyed. He is a moral homicide, a self-murderer. *"O Israel, thou hast destroyed thyself!"* This is the first lesson the renewed creature learns. He learns that he is sinful, and a sinner before God. That he has no righteousness, no goodness, no worthiness, no strength; that he stands in God's bankruptcy court, owing ten thousand talents, and having nothing to pay. Oh, blessed truth this to learn under the teaching of the Holy Ghost—our poverty, emptiness, impotence, and nothingness ! But this is not all. As there is no creature so conscious of his weakness, so there is none so conscious of his strength as the *renewed* man. Taught his dependence, he has also been taught upon whom he is to depend. Instructed in the knowledge of his weakness, by the same Spirit he has been instructed wherein his great strength lies.

Hitherto the petitions taught us by our Lord in this, the disciples' incomparable prayer, have borne exclusive reference to the adoration, glory, and empire we ascribe to God. In this order we trace the infinite wisdom of our Great Teacher, who, in a subsequent part of His sermon on the mount, instructs us to *"seek* FIRST *the kingdom of God and His righteousness, and that all things else should be added to us."* God first—His being, His glory, His empire. Man second—his prayers, his wants, his supplies; that thus God in Christ might in all things have the pre-eminence. Turn we now to the petition itself: *"Give us this day our daily bread."*

There are four kingdoms—as we have seen in a preceding chapter—over which the sovereignty of God extends,—the kingdoms of nature and providence, of grace and glory. These are not separate and independent sovereignties, but are parts of one perfect whole—divisions of one great empire, God's sceptre ruling alike over each and all. We may confirm and illustrate the *unity* of God's empire, by the spiritual conversion of His people. In their first, or abnormal state, they are found in *the kingdom of nature,* knowing nothing more of God than is learnt in, and presenting nothing more to God than is culled from, the natural world. Their religion is that of Cain—the religion of nature, the religion of fruit and flower. The bloomed-grape and the fragrant *bouquet* are all the sacrifice they present. *"And Cain brought of the fruits of the ground an offering unto the Lord."* In this offering there was no recognition of God's spiritual being, and no acknowledgment of his own sinfulness. *"Abel he also brought of the firstlings of his flock, and of the fat thereof And the Lord had respect unto Abel and his offering: but unto Cain and to his offering He had no respect."* The difference between these offerings was essential, and it was this. The offering of Cain was that of the *natural* man; the offering of Abel was that of the *renewed* man. The one was without an atonement for sin; the other was atonement itself. The one was a recognition of God's goodness; the other was an acknowledgment of God's holiness. The one honoured God in His natural, the other in His moral perfections. The one embodied the self-righteousness and language of the Pharisee, the other the penitence and confession of the publican. Look well to your religion, my reader! is it that of Cain, or of Abel? But, bent upon His purpose of love, God leads His people from the kingdom of nature into the *kingdom of providence.* Here they become the subjects of His wonderful works with the children of men. Perhaps, by the decay of health, perhaps by the loss of property, perhaps by the sorrow of bereavement, or by adversity in some of its countless forms, God at length brings them into the *kingdom of grace.* Taught in this kingdom their sinfulness, emptiness, and poverty; led to believe in the Lord Jesus, and to accept Him as all their salvation and all their desire; instructed, tried, tempted, sanctified, they are, at length, transferred from the kingdom of grace into the *kingdom of glory,* where they live and reign with Christ for ever. Thus, the four kingdoms constitute one grand monarchy, of which Jehovah is the great King. Now, it is in the kingdom of grace that this petition finds its most fervent and most emphatic utterance.

Turn we to the petition itself. *"Give us this day our daily bread."* How rich and comprehensive the meaning of this simple and brief prayer! How it expresses the need of all classes and conditions of men! How worthy the wisdom and the benevolence of Him who taught it! It adapts itself alike to the simplicity of the child, and to the wisdom of the sage; to the guilt of the sinner, and to the spiritual aspirations of the saint! All, of every age, and clime, and state alike, find a vehicle of utterance for their wants in this single and sublime petition, *"Give* us *this day our daily bread!"*

The first consideration is, *the Source of the supply*. Jesus, having first taught us that God was our Father—then to approach Him in the spirit of adoption as children—now instructs us to look up to Him for the supply of our wants; it being the province of a parent to provide for the necessities of his children. In this sense God is the universal Parent of the race. As all life emanates from God, so all life is sustained by God. *"The eyes of all wait upon Thee; and Thou givest them their meat in due season. Thou openest Thine hand, and satisfiest the desire of every living thing." "He giveth to the beast his food, and to the young ravens which cry."* Wonderful Parent! bountiful Benefactor! Every living thing attracts Thy notice, and receives its supply at Thy hand. From the tiny insect traversing the rose leaf, up to the highest form of animal life, all draw their sustenance from Thee. All receive from Thy bounty their daily bread. But how much more the children of Thy electing love and converting grace! The very existence of God as our Father involves the certain supply of all our need. Assured that we are His children—confirmed and sealed by the Holy Spirit—it were the veriest unbelief to doubt for a moment the truth that all our wants will be met by His outstretched, full, and overflowing hand. Oh, get this assurance that God is your Father, and then faith may grasp the pledge which this fact involves, that He will supply your daily need. How earnest and loving was Jesus in seeking to emancipate the minds of His disciples from all anxious, earthly care, by expounding to them the care of their Father in heaven. *"Your heavenly Father knoweth that ye have need of all these things."* Inexpressibly tender, soothing words! With what music do they fall upon the ear of the straitened, tried, care-oppressed child of God! *"Your heavenly Father knoweth."* Each dissected word in this consolatory passage embodies a distinct and precious thought. *"Your HEAVENLY FATHER,"*—it is a Father's knowledge, a Father's care, a Father's wealth. With such a Father, what want can He not, will He not supply? Again, *"YOUR heavenly Father!"* Yours by adopting love, yours by free grace, yours in a changeless covenant, yours individually, inalienably, and for ever yours—as if you were His *only* child! Again, *"Your heavenly Father KNOWETH"*—knoweth your person, your name, your relation; knoweth your circumstances, your straitened position, your tried faith, your assailed integrity, your tempted spirit, your sad and drooping heart. He knows it all with the knowledge of a loving Parent. Yet again: *"Your heavenly Father knoweth that you have NEED"*—your necessity; every want that exists, every demand that is made, every emergency that presses upon you, He knows. It is not what you desire, or think needful, but what you really and truly require, He recognises and provides for. This was the apostle's limit on behalf of the saints, *"My God shall supply all your NEED;"* not your imaginary or your luxurious wants, but what you necessarily and absolutely *need.* Once more: *"Your heavenly Father KNOWETH that ye have need of all THESE THINGS.* What things? food and raiment, things convenient for you; the temporal requirements of this present life. *"Godliness hath the promise of the life that now is."* With this divine, this full assurance, breathing so kindly from the lips of Jesus, how should every doubt be removed, and every fear be allayed as to the present and ample supply of our temporal wants! What a gentle, loving, yet searching rebuke of our unbelieving distrust of God! He who openeth His hand and supplieth the wants of every living thing, will He close that hand to you? He who hears the ravens when they cry, will He be deaf to you? He who guides the sparrow to the spot where the tiny seed awaits its morning's repast, will He not provide for you? O thou of little faith! wherefore dost thou doubt? Look round upon this wide, this rich, this fruitful world—it is all your Father's domain. The cattle browsing upon its hills—the golden corn waving in its fields—the capacious granaries clustering around its homesteads—the precious gems embedded within its mines—all, *all* is yours, because all is His. Truly we have a wealthy Parent, the Proprietor of the universe; *"for the earth is the Lord's, and the fulness thereof."* And He preserves its existence, fertilises and blesses it for the provision of the many sons He is bringing home to glory. Let us not, then, yield to despondency or sink in despair when the barrel of meal and the cruse of oil are well-nigh exhausted. God often permits our stores to come almost to their end ere He interposes His supply, that we may all the more distinctly trace His love and gratefully acknowledge His hand. It is through many sharp trials that faith has to travel ere it brings glory to God. The spirit of *dependence* is the essence of *faith*. Faith would remain a concealed, undeveloped, and unshapen grace, with no form, nor beauty, nor power, but for the severe tests, the stern discipline of service and of suffering to which our God often subjects it. We can speak fluently and boastfully of our trust in God, so long as sense traces the way and eyes the supplies, and leans upon a creature prop. But oh, when all this fails us; when resources are drying, and supplies are lessening, and props are breaking, and want, difficulty, and involvement stare us in the face, and we are brought to our wits' end, then we discover how slender is our hold upon God, how doubtful our trust in His word, how feeble and dwarfish our faith. And yet, small in degree as is that faith, it is priceless and imperishable. It may be sharply tried, severely winnowed, brought to its lowest ebb, its last resource; yet, such is its heavenly ascendancy, from the lowest depths it will shoot its arrows straight into heaven, send up its cry direct unto God, exclaiming, *"Though He slay me, yet will I trust in Him."* Precious faith! that can support when nature sinks; can call God Father when He smites; can dissect a smile from a frown; can discover some rays of light in the darkest cloud; empties the heart of sadness and care, and fills it with joy, confidence, and hope. The faith of God's elect, in some of its actings in the soul, resembles the feeble tendril. Following the instinct of its divine nature, faith climbs the wall of the exceeding great and precious promise, clasps in its arms the "tree of life," and so gradually ascending into the fulness of Christ, and bathing its towering head in the calm sunshine of God's love, it smiles at the tempest and defies the storm.

Thus are we directed by the petition to look to our heavenly Father for the supply of our daily temporal necessities. This He does in various ways; and it is pleasant to trace His hand in all.

He grants strength of body, resoluteness of will, and perseverance of effort in toil—and so gives us our daily bread. He clears and sustains our mental faculties, counsels our perplexities, and preserves us from, or extricates us out of, the difficulties of our path—and so gives us our daily bread. He suggests our undertakings, prospers our enterprises, blesses the work of our hands—and so gives us our daily bread. He knows our need, anticipates our wants, and times His supply to our necessities— and so gives us our daily bread. He unveils hidden sources of wealth, raises up improbable and unexpected agencies, opens the hand and inclines the heart of kindness, affection, and sympathy— and so gives us our daily bread. Thus does our heavenly Father; and by the wonder-working of His providence, often most astounding and unlooked for, feeds and clothes us. Promising that our basket and our store shall not diminish, that our bread and our water shall not fail, day by day He spreads a table for us in the wilderness, raining down the bread that sustains us with the morning's light and with the evening's shade. Could the simple annals of God's tried and straitened saints be written, what numberless instances of His providential care might be cited! scarcely less striking and touching than the most remarkable penned by the sacred historian. The cases of the prophet Elijah, of the widow of Sarepta, of the disciples for whom Jesus provided the morning's repast after their night of fruitless toil, of the multitudes whom, from the scanty supply, He more than fed in the wilderness, would all, in some one essential feature, seem to live over again. Ye, who, when temporal circumstances are straitened, whose barrel of meal and cruse of oil are brought very low, whose minds' anxieties are corroding, whose hearts' fears are sinking, to whose eyes want and dependence appear in terrible form—turn this petition into the prayer of faith, and send it up to your heavenly Father, who knows your need, and whose love, faithfulness, and power are pledged to meet it. *"For He hath said, I will never leave thee nor forsake thee. So that we may boldly say, The Lord is my Helper, and I will not fear."*

But we must present this petition in its *spiritual* teaching. That our Lord included this as its chief burden there cannot be a doubt. How familiar, significant, and precious His own words bearing on this truth, and supplying the most full and impressive comment on the petition—*"I am the* BREAD *of* LIFE." *"I am the* LIVING BREAD *which came down from heaven: if any man eat of this bread, he shall live for ever: and the bread that I will give him is my flesh, which I will give for the life of the world."* No truth stands out from the page of God's word more gloriously than this. Jesus is our life; and in this the figure He condescendingly employs—like all the types, similitudes, and emblems which set forth the Lord Jesus Christ—falls below the spiritual truth it was intended to illustrate. Natural bread does not *impart* life, it only *nourishes* and *sustains* it. But Jesus, as the Bread of Life, *gives life;* he that eateth of Him *lives.* "I have come that *they might have* and that they might have it *more abundantly."* This "Bread" possesses both divine life and mediatorial life, and both are essential to the salvation of the soul. Oh, who can ever tell what our Lord passed through in order to become available as the life of His people! *"Bread-corn is* BRUISED." How affectingly true was this of Jesus, as the living bread of His Church! In every sense and from every quarter He was *bruised.* *"It pleased the Father to* BRUISE *Him, He hath put Him to grief."* He was bruised by Satan and by man—He was bruised by sin and by sinners—He was bruised by friends and by foes. Who can describe the terrible process through which the fine wheat from heaven passed ere we could eat by faith of this bread and live! What clue have we to this mystery of mysteries, what solution of this profoundest of problems—Christ's sufferings—Himself sinless and innocent—but that which the theory of a *substitutionary sacrifice* supplies? *"Christ hath loved us, and hath given Himself for us, an offering and a sacrifice unto God for a sweet smelling savour."* This explains it all. His death was expiatory. It was for sin. *"Who His own self bear our* SINS *in His own body on the tree."* *"When He had by Himself purged our* SINS." *"He is the propitiation for our* SINS." *"The blood of Jesus Christ His Son cleanseth us from all* SIN." Hold fast this doctrine of Christianity! It is more than this—it is Christianity itself. It is the life-blood of our religion, it is the life of our souls. Contend for it unto the death. Maintain your belief of the Atonement at any cost; sell it at none. It admits of no dilution, of no reservation, of no compromise. Received fully, and believed simply, and lived holily, the end, in this world, of your faith, will be a happy, hopeful death, and in the world to come life everlasting. As a mortal soon to die, as a responsible being soon to give an account, as a sinner soon to appear before God, as an immortal linked with an endless destiny, the ATONEMENT of the Son of God is *everything* to you. It cannot be questioned, denied, ignored, but at the peril of interests more precious, and of an eternity more solemn than the universe!

You inquire, perhaps, in view of this impressive and emphatic statement, How may I obtain an interest in the atonement of Christ? Your question is of infinite moment. No profound reasoning or elaborate disquisition is necessary to its answer, as no laboured process or weary pilgrimage is required for its attainment. God has made *faith* the receptive grace of salvation. The gospel terms are—not him that worketh, nor him that runneth, nor him that deserveth—but, "him that *believeth.*" The whole edifice of your salvation rests upon the simple reception in faith of a personal Saviour. The words of that Saviour are, *"Verily, verily, I say unto you, He that BELIEVETH on me hath everlasting life."* With this agrees the teaching of His apostle, "BELIEVE in the Lord Jesus Christ, and thou shalt be saved." What terms could be more simple, what mode of bringing you into the full reception of salvation, with its priceless, countless blessings of peace, joy, hope, more appropriate? But even at this, perchance, you stumble! The very *simplicity* of God's mode of bringing you into the experience of the costliest gift in His power to bestow, is your bar to its possession. But let a wise and holy witness testify:—"Sin gives you the first title to the Friend of sinners; a simple, naked faith the second. Do not puzzle yourself about contrition, faithfulness, love, joy, power over sin, and a thousand such things which the white devil will persuade you you must bring to Christ. He will receive you gladly with the greatest mountain of sin; and the smallest grain of faith at Christ's feet will remove that mountain. At the peril of your soul, desire at present not peace nor joy, nor puzzle yourself even about love; only desire that that blessed Man may be your Bridegroom, and that you may firmly believe that He is so, because He hath given you His flesh and blood upon the cross. You have nothing to do with sin and self, although they will have much to do with you. *Your business is with Jesus*—with His free, unmerited love, with His glorious promises. Strongly expect nothing from your own heart but unbelief, hardness, and backsliding, and when you find them there be not shaken nor discomfited; rather rejoice that you are to live by faith on the faithful heart of Christ, and cast not away your confidence, which hath great recompense of reward."*

> "Faith is not what we feel or see;
>   It is a simple trust
> On what the God of love has said
>   Of Jesus, or the 'Just.'

> "What Jesus is, and that alone,
>   Is faith's delightful plea;
> It never deals with sinful self,
>   Or righteousness in me.

> "It tells me I am counted dead
>   By God in His own word;
> It tells me I am 'born again'
>   In Christ my risen Lord.

> "If He is free, then I am free
>   From all unrighteousness:
> If He is just, then I am just;
>   *He* is my Righteousness."

Behold, then, this "living Bread"—giving life, sustaining life, and crowning life with the diadem of life eternal. It has in it all the ingredients of spiritual life,—the pardon of sin, peace of mind, joy of heart, holiness of walk, and hope beyond. There is everything that your soul needs in Jesus. Make an inventory of your wants—add up the sum total, sign it with "poverty," "bankruptcy," "sinner the chief," "hell-deserving," and take it to Jesus, and from His full,

---

* Fletcher.

overflowing, free-flowing redundancy of all grace He will meet your need, honour your draft, and dismiss you from His presence your heart thrilling with joy unspeakable and full of glory.

"GIVE us." God's blessings are gifts. Divine, priceless, and precious they are beyond all purchase. They have indeed been purchased, but the purchase-price was not that of man's finding, but of God's—even the price of Christ's most precious blood. We come not, then, to God with the petition, "*Sell* us," but, "*Give* us." Out of Thine overflowing heart, from Thine infinite sufficiency and most free favour, give us the blessings of Thy providence and grace. "I come, Lord, with an outstretched hand, with an empty palm, stricken with hunger, famished and ready to die. I have heard that there is bread enough in my Father's house and to spare. Lo! I come, not worthy to be called Thy son, asking but the portion of a slave. Give me this day my daily bread." Oh, what a charm, what a sweetness does the freeness of grace impart to the blessings bestowed upon us by God! All who cluster around His table and eat of this bread appear there as the pensioners of His most free grace. They are invited as a sovereign asks his guests to *receive* the hospitality of his princely home. What an affront would it be to that sovereign to offer to *pay* for the banquet to which he had graciously invited you! A greater affront cannot be offered to the free grace and love of God than to imagine that He will *sell* His favours, that He requires you to *pay* for your admittance into His kingdom of grace and glory. True, solemnly true, He expects a *return,* and a *large* return too, but it is such a return of love and thankfulness, of obedience and service, as His own Spirit working in our hearts enables us to make. Thus, when grace finds us God's beggars, it leaves us His debtors, laying us under the obligation— oh, sweet and holy bond!—of yielding ourselves, body, soul, and spirit, an unreserved surrender.

"THIS DAY"—"day by day." God will have us live upon His bounty by the day. We have no inherent, independent resources, no reserved and treasured supplies. The manna rained down by God around Israel's camp was a striking type of this truth. It was the Lord's Prayer of the Old Testament saints. In it they were taught

to ask and to expect from God their daily bread. It was a morning
and an evening supply. They were commanded to lay up nothing
for the morrow. If they disobeyed this injunction, the manna
decomposed and was unfit for use. There was no surplus, no waste,
nothing superfluous. *"As it is written, He that had gathered much
had nothing over; and he that had gathered little had no lack."*
What a divine lesson was Israel here taught! And what a gospel,
spiritual truth it teaches us! We are here taught the great mystery
of a life of daily faith. And oh, what may be the need, what the
history of one single day! What its demands, its pressures, its
trials. One short day may give its mould and complexion to a man's
endless being. What events, what changes, what disappointments,
what sorrows, what new and startling pictures in life's ever-
shifting panorama may revolve! The sun which in the morning
rose so gorgeously may at evening set in darkness and in storm.
But oh, how precious is this truth—God is prepared in response
to our morning's prayer, to give us all that the day shall need. In
anticipation of its daily toil, its mental anxiety, its physical
demands, its trials of affection, its tests of principle, its endurance
of suffering, its experience of grief, its losses, its crosses, its
partings, you may perhaps enter upon it as the disciples entered
into the cloud on Mount Tabor, with fear and trembling. But behold
your promise! "Give us THIS DAY our daily bread." You thus begin
your day with looking up. You commence it with God. Ere you enter
upon the day's battle of life, you repair to the Strong One for
strength, to the Divine Counsellor for wisdom, to the full Saviour
for grace, to your Heavenly Father for the day's supply,—and with
your urn thus filled from the infinite source of all blessing, you go
forth from your chamber as a strong man to run a race, fed,
nourished, invigorated, with the daily bread God has so kindly
and so profusely snowed around your camp. Thus will God have
us live a life of daily faith upon His bounty. If we would live amid
the daily conflict of the flesh a life of holy victory, we must live a
life of daily faith upon Jesus, a life of daily waiting upon God.
"This day, my Father! The supplies of yesterday are exhausted;
those of tomorrow I leave with Thee: give me this day all that its

circumstances may demand. Give me the clearness of judgment, the soundness of decision, the resoluteness of will, the integrity of principle, the uprightness of heart, the moral courage, the Christ-like meekness, the holy love, the watchfulness and prayerfulness, the circumspection and consistency its yet unshaped history may require. I know not to what temptations I shall be exposed, by what foes I shall be assailed, through what trials I shall pass; what clouds will shade, what sorrows will embitter, what circumstances will wound my spirit. Lord, give me grace, strength, love, guidance, faith; give me this day my daily bread." What a holy, happy life is this! It removes all care from the mind but the present, and for that present the believer hangs upon a Father's care. In this we trace a beautiful and perfect harmony of the Old and the New Testaments. The *promise* to the Old Testament saints was, *"As THY DAYS, so shall thy strength be."* The *prayer* taught the New Testament saints is, *"Give us THIS DAY our daily bread."* And so we learn that God is the Author of both the Old and the New Testaments; and these two divine witnesses unite in testifying to His love, bounty, and faithfulness to His people. Thus begin and continue your day with God. Its history, as I have reminded you, is all undeveloped, uncertain, and untraced. You cannot foresee one step, antedate one circumstance, or control one event. Let your prayer be—"Give me, Lord, all supplies for this day. I may have trials—trials of my judgment, trials of my affections, trials of conscience, trials of my principles, trials from those I most tenderly love—Lord, be with me. Guide me with Thy counsel, hold up my steps that they slide not, and, in the multitude of my thoughts within me, let Thy comforts delight my soul."

And mark the *unselfishness* and *sympathy* of this petition. It is not "give *me*," but "give us." There is a largeness of heart, a breadth of supplication here worthy of Him at whose feet we learn the prayer. Christ had come to bless the race. Self was its idol, and selfishness its sin. He had come to dethrone the one and to annihilate the other. By the "expulsive power of a new affection"— the love of God in the heart of man—He sought to unlock the affections, unseal the sympathies, and expand the powers of the soul; and by reinstating man in his filial relation to God, to reinstate him in his fraternal relation to his brother. Thus are we taught by Jesus to cast from us all selfishness in prayer, and in asking of our Heavenly Father—the ONE Father of His people by grace, and the one Parent of the race by creation—daily bread for ourselves, to ask also daily bread for others. Give us—the rich and the poor, the saint and the sinner, he who owns and he who tills the land—give *us* our daily bread. Drinking into the spirit of this petition, we shall resolve with Job not to *"eat our morsel alone, the fatherless not eating thereof,"* (Job xxxi. 17.) A yet higher example of generous sympathy will influence us—the example of Christ himself. Followed into the desert by the populace, eager to hear His words and to see His works, they were three days with out food. His disciples would have dismissed the multitude to their homes famishing and fainting by the way. Not so the Lord. Himself often an hungered for the very bread He so generously provided for others, He resolved upon meeting the present need. Taking in His hands the scanty supply, He sought His Father's blessing, then break and distributed, and by the exercise of His own divine power, so multiplied the few and increased the little as satisfied to the full the wants of *"about three thousand men, besides women and children."* Who will say that our Lord was indifferent to the *temporal* necessities of man? That, because His first and chief mission was to bring down the bread of heaven to a fallen, sinful world, He would be slow to make an equal provision for the body; that body which, by the renewing of the Holy Ghost, was to become the sacred temple of God through the Spirit! The practical lesson, then, we learn from this memorable and instructive incident of our Lord's life is, *to remember the poor.* It is God's will that *"the poor shall never cease out of the land."* They are His special clients. *"He shall judge the poor of the people." "He shall stand at the right hand of the poor to save him from them that condemn his soul."* Poor and dependent Himself; it was amongst this class of society Jesus the most frequently mingled, and to whom He more especially addressed His ministry of grace, and among whom, for the most part, He wrought His miracles of power. The common people heard Him gladly, and to the poor the gospel was preached. Imitating our Lord, we shall not deem the poor and the needy— especially those of the "household of faith"—beneath our regard, or beyond the pale of our sympathy and succour. Blessed ourselves with daily bread, we should share our loaf with our less amply supplied and more necessitous brother, and in this way be instrumental in answering the petition sent up to his Father— "Give me day by day my daily bread." Oh, it is a high honour and a precious privilege to be God's almoner to the poor! Has He given us *more* than our daily bread? It is that we might give of our superfluity to others! The *excess* of our supply is to augment another's *deficiency*. Not the crumbs that fall from our table, but of its groaning abundance, are we to give. *"There is that scattereth, and yet increaseth; there is that withholdeth, and it tendeth to poverty."* The manna we selfishly refuse, or niggardly dole, or covetously hoard, shall breed its own devouring worm and emit a noisome savour. This suggests another and an important thought.

Let us not suppose that the question of the supply of the poor and the needy is a national, ecclesiastical, or class question. It is purely a Christian and humane one. The pauper of every clime and religion and grade is a 'brother' and a 'neighbour,' asking and claiming our recognition, sympathy, and aid. How nobly did our American brethren illustrate this fact, during the recent Irish famine, when they opened their granaries and despatched their ships freighted with corn to a people suffering from the blight of their crops, three thousand miles distant from their shores! All honour to a great nation true to the instincts of humanity, noble in character and illustrious in religion! Few questions of political economy have proved of a graver and more perplexing cast, and have tasked and tested to the same extent the power and skill of a nation's statesmanship, than the mode of meeting the necessities of the poor. Pauperism exists in every land; but England has nothing to be ashamed of in the mode by which it has been met. The Christianity of the nation—its religion and its Protestantism—has nobly grappled with the "Bread Question," generously originating and wisely directing its supplies. The contrast of pauperism, as it both exists and is met in Protestant and in Papal countries, is so forcibly put by an American divine—an original and eloquent thinker—that I am tempted to quote his remarks *in extenso.* "Pauperism," he writes, "must be, and should be fed; but who? Catholicism taunts Protestantism with the pauperism of England, as if it were chargeable on the rejection of the Roman faith. But in answer to this, it is sufficient to say that the pauperism of British countries is found mainly in the class who are not church-goers. The artisan and ploughman who have become imbruted and sceptical, who keep no Sabbath, and read no Bible, and never enter the sanctuary, are in Protestant England the chief burdens on the poor fund. Those who visit the Sabbath-school, and the chapel or the church, both in the mining and manufacturing districts, are less grievously and less often the victims of want. But in Catholic countries it is the church-going—those who haunt the porch, and the altar, and the confessional, and keep the church-holidays, that are the most shameless and importunate in their mendicancy. The poor of the Protestant countries are by their religion kept mainly from the worst woes and vices of the pauperism around them, which preys mainly on the rejecters or neglecters of their religion. But the poor of Catholic countries are made such and kept such *by their faith;* by its festivals, fostering idleness; by the mendicancy of many of its religious orders of friars, and by the mortmain engrossment of large portions of the nation's soil and the nation's resources in the support of monastic establishments, which consume but do not produce. Again, the pauperism of Protestant England is not either as deep or deplorable as that of Catholic Ireland; nor that of the Protestant cantons in Switzerland like that of Catholic Savoy. We say this but in passing, and in reply to an unjust impeachment which the Roman Catholic often brings. But wherever population has become dense, and labour difficult to be obtained, pauperism has grown into a formidable evil. It is in many lands the great question of the times. The gaunt and hollow-eyed class of the 'Wants' are confronting the more sleek but the less numerous and the feebler house of the 'Haves.' Shall the sinewy grasp of famine's bony hand be laid on the pampered throat of luxury, and a violent social revolution assay the right for a time the dread inequality? We believe that to the lands which honour not or scorn the gospel, there are few enemies which they have more cause to fear than this famishing multitude—fierce, unrestrained, and illiterate—a Lazarus without a gospel and without a God, turning wolf—like in the blindness of its misery and its brute strength on a Dives without conscience and without mercy. The poor must be relieved, but not in indolence. That gospel which is so eminently a message for the poor, yet declares that if any man will not work neither shall he eat. Society must not overlook her destitute children, but she must not nurse and fatten them in sloth. If, on the other hand, she undertake to supply and direct all their labour, she would restrain rather than foster enterprise and industry. If she compel work, she must have despotic powers to extort it. If she resolutely cling to free institutions and reject despotism, she must forego the compulsory requirement of the labour; and then is it charity to bestow the unearned pay, and whilst the sluggard folds his arms to thrust alms betwixt his teeth? We do not see in association or social revolution, or in any system of mere political legislation, the full remedy of this. The gospel must come in, and by its influence on personal conscience and on individual character, teach the poor self-respect, diligence, economy, and content; and require of the rich sympathy, compassion, and bounty for their more necessitous brethren. Christ is needed, not only as an Interpreter and a Daysman betwixt man and God; He is needed also in the daily business of the world as a Daysman betwixt the several classes of society that now eye each other askance— each endeavouring to abridge its own duties and exaggerating its demands upon the class opposed to itself. And ought the wealthy to forget ever the bonds of sympathy that bind them, amid their opulence and in their ceiled houses and their elegant leisure, to the multitudes around? Are they wealthy? The poor man aided in building, storing, and sailing their argosies, and in rearing and guarding their sumptuous abodes. The poor man takes, to protect their slumbers, the watchman's weary beat and the fireman's noble risks. Every grain of sugar and every lock of cotton that passes through their warehouses is the fruit of the labour of some other of the great household—their kindred, and their duty to whom they may not justly disavow. The purple and fine linen passed through the poor man's hands at the loom and the vat; and not an ornament or a comfort decks or gladdens them in their persons or in their houses on which the horny palm of WANT has not at some time wearily rested. In one apartment there have met the toils of the colliers of Northumberland and of the potters of Staffordshire. Upon one and the same table are grouped the offerings of the Mexican mines and of the British cutler, of the Scottish weaver and the Irish cottar, of the tea-gatherer of 'far Cathay' and of the whale-fisher of their own Nantucket. *'We are members one of another.'* We cannot forget it with impunity. If each member of the great brotherhood of the nations were to come and claim back his contributions to our daily comforts, how poor and forlorn should we be left! Our common Father would not have us overlook it, in the benefits it has brought and in the bonds which it imposes. We owe much to our fellows, and we owe more to Him. To Him, the wealthiest capitalist who rules the exchanges of a nation owes as much of hourly obligation for life, and food, and health, and competence, as did Elijah the prophet, in the sore famine when God was feeding him by daily miracle at the brooks, and ravens were his purveyors, or in the house of the widow of Sarepta. Now, one mode of acknowledging gratefully our indebtedness to God is by the fraternal acknowledgment of obligation to our brethren, whom, as His pensioners, He transfers to our care. The rich, then, are not entitled to be profuse and wasteful, and thus to empty the granaries, as it were, of many coming years and of many needy households in selfish rioting and prodigality. We do not call for the enactment of sumptuary laws, but we suppose Christianity to require of its individual disciples that *'their MODERATION should be known to all men.'**

Remarks fraught with such practical wisdom, and from the pen of a foreign writer, whose European travel betrays so much shrewd and impartial observation, strongly commend themselves to the study of every Christian, of every Christian statesman and political

---

* "Lectures on the Lord's Prayer, by William R. Williams, D.D., New York, pp. 115-119. Boston, U.S."

economist. Christianity alone supplies the true solution of the problem—How is pauperism to be met? It alone throws upon the canvas the different shades into which pauperism resolves itself— the pauperism that is the result of indolence and improvidence, or that which is engendered by a religious system spurious and superstitious, or that which is the natural offspring of unwise political legislation, or, yet more, that which is produced, in the providence of God, by social and national calamity. While the gospel thus clearly defines pauperism, it as clearly instructs us how to meet it. It teaches the lesson of prudence, frugality, and economy, and it inculcates the precepts of self-denial, sympathy, and benevolence. It bridges the chasm between the rich and the poor, moulds the race into kin, and by its regenerating influence unites the kin into a family, and teaches us that he is my neighbour and he my brother who, wounded, in suffering, or in want, needs my sympathy and asks my aid.

Cheerful *contentment* with God's measured supplies, is taught us by this petition. How uniform is the teaching of the Bible on this point of Christian duty! It nowhere promises superfluities, or encourages peevish discontent with God's restricted supply. Not what we *wish,* not what we *ask,* but what we *need,* is insured to us. While God is infinitely rich and boundless in His resources, and often profuse and luxurious in His supplies, this is not the rule, but the exception, of His dealings with men, and especially with the saints. The *promise* is, *"Your BREAD and your WATER shall be sure."* The *precept* is, *"Be CONTENT with such things as ye have."* The *limit* is, *"God shall supply all you NEED."* The *exhortation* is, *"Having FOOD and RAIMENT, therewith to be content."* The *desire* is, *"Neither poverty nor riches."* The *prayer* is, *"Give me this day my daily BREAD."* Such was the lowly fare of Him who came to work out our redemption from eternal woe. Be often hungered, yet supplied others with bread; thirsted, yet gave others drink; wearied, yet gave others rest; sorrowed, yet gave others joy. Oh, what a self-abjuring, self-sacrificing, man-loving life was Christ's! Not a breath of murmur, not a syllable of discontent, not a word of impatience ever passed His lips. Contentment was enthroned upon

His brow, meekness was reflected in His countenance, love beamed in His eye, kindness, gentleness, and compassion breathed in His every word. What was carnal enjoyment, the dainty table, the soft couch, the luxurious raiment, the splendid hall, the exquisite music, to Him whose kingdom was not of this world?—who came to live a life of poverty—to toil as a mechanic—to be evil entreated, maligned, and traduced; and then, to close His career, condemned as a felon and crucified as a slave—all for LOVE to man! With such an example of moderation, contentment, and patience; with such a model of unearthliness, unworldliness, and heavenliness; with such a CRUCIFIXION to the world ever before us,—when *"the lust of the flesh, and the lust of the eyes, and the pride of life,"* would allure is from the simplicity that is in Christ Jesus,—what true disciple of the Saviour is not content with the needful and the moderate provision which a faithful and a loving Father is pledged daily to supply? Confronted by this truth, shall we allow any allurement of the world, any temptation to wealth, or any proffer of daily sustenance to overcome our loyalty to conscience, to Christ, and to God? Shall we be tempted to profane the Sabbath, to embark in an enterprise injurious to our fellow-creatures—to take a step unjust and dishonest, selfish and questionable, to gain our livelihood, to win our daily bread? God forbid! Better, far better, eat your moulded crust, and slake your morning and evening thirst at the pure spring, and so make your daily repast, than to luxuriate and fatten upon the *"wages of sin."* Is God your Father?—*trust Him.* Was He the God of your parent?—*trust Him. "I have been young, and now am old; yet have I not seen the righteous forsaken, nor his seed begging BREAD."*

See through what channel all our blessings, temporal or spiritual, flow—the divinely appointed channel of *prayer. "ASK, and ye shall receive." "If ye then, being evil, know how to give good gifts unto your children, how much more shall your Father which is in heaven give good things to them that ASK HIM?"* And how corresponding and encouraging the apostle's exhortation, *"Be careful for nothing; but in everything by prayer and supplication, with thanksgiving, let your REQUESTS be made known unto God."*

That want is enriching, that sorrow is joyful, that burden is uplifting, that care is lightsome, that trial is precious, that discovery of indwelling evil is sanctifying, that leads us to the throne of grace, that shuts us up to God in prayer. Oh, for what intent a Father's smiting, a Father's rebuke, a Father's rod, a Father's blessing, but to open our heart in prayer, and to unseal our lips in praise! *"Let me hear Thy voice; for sweet is Thy voice, and Thy countenance is comely."* In this loving, holy light, interpret all the dealings of your Father God.

Be earnest and covetous in your seeking after the *"Bread of life."* Here lay no restraint upon your desires, put no limit to your requests. *"Open thy mouth wide, and I will fill it."* You cannot approach with a basket too large, with a vessel too empty, with a frequency too often, nor with a request too importunate. God has given you Christ. This DIVINE LOAF, prepared by God in heaven, has come down to earth, of which you are invited to partake, freely, abundantly, daily, and live. All that Christ is—all that Christ has done—and all that Christ is now doing—is *yours*. Every pulse of His heart beats for you; every drop of His shed-blood was for you; every grain of His treasured grace is for you; every breath of His intercession in heaven is for you—all is yours; for you are Christ's, and Christ is God's. Day by day is the life of faith you are to live upon Jesus. It is DAILY BREAD. Jesus for each and for every day. Jesus for each day's wants—Jesus for each day's trials—Jesus for each day's sins—Jesus for life—Jesus for death—JESUS FOR EVER!

CHAPTER VIII.

THE PENITENTIAL SPIRIT OF
THE LORD'S PRAYER.

"Forgive us our debts."—MATT. vi. 12.

RAYER for divine forgiveness, springing from penitence for conscious sin, is the burden of this petition taught us by our Lord. It is proposed to consider both of these states in the present chapter. We, of course, begin with the essential grace of repentance, seeing that this is God's order in conversion. Contrition for an offence must precede the pardon of an offence. In social life, in the family government, in the Church, and in the State this is an acknowledged and invariable law. The debtor would be incapable of appreciating the clemency which cancelled the debt, so long as he denied either the existence or the justice of the claim. Unconscious of the obligation, he would be insensible to the grace that remitted it. In a higher and more impressive sense does this hold good between the sinner and God. The forgiveness of sin is too divine and costly a pearl to cast before swine. In other words, God holds this His own and sole prerogative at too high a rate to exercise it in behalf of a sinner blind to, and the willing slave of, his sins. Repentance is in His eye so divine and gracious a work, the humble and contrite heart so spiritual and precious a sacrifice, that to this man, and to him alone, will He deign to look with an eye of forgiving love and complacent delight; and upon him and him only will He bestow the costliest blessing that He can give or we receive—the pardon of sin. Can we for a moment suppose that God will bind this precious jewel upon a brow that has never bowed before Him in penitence, confession, and prayer? Will He confer so costly a boon upon a soul incapable of knowing its worth or of tasting its sweetness, and not even asking or desiring its bestowment? Assuredly not! God will never pour the grace of His pardoning mercy and love but into the vessel of a broken heart. But the prayer, "Forgive," is the breathing of a penitent soul. It expresses the conviction and is an acknowledgment of sin. It is a prayer that could only arise from a heart sorely conscious of its misery and plague. It is the language of a self-arraigned, self-convicted soul. Standing at the bar of its own conscience, and trying itself, as if in anticipation of the great judgment, and passing the sentence of self-condemnation, it appeals to God the Judge of all—"Forgive!" And yet it is also the prayer of a *forgiven* soul. Forgiveness is a past, present, and future act of sovereign grace. This prayer, as it is the first and earliest, so is it the last and latest breathing of a pardoned and gracious man. All through the divine life—as we shall presently show—there is a daily renewal of pardon, a constant application of atoning blood to the quickened conscience. And prayer may ascend to our Heavenly Father for forgiveness with a firm faith in His precious assurance—"I HAVE *pardoned*"— until prayer for pardon shall terminate in its eternal praise.

Let us now direct our attention to the petition—*"Forgive us our debts."*

There is a close and beautiful connexion—the links of which are so delicate as to be visible only to the spiritual eye—between the present and the preceding petition. The prayer for daily bread finds its best exposition in the prayer for daily forgiveness. The true, the heavenly bread has in it this divine and precious element, and it is no bread to me apart from it. What is *mere* bread to a man under the sentence of death, but the bread of condemnation? You who are still under the law, dead in trespasses and sins; you who have no righteousness but your own works, no Saviour but yourself; you whose heaven is earth, whose God is your belly, whose possessions are beautiful parks, and pleasant pictures, and costly jewels, and domestic comforts, and luxurious enjoyments, and gay delights, so long as you are unconverted and under the condemnation of God's holy law, you but eat the bread of the convict who tomorrow is roused to his last meal ere he is led forth to die. Awful state! the daily bread you coldly ask, yet munificently receive, is the bread of *death,* not the bread of *life!* There is in it no ingredient of God's forgiveness of sin, no sweetness of Christ's love to the sinner, no foretaste of a heaven of glory, no nourishment for a soul that is to live for ever,—it perishes, and, inevitably and eternally, you perish with it! And yet you exist on, and dream on, and trifle on, profoundly unconscious of your perilous condition, totally insensible to the dread world to which you hasten.

Turn we now to the petition before us. It portrays God as a Creditor, man as the debtor, and the attitude of the soul as that of a humble penitent suing for the forgiveness of the debt. Before you proceed or read further, will you, my reader, pause upon the threshold of the subject, and lift up your heart in silent prayer to the Holy Spirit for His enlightening, quickening grace, that the great and vital truths about to be unfolded may be the power of God unto your salvation, and, if saved, for your more abundant sanctification, comfort, and meetness for glory.

Man is God's debtor in a thousand ways. We commence with *his being.* He made us, and not we ourselves. As *"none can keep alive his own soul,"* it follows that not having the power to *preserve* life, no creature has power to *give* life: so that we are neither self-created nor self-preserved. God made us. It is a proper and beautiful acknowledgment of the Episcopal service, "We thank Thee for our *creation."* Will any intelligent individual assert that he is under no obligation to God for his bodily existence, his intellectual faculties, his moral powers, his soul capable of such high enjoyment now, and, if saved, destined to a happiness inconceivably great and eternal hereafter? This is a debt. We owe all we are to Him who has said, *"I have created him for my glory."* We are not self-proprietors, we belong not to ourselves, we are not our own. We may not employ our members, nor use our faculties, as we list. Our physical, intellectual, and moral nature belongs to God. Made originally in His image, it was made exclusively for His glory. The inventor of a curious piece of mechanism must of necessity be its sole proprietor. The mechanism has no natural, invested, and inalienable right to itself, simply because it displays such inventive genius and possesses such marvellous action. The argument of Locke is as logically sound as it is theologically correct—that, God has a *right* to His workmanship. It is His own. He made us at His will, and at His will He can destroy us. Admit that man has property in himself, and you must admit that his responsibility ceases. The moment he ceases to be a dependent being, he ceases to be a responsible being. He then becomes—awful conclusion!—a deity to himself. To himself he is alone accountable how he uses the members of his body, how he employs the faculties of his mind, how he lays out the powers of his soul, how he disposes of his earthly substance. A god to himself he owns no other allegiance, acknowledges no other authority, recognises no other right to rule and to possess him than his own! But no sophistical reasoning, no fine-drawn infidelity, can contravene the fact or release him from the truth that, the creature must be the absolute, undivided, indefeasible property of the Creator; that this involves his *responsibility;* and that as a responsible being *"every one of us must give account of himself to God."* Such is the natural debt you owe to God, my reader. You owe to Him as your Maker every member of your body, every faculty of your mind, every power of your soul. To Him you must give account of your body, how you have used it; of your talents, how you have employed them; of your soul, how you have cared for it; of your rank, wealth, influence, time, how you have laid out all for God. Do you acknowledge the debt? Do you recognise the claim by a holy, cheerful, unreserved surrender? God has power to assert His claim, and He will assert it for time and for eternity.

But we are God's *moral* debtors. The existence of a moral government implies the existence of moral law; and the existence of law implies the existence of moral obligation on the part of the subjects of that government. Every human being is a subject of

God's moral government, and is under the most solemn
obligation—an obligation enforced by rewards and punishments
the most holy and inflexible—to obey. God, as the Great Ruler of
the universe, has a right to prescribe rules of action to His
creatures, and to connect those rules with promises and
threatenings. Let it be borne in mind that His enactings are not
simply *commands,* but in the strictest and highest sense, *laws.*
Commands and laws are two different things. It is true that every
law involves a command, but every command does not involve a
law. A command must be *rightful* in order to be a law, and not
merely rightful, but he who issues the command must have
authority so to do, and those to whom the command is given must
be *bound* to obey; on these conditions only does a command become
a law. Hence we learn what *sin* is. Sin is a deviation from the law
of God. In the language of jurists this would simply be called a
crime, but in the language of Scripture it is called SIN. *"Sin is the
transgression of the law."* We come now to the subject of man's
obedience to God. It is illustrated by the idea of the payment of a
debt. The stern, unbending language of the law is, *"Pay me that
thou owest."* From this demand there is no release. The claim must
be met, the obligation cancelled, or the penalty endured, either in
the person of the actual debtor, or in the person of an equivalent
surety equal to the justice and extent of the demand. It is here
the mediatorial scheme presents itself. In default of man's
obedience—his original violation of God's law, and, as a
consequence, his utter inability to keep one single precept—the
Son of God came into the world, was born of a woman, and was
made under the law; and by His perfect obedience He became the
end of the law for righteousness to every one that believeth. How
divine is the gospel plan! With whom but with God could it have
originated? What mind could have conceived, what heart devised,
what power have executed the salvation of man but His? The entire
scheme is so befitting and marvellous. It meets all the
requirements of God's government, and all the necessities of man's
condition. On the part of His elect people the Lord Jesus has *paid*
this great debt of obedience. He obeyed in their stead and as their

substitute, and His obedience—the obedience of the God-man Mediator—becomes virtually the righteousness in which they stand delivered from condemnation and accepted of God. *"By the obedience of one many* (a number which no man can compute) *are made righteous."* Take hold in simple faith of this righteousness, my reader, and you are fully, freely, and for ever justified. In other words, take hold of CHRIST, who is the *"Lord our Righteousness,"* for, *"by Him all that believe are justified from all things."* Through no other door can you enter heaven but this.

3) We owe *supreme love to God.* The terms of the law are clear and explicit—*"Thou shalt* LOVE *the Lord thy God with all thy heart, and with all thy soul, and with all thy mind. This is the first and great commandment."* The law requires us to love God with all the powers and faculties of our being—the will, the understanding, the affections. This love must be paramount to all objects whatsoever—simply, singly, supremely. In man's innocence this law was implicitly obeyed, his state of original and perfect holiness rendering him as capable of, as he was happy in, so doing. His fall, however, has rendered him utterly unable to perform it. So far from loving God with all his soul, he has no true love to God whatever, but sad, awful hatred to God and to everything that belongs to Him. *"The carnal mind is* ENMITY *against God."* The use of the abstract term *enmity,* instead of the concrete *enemy,* in this passage, is remarkably striking and solemn. In our description of character we always make choice of the latter. We say of a person that he is *friendly,* not *friendship;* that he is *lovely,* not *love.* But this mode of speaking would not do justice to the present case. Man is not only an *enemy* to God, but he is ENMITY itself against God. Hatred to God is not a mere quality or attribute of man, something which exists in him; it is his very nature, it is himself. We owe, then, to God this debt of supreme love. It is the law of His moral government that we give to Him—the Supreme Good—the supreme affection of our soul, of which He is worthy. Were there a being higher than God—we recoil instinctively from the bare supposition—then it were an unrighteous law that challenged for God our single and supreme love. But since the Lord our God is one Lord, and that He is the eternal, self-existent

Jehovah, the Creator of heaven and earth, man's divine Maker, and the moral Governor of the universe, it is a most righteous law that demands from the creatures He has made their single, undivided, supreme affection. No inability to render this single affection releases us from the duty. The obligation is still the same—irrevocable, irrefragable, eternal. Do you love God, my reader? I drop the cold expression which presents your obligation as a duty. I speak of it rather as a precious *privilege*—the highest privilege belonging to man—Is God the chief object of your supreme affection? Inquire of your conscience, examine your heart, look into your life, and ask yourself the solemn question—Do I love God? Have I returned to Him the affection His law requires, His nature demands, my being justly owes? What traces are there in my conduct, what evidences in my life, of love to Christ? Do I exhibit any of the marks of genuine affection to my Maker, Preserver, and Benefactor? Have I believed in Christ, have I accepted God's plan of salvation, am I regulating my life by His word, am I warring with sin and striving after holiness? If I do not love God with all my soul, then whom do I love? And if I die with this debt of love uncancelled, what awaits me save the prison from whence there is no release until I shall have paid the uttermost farthing.

But how sacred is this obligation, how precious this privilege to a child of God! Love to God is the sweetest debt you pay. What are your happiest moments? Are they not when, floating upon the wings of affection, your soul mounts towards the Fountain of life, the centre and source of love, and you find yourself approaching nearer and still nearer the ineffable glory of God?

And here again the Lord Jesus Christ, as the great paymaster of His people, graciously appears. In default of their ever reaching this standard of perfect love to God required by the law, Jesus presents Himself on their behalf. He came, as I have just shown, to keep every precept of the law in their place—and this the chief one of all—for *"love is the first and great commandment,"* and, *"love is the fulfilling of the law."* He loved God with a perfect love. He loved Him with all His heart, and with all His mind, and with all His soul; and so, as the substitute and surety of His elect Church, He honoured and magnified the law in this its highest and chief requirement. How delightful to study the whole life of Jesus as the life of love—love to God and love to man! Love explains the great mystery of His marvellous incarnation. Love admits us to the secret of His life of unreserved devotion to man. Love explains the marvel of His unparalleled sufferings and His ignominious death. Love elucidates the great truth of the gospel—the Innocent One suffering for the guilty, the Just One for *the unjust*. I ask philosophy, I challenge every system and religion invented by man, to explain this mystery of SUBSTITUTION in the moral government of Jehovah— the holy Son of God suffering and dying in man's stead—and all is silence! There is no solution, there is no clue but His LOVE—His own divine and eternal love supplies it. Oh, yes! all His life was love— love to His Father, love to His commands, love to His honour, love to His truth, love to His people, love to man, love to sinners the vilest, to rebels the greatest, to enemies the bitterest, to His murderers the fiercest—love which constrained Him to lay down His sacred life, to give Himself an expiatory offering and an atoning sacrifice unto God for man's salvation. This one single, magic word— LOVE—is the great principle of all that is most stupendous, mysterious, and sublime in our religion. This reveals the Mind where all originated, and unveils the bosom where all centred. The grand secret of heaven is now made known! And yet it is the substitution of one mystery for another. If love explains His mission and defines His work, what shall explain His love itself? Truly, "the love of Christ PASSETH KNOWLEDGE." But in the embrace of this mystery I am willing for ever to dwell. Conscious that His almighty arms are around me, I ask, I desire no more than the assurance that "He hath loved me, and hath given Himself for me." I fall before Him in the dust, I kiss the border of His robe, I bathe His feet with tears, till at length, oppressed with the weight of such amazing love, my cup running over, my soul filled to its utmost capacity of emotion, I exclaim, "I am sick of love. Turn away Thine eyes from me, for They have overcome me. Withhold Thine hand, or take me up into Thy presence, where there is fulness of joy; and raise me to Thy right hand, where there are pleasures for evermore."

"Oh, unexampled love!
Love nowhere to be found—less than *divine.*"

Thus what a debtor is the child of God! Ask the believer in Jesus for what he is indebted, how much he owes! He replies, "I am indebted more than I can ever pay. I owe my happy being to God, my ransomed soul to Christ, my new-born life to the Holy Ghost. I owe my body, soul, and spirit to my Saviour, for He purchased all with His own most precious blood, saved me from death, ransomed me from condemnation, rescued me from hell. I am a debtor to sovereign grace, but for which I had never come as a poor sinner to the feet of Jesus, but had lived and died and had been eternally lost in my sins. I am daily, hourly, a debtor to the restraints of divine grace, to the constraints of divine love, to the consolations of divine sympathy, and to that divine power which keeps me from falling and preserves me unto His heavenly kingdom." Such is the grateful acknowledgment of every child of God, of every sinner saved by grace. Beloved, evidence your indebtedness by your cheerful obedience, your holy walk, your unreserved surrender. If you love Him, keep His commandments. If you would confess Him, bear His cross. If you would imitate Him, die to sin and to the world. If you would glorify Him, "present your bodies a living sacrifice, holy, acceptable unto God, which is your most reasonable service."

"LORD, when my thoughts delighted rove
Amid the wonders of Thy love,
Thy sight revives my drooping heart,
And bids invading fears depart.

"Guilty and weak, to Thee I fly,
On Thy atoning blood rely;
And on Thy righteousness depend,
My Lord, my Saviour, and my Friend.

"Be all my heart, be all my days,
Devoted to Thy single praise
And let my glad obedience prove,
How much I owe, how much I love."

But what is the import of this petition—"Forgive us our debts?"

Let us examine it. It at once confronts us with the sin-forgiving God. It presents Him to our view exercising one of the most divine and glorious prerogatives of His nature, the prerogative of pardoning sin. Against whom is sin committed? Against God. Then in whose hands alone is the prerogative and power of pardon lodged? In His against whom the sin is committed. This single and simple argument overthrows entirely the Popish figment of priestly absolution: that is, the confession of sin to, and the exercise of forgiveness by, man. Such a doctrine resolves the whole matter of salvation into mere human agency. In the Romanistic scheme, the power of the priest is everything. He is a confessing priest, a forgiving priest, a sacrificing priest, and, I may add, a ruling, despotic priest. Man is everything, and Christ is virtually nothing. But this petition, taught us by our Lord, brings us through the true Priesthood into the presence of the only sin-pardoning Being in the universe. Pardon is lodged with God, and it being the most godly exercise of His divine sovereignty, He delegates it to no other. It is His divine right, His exclusive property, and He has fenced and vindicated it with the most holy and jealous care. See how early in the history of the race God stepped forward, as it were, invested with this divine and august robe. "The Lord passed by Moses, and proclaimed, The Lord, the Lord God, merciful and gracious, longsuffering, and abundant in goodness and truth, keeping mercy for thousands, forgiving iniquity, and transgression, and sin," (Exod. xxxiv. 6.) Here we have the very marrow of the gospel at the very commencement of the Bible. Indeed, what is the Bible, the whole Bible, but a record of the *"glorious gospel of the blessed God?"* It is a gradual development of God's plan of salvation by the revelation of Jesus Christ. We have in the prophet Micah another remarkable unfolding of God's sin-forgiving character,—*"Who is a God like unto thee, that* PARDONETH *iniquity, transgression, and sin."* And why does He pardon? It is written, *"Because He delighteth in mercy."* When God is spoken of in His word as *delighting* in any one especial perfection of His nature—for He must delight in all—we have the most transcendent view of the greatness, the glory, and the preciousness of that perfection. Now, God is said to "DELIGHT IN

MERCY." It is a natural, essential perfection of His being. It is the spring from whence pardon flows through Christ's atoning blood; and pardon is the channel through which streams of peace, and joy, and hope flow into the soul. <u>Every spiritual blessing comes through the door of forgiven sin</u>. We reach, then, a most precious and encouraging view of this subject—the delight with which God exercises this divine prerogative of pardon. Oh, how low are our thoughts of the *readiness* with which He meets the penitent sinner with the sentence of forgiveness! Listen to those words of sweetest music breathing from Isaiah's harp:—*"Let the wicked forsake his way, and the unrighteous man his thoughts, and let him return unto the Lord; for He will have mercy upon him, and to our God; for He will ABUNDANTLY pardon."* What says Nehemiah? *"Thou art a God READY to pardon."* Such is God's character. Such is the Being with whom we have alone to do in the great and momentous matter of our *sins*. Mercy is the brightest jewel in the diadem of God; and mercy rejoiceth against judgment. In this respect the government of God and the government of man essentially differ. In the Divine Government, mercy is central and justice incidental, In the human government, justice is central and mercy incidental. God, in His dealings with the sinner, works from the centre of love to the circumference of justice; man, in his dealings with man, works from the centre of justice to the circumference of mercy. Thus God ends where man begins. Not until love, as it were, has exhausted all its resources; not until mercy has uttered her last and latest appeal to the sinner to repent and return, does justice step forward to arrest the criminal and hail him to judgment. Can we, then, hesitate to throw ourselves at the feet of His pardoning mercy who has said, *Come, now, and let us reason together, saith the Lord; though your sins be as scarlet, they shall be as white as snow, though they be red like crimson, they shall be as wool."* Who shall interdict you when God invites your approach? who shall say nay, when He has said yea? Who shall affirm that your sins are too enormous, your iniquities too aggravated, your transgressions too many, to be forgiven? Bring the great, the measureless, the long-standing and accumulated debt, and in penitence and faith, cast it down at the footstool of mercy, and see if God will not be true to His word,—*"If we confess our sins, He is able and just to* FORGIVE US *our sins."* The order in which the Holy Ghost in this passage places the precept and the doctrine, is worthy of remark. First, the *confession* of sin; second, the *forgiveness* of sin. God has laid great stress in His word upon the *confession* of sin. How touching His language addressed to His backsliding people, whose backslidings were of a most aggravated character,—than which none could have been of deeper guilt, seeing that they had committed the sin of *idolatry!*—*"Only* ACKNOWLEDGE *thine iniquity."* This was all that He required at their hands. *"*ONLY *acknowledge."* Poor penitent soul, bending in tears and self-reproaches over this page, read these words again and again, and yet again, until they have scattered all your dark, repelling thoughts of this sin-forgiving God, winning you to His feet as His restored and pacified child,—"ONLY ACKNOWLEDGE THINE INIQUITY." "What! Lord! after all that I have done, after my base returns, my repeated wanderings, my aggravated transgressions, my complicated iniquity, my sins against conviction, light, and love, dost thou still stretch out thine hand to me, a poor, wretched wanderer as I am? Dost thou go forth to meet, to welcome, to pardon me? Dost thou watch the first kindling of penitence, the first tear of contrition, the first word of confession—Father, I have sinned! Lord, I fall at Thy feet, since Thou dost say, 'Only acknowledge thine iniquity,' the greatest of sinners. Thy power has drawn me, Thy love has subdued me, Thy grace has conquered me!" Such was the royal penitent's experience *"I said I will* CONFESS *my transgressions unto the Lord, and Thou* FORGAVEST *the iniquity of my sin."* My beloved reader, God only writes the sentence of forgiveness upon a contrite, sin-confessing heart. The confession of sin, to be real and acceptable to Him, must not be in the abstract, but minute and in detail. There is a great and fatal danger of merging what are falsely termed "little sins" into great ones; of allowing the major to absorb the minor. We overlook, in our confessions to God, the sins of the heart, the thoughts, the imagination, and the tongue. We take not into account the sin of indolence, extravagance, wasted time, lost opportunities, neglected privileges; worldliness of dress, of living, and of recreation; covetousness, meanness, selfishness, uncharitableness, malice, slander, unkind and false insinuations. These are sins which exist to a great enormity, and yet seldom enter into our confessions, or lay our mouths in the dust before God. "Oh," as a holy man of God has said, "there is nothing more heartless than some of those general confessions that come from the lips of man."* Such, then, is the nature of that confession of sin, which He to whom alone confession is to be made, and with whom exclusively belongs the prerogative of pardon, demands. The Lord lay it closely upon our hearts!

The remaining portion of this chapter must be devoted to a yet untouched, but important part of our subject—the *daily* application for divine forgiveness.

With regard to this point, there occurs a most remarkable and instructive, yet much misunderstood passage, in the exquisitely touching narrative of Christ's act of washing the disciples' feet. The words are these: *"Jesus saith to him, (Peter,) he that is washed needeth not save to wash his feet, but is clean every whit."* The proposal of our Lord to wash the feet of His disciples, although in perfect harmony with every previous act of His holy life, was perfectly unique and startling to the high-minded, impulsive apostle. Recoiling from a proposal so menial and condescending on the part of his Master, he exclaims, *"Thou shalt never wash my feet!"* He had yet to learn the lesson that, *"to obey was better than sacrifice."* Such, in effect, was the teaching of his Lord when He uttered the significant words, *"If I wash thee not, thou hast no part with me."* Startled by this solemn warning, and with an impetuosity characteristic of this disciple, he rushes to an opposite extreme, and exclaims, *"Lord, not my feet only, but also my hands and my head."* Thus difficult is simple obedience—self-will, refusing, on the one hand, what Christ demands, and demanding, on the other hand, what Christ does not offer. It was this passage of arms between the Lord and the disciple that elicited the

* James Harrington Evans.

declaration, to which once more I call the reader's attention, *"He that is washed needeth not save to wash his feet, but is clean every whit."* Our Lord, in the first place, refers to the GREAT washing, as a thing past and done; not to the washing of baptism, whether received in the unconsciousness of infancy or with the intelligence of faith, but the washing of ATONING BLOOD, even His own blood, shed for the cleansing "of sin and uncleanness." The true believer has already passed through this washing; he is now and entirely washed; he is now and fully pardoned; his is the condition of a present, a complete, and irrevocable forgiveness. How emphatic the terms used by the Lord—"He that IS WASHED!" Corresponding with this, how decided the language of the apostle, who will not be suspected of any trimming in a truth so vital and precious as this—*"Such were some of you, but ye ARE WASHED."* Mistake not, my reader, as some have done, the present and perfect washing here referred to. There are preachers and writers who speak boldly of "holy baptism," of the "laver of baptism," of "baptismal purity," as if there existed in God's word an idea, or the phraseology expressive of the idea, so derogatory of the work of the Holy Spirit, and so fatally imperilling the deathless interests of souls. Woe be to us if we either add to, or take from, what is written in God's word! The terrible threatening with which the sacred canon closes, at once affirms the completeness, and fences the integrity of the Bible while it solemnly warns us of the crime of denying the one and of tampering with the other.

But the only baptism referred to in these remarkable words of the Lord Jesus is, THE BAPTISM OF HIS OWN BLOOD. Thus interpreted, how significant and precious the truth, "HE THAT IS WASHED." The atoning blood of the Saviour, the "precious blood of Christ, as of a Lamb without blemish and without spot," is the divine, the only laver in which the penitent and believing soul is now washed, entirely washed, for ever washed, from ALL sin. *"By one offering He hath perfected for ever them that are sanctified."* This is the first, the great and indispensable washing: *Without the shedding of blood there is no remission."* Unwashed, uncleansed in His blood through faith, our sins are yet unpardoned, our guilt is yet uncleansed, our debt is yet unremitted. But if we, on the other hand, have by faith approached His blood, have plunged into this open Fountain, have bathed in this divine laver, and have thus been *baptized in blood,* our present and high position is that of a sinner all whose sins are forgiven, all whose guilt is cleansed, and whose person appears before God washed whiter than snow. Seek, my reader, to ascertain your true standing, your real position as before God. Remember, no altar but the cross, no sacrifice but Christ, no laver but His blood, can avail to snatch you from endless condemnation, to save you from the worm that never dies, from the fire that is never quenched.

And yet a great truth is enfolded in the condescending act of our Lord when He *"took a basin of water, and washed His disciples' feet."* What was the moral significance of this lowly act? what the evangelical interpretation of this expressive symbol? Most clearly and undoubtedly Christ taught us the necessity of *daily* repentance, washing, and forgiveness. The "feet" are those parts of the body which are the most exposed to the dust and defilement of earth. The head may teem with lofty thoughts, the heart pulsate with pure affections, the hands overflow with generous actions, the eye roam amid countless beauties, and the whole soul live in a delirium of delight, while the *feet* press the dust from whence we sprang and to which we return. Does there exist, then, no necessity, palpable and impressive, of daily ablution? What, in eastern climes, is a literal and indispensable act—the constant laving of the sandaled feet—in the divine life is a spiritual and not less necessary one. The Christian's weary travel is through the dusty lanes, and defiling paths, and across the sandy desert of a world *"lying in the wicked one."* And whether he be engaged in recreation, in business, in social intercourse, or in duty, although the soul is *"washed, and is clean every whit,"* the *feet* still need continuous washing in the *"water and the blood"* which issued from the Saviour's pierced side. If it be true, as an eminent divine has remarked, that "the devil lets no saint of God reach heaven with unsoiled feet," it is equally and yet more divinely true that Christ came into the world to *"destroy the works of the devil,"* and this among them, by providing for the believer's daily repentance and remission of sin. With this petition, then, and *"having boldness* (or liberty) *to enter into the holiest by the blood of Jesus,"* let us, day by day, *"draw near with a true heart, in full assurance of faith, having our hearts sprinkled from an evil conscience, and our bodies washed with pure water,"* breathing in our heavenly Father's ear the petition taught us by His Son, "Forgive us our trespasses. Forgive my daily failures, negligences, and carelessness of my religious life. The omissions of duty,—the shortcomings of practice,—the waste of time,—lost opportunities,—the neglect of my Bible and my closet,—the excuses for sin,—the parleying with the tempter,—the self-seeking,—the subtle shades of evil blending with my commercial, professional, sacred calling. Forgive all my ebullitions of temper,—my evil speaking,—the wounds I have inflicted, the injury I have done,—the stiflings of conscience, and the grieving of the Holy Spirit. Pardon mine iniquities, O Lord, for they are many and great."

And in this daily washing of the feet, may there not be a pointed reference to the constant application *of the sanctifying influence of the Holy Spirit?*—"the body washed with *pure water.*" This was strikingly shadowed forth in the type of the laver placed by God's command between the congregation and the altar, which was to be filled *with water,* in which those who approached the altar were first to wash. *"And he set the laver between the tent of the congregation and the altar, and put* WATER *there, to wash withal. And Moses and Aaron, and his sons, washed their hands and their* FEET *thereat: when they went into the tent of the congregation, and when they came near unto the altar, they washed; as the* LORD *commanded Moses,"* (Exod. xl. 30-32.) They had already worshipped at the *"altar of burnt-offering by the door of the tabernacle,"* and had *"offered upon it the burnt-offering and the meat-offering."* But now, penetrating into the tabernacle, and coming near the altar of incense, they were intercepted by the laver *filled with water,* which stood between the tent and the altar, in which they must wash their *hands* and their feet—not the whole body—before they came near unto the altar. Did not this signify that, not only does the believer need Christ's blood of atonement, but also the sanctifying grace of the Holy Spirit in its daily application to the feet—the earth-soiled, earth-wounded, earth-weary feet — of his homeward travel? <u>Thus are we taught our daily need of the Holy Spirit, not only to guide and comfort us, but what should be still more deeply the yearning of our heart, that He might *sanctify* us.</u> As the Spirit of holiness, He makes us holy; as the Sanctifier, He promotes our progressive sanctification. This He does by developing the divine nature within us, by curbing our strong propensities to evil, and by leading us continually to the blood of atonement. And when our Lord filled the basin with WATER, and washed the disciples' feet, by that lowly yet significant act He seemed to say, "He that is washed in my blood is clean from the guilt and condemnation of sin every whit, yet needeth afterwards the daily sanctifying grace of my Spirit." Thus constantly approaching the altar of sacrifice and the laver of purification, Enoch-like, we shall *"walk with God."* Living in perpetual sunlight, our path to glory will be one of progressive lustre, even that of the just, which shineth more and more unto the perfect day.

There is an *unselfishness* in this petition, as taught us by Christ, which we have need to learn. *"Forgive* US *our debts."* <u>We are to be concerned on account of, to mourn for, and to confess penitentially, the sins of others.</u> And although no individual can repent and believe, be pardoned and accepted on behalf of another, yet, while we are commanded *"not to be partakers of other men's sins,"* at the same time, like Nehemiah and Daniel, we are to confess the sins of our families, of the Church, and of the nation, and humble ourselves before God because of them, and to intercede for His pardoning mercy. Did not Moses, throw himself in the breach, and more than once, by his intercessory supplications, avert the Divine judgments from the children of Israel? *"Pardon, I beseech Thee, the iniquities of this people, according unto the greatness of Thy mercy;" "And the Lord said, I have pardoned according unto thy word,"* (Neh. xiv. 19, 20.) How earnest and touching the prayer! how quick and gracious the response! Such, too, is the teaching of the apostles: "I exhort that supplications, prayers, intercessions, and giving of thanks be made for all men," (1 Tim. ii. 1.) Pardoned ourselves, let us wave before God our censer of intercession for the pardon of others—our parents, our children, our kindred, our friends—while the jubilee sound of debts forgiven through Christ still rolls its echoes round a world needing God's forgiveness.

> "When this passing world is done,
> When has sunk yon glaring sun,
> When we stand with Christ in glory,
> Looking o'er life's finish'd story,
> Then, Lord, shall I fully know—
> Not till then—how much I owe.
>
> "When I hear the wicked call
> On the rocks and hills to fall,
> When I see them start and shrink
> On the fiery deluge brink,
> Then, Lord, shall I fully know—
> Not till then—how much I owe.
>
> "When I stand before the throne,
> Dress'd in beauty not my own,
> When I see Thee as Thou art,
> Love Thee with unsinning heart,
> Then, Lord, shall I fully know—
> Not till then—how much I owe.
>
> "When the praise of heaven I hear,
> Loud as thunders on the ear,
> Loud as many waters' noise,
> Sweet as harp's melodious voice,
> Then, Lord, shall I fully know—
> Not till then—how much I owe.
>
> "Even on earth, as through a glass,
> Darkly let Thy glory pass,
> Make forgiveness feel so sweet,
> Make Thy Spirit's help so meet,
> Even on earth, Lord, make me know
> Something of how much I owe.

"Oft I walk beneath the cloud,
Dark as midnight's gloomy shroud;
But, when fear is at its height,
Jesus comes, and all is light;
Blessed Jesus! bid me show
Doubting saints how much I owe.

"When in flowery paths I tread,
Oft by sin I'm captive led;
Oft I fall—but still arise—
The Spirit comes, the Tempter flies;
Blessed Spirit! bid me show
Weary sinners all I owe.

"Oft the sights of sorrow reign—
Weeping, sickness, sighing, pain;
But a night Thine anger burns,
Morning comes, and joy returns;
God of comfort! bid me show
To Thy poor how much I owe."*

* M'Cheyne.

CHAPTER IX.

THE FORGIVING SPIRIT OF
THE LORD'S PRAYER.

"As we forgive our debtors."—Matt. vi. 12.

O *forgive*, it has been remarked, is divine. If the forgiveness of sin is the sole prerogative of God, the highest and most gracious franchise of heaven, then, man's forgiveness of the wrong done him by his fellow bears a close resemblance to the divine. It was only by God that this precept of forgiveness of injury could be revealed, and it is only beneath the cross of the incarnate God it can be properly learned. It is in the region of our own forgiveness we learn the Christian precept of our forgiveness of others. As believers in the Lord Jesus, we stand before men discharged bankrupts. Passing out of God's court of justice, released from a debt of "ten thousand talents," we, perhaps, confront upon its threshold a fellow-servant owing us a "hundred pence." The line of conduct towards our debtor is obvious and imperative. A pardoned sinner, all whose transgressions against Jehovah are fully and eternally forgiven, the great debt wholly cancelled, my duty to my fellow-sinner is written as with a sunbeam. Instead of grasping him by the throat, exclaiming, "Pay me that thou owest," I am to deal with him as my Lord has dealt with me—fully releasing him from the claim. *Forgiven*, I am to *forgive*. How can I justly, or with any degree of assurance, put in a claim to be forgiven myself of God, while cherishing in my heart the spirit of unforgiveness towards man? This is Christian logic, Christian precept, yea, it is Christianity itself. Such is the *spirit* of the petition we now consider.

That there exists a great and wide *necessity* for the exercise of this godlike precept of forgiveness is obvious. Our Lord forewarned us of it when He said, *"It must needs be that offences will come."* The present admixture of good and evil, the imperfect state of the Church, the existence of so much that is totally unrenewed in the unbeliever, and of so much that is but partially renewed in the believer, presents a wide field for the exercise of this divine grace. In the various Christian communions, in the domestic circles, in the social intercourse of life—among fellow-Christians, friends, relations, and neighbours—these sad debts between man and man are constantly occurring; misunderstandings arise, offences are given, injuries are inflicted, breaches are made, hearts are alienated, friendships are forfeited, demanding a perpetual recurrence to the divine precept, *"Forgive us our debts, as we forgive them that are indebted against us."* Such a state of things is one of the most lamentable occurrences of life. One-half of its beclouding and its bitterness, arises from the existence of this element of evil. What perpetual sweetness, what undimmed sunshine would there be in many a domestic home, in many a social circle, in many a Christian community, were there more union of heart, concord of judgment, outflow of sympathy and love! To cite but one illustration of this— the *family circle.* How many families are there which, like the sweet apple, has a worm feeding and fattening at its core! The *domestic* is the most important, as it is the sweetest, earthly constitution. And yet, where you expect to find love on its loftiest throne, charity in its sweetest flow, confidence in its firmest hold, sympathy in its tenderest exercise, we often find nought but weakened ties, alienated affections, divided interests, and even anger, animosity, and litigation. No spectacle presents our humanity in a more painful and humiliating aspect. To see *brothers,* dandled on the same paternal knee, nourished at the breast of the same fond mother, divided in their tastes, dissonant in judgment, alienated in affection, and even confronting each other in hostility; to see *sisters* possessed of the pure sentiments, the tender sensibilities, the deep love and gentleness of the sex, regarding each other with coldness of affection, unsympathising manner, living in secret irritation of mind, if not in open ill-will and animosity, presents a spectacle at which strangers are shocked, and over which angels might weep. Surely in such a sphere the Christian grace of *forgiveness* finds its proper and its noblest exercise!

Now it is clear from this petition taught us by the Saviour, that God's forgiveness of us is to be the *rule* and the *measure* of our forgiveness of others. We cannot for a moment suppose that there exists anything like equality with, but simply conformity to, God's forgiveness. Still less does our forgiveness of man involve any meritorious plea wherefore God should forgive us. Nor does this exercise of forgiveness suppose the existence of insensibility to injury. Never was Jesus so sensible of the injustice and the wrong done Him by man than when impaled upon the tree for man He prayed, *"Father, FORGIVE them!"* *"It is the glory of a man to pass over a transgression"*—that glory beamed around the dying head of Jesus when from the cross He breathed this prayer. And yet, as I have remarked, God's forgiveness of us is to be the *rule* of our forgiveness of others. No canon less divine, no model less godlike, is to govern and guide us in this Christian duty. Our forgiveness of an offending yet repentant brother may not be equal, yet it must be *like*, God's forgiveness of our offences. How, then, does God forgive?

God forgives us *immediately*—so ought we to forgive those who have trespassed against us. "Thou art a God *ready* to forgive." Is there any demur, any, the least, hesitation on the part of God in remitting the sins of the penitent, in cancelling the debt of the contrite sinner? None whatever! Listen to the language of David, already quoted, *"I said I will confess my transgressions unto the Lord; and Thou forgavest."* Not a moment's hesitation! The royal penitent but acknowledged his sin, and immediately the sin-forgiving God pardoned it. Moses prayed, *"Pardon, I beseech thee, the iniquity of this people."* "And the LORD said, *I have pardoned.*" As if God had anticipated His servant's request. To cite once more the case of David. In the matter of Uriah the Hittite, how did God deal with him? By the same messenger who told him of his sin God sent the message of His forgiveness. *"And David said unto Nathan, I have sinned against the Lord. And Nathan said unto David, The Lord also hath put away thy sin; thou shalt not die."* Not a moment's agonising suspense intervened between the indictment and the pardon. And shall we not deal thus with our fellow-men? Shall we demur, hesitate, and debate in our minds the question of forgiveness, and then go to God and ask Him to forgive us as we forgive others? Hesitate to forgive a brother, and then, if you can, ask God *so* to pardon you. Remember God forgives *at once!*

God forgives *fully—so* must we forgive our fellows. A partial forgiveness of sin would be no real forgiveness to us whatever. Were the ten thousand talents, save one, all paid, and that one were left for us to pay, we should be for ever exiles from the land of the blest. All the demands of the law of God must be met, and the full penalty of justice must be endured either by ourselves or by our Surety, if ever we are saved. In default of our utter inability to meet these claims, the Lord Jesus, on behalf of His Church has, *"by one offering perfected for ever them that are sanctified."* On the cross the Son of God paid the bond, and at the grave the Father ratified it. *"He was delivered for our offences, and was raised again for our justification."* And now Jesus saves to the *uttermost* all that come unto God by Him. Nothing stands between the greatest sinner and his full and eternal salvation. Believing in the Lord Jesus, he passes out of the court of Divine justice not simply protected from arrest, but fully, honourably, eternally discharged, Christ having done all. Believer in Jesus I realise this to be your present standing before God. Your great concern is, not with your sins, but with the Atonement that has put them away; not with the debt, but with your obligation to Him who paid it. Oh, see into what a blessed state the atoning blood of Christ places you! It has put away your *sins* from God,—oh, how far!—but it has brought *you* nigh to God,—oh, how nigh! *"Now in Christ Jesus ye who sometimes were far off are* MADE NIGH *by the blood of Christ."* Such must be our forgiveness! It must be like God's, full, complete,

<u>unreserved.</u> How can we repair to the throne of grace, and pray, "Forgive me my debts as I forgive them that are indebted to me," while we have refused an offending brother or sister a full, frank, ingenuous forgiveness? <u>The offence must be entirely forgiven, the debt wholly cancelled, if we would deal with our fellow-servant as his Master and ours has dealt with us.</u>

God's forgiveness of us is a *hearty* forgiveness—so must be ours—sincere, cordial, hearty. Oh, there is no coldness, nothing begrudged, in God's pardon of our sins. It is, as I have said, with all His heart. And remember that the heart of God is *infinite!* What, then, must be the sincerity, the love, the cordiality with which our heavenly Father has forgiven us all sin! Let this whole-heartedness be seen in the forgiveness which *we* extend to a sinning brother. Let him see that our hand is not outstretched reluctantly, half-way only; but that, with our heart in our hand, we extend to him a like forgiveness God has extended to us—the forgiveness of the HEART!

God *forgets*, as well as forgives, our debts. So entirely are the sins of His people effaced that, speaking after the manner of men, God says, *"I will remember them no more for ever."* And again He says, "I have *blotted out* thy transgressions as a cloud, and thine iniquities as a thick cloud." Blotted from the book of His justice, and of His law, and of His remembrance. This same truth comforted Hezekiah, "Thou hast cast all my sins *behind Thy back."* How like our God is this—magnificent, stupendous, divine! Can God *forget?* He cannot. And yet so entirely has He cancelled out our debt; at so infinite a distance has He cast our transgressions, they are to Him as things out of mind, buried in the fathomless depths of Divine oblivion. I think that this truth supplies an argument in favour of another, that the sins of the believer will not be *adjudicated* in the last day as the sins of the ungodly. The saints will already have been judged and condemned in the person of Jesus their Great Surety, and in Him punished to the utmost extent of the demands of Divine Justice; their sins, therefore, will have been sunk into the fathomless depths of the sea of His blood, never more to come into remembrance. *"Thou wilt cast all their sins into the depths of the sea,"* (Micah vii. 19.) I cannot but conclude, therefore, that the trial of the saints in the great assize will be nominal rather than actual; that they will be subpœned, not for scrutiny, but for discharge, not for adjudication, but for acquittal. Remember that their *Surety* will be the *Judge!* What a shadow upon His own finished work would be the same judicial process of the saints as that through which the *ungodly* must finally and inevitably pass! The great debt of the Church once paid will not a second time be brought into court.

Such should be the spirit of our forgiveness, which is the spirit inculcated by our Lord in His prayer taught the disciples. But, universal as is the belief and adoption of this prayer, is the forgiving spirit which it breathes equally so? Alas! that it should *not* be! "I can *forgive,* but I cannot *forget,"* is too frequently the haughty and sullen language of an offended brother. But what does this rankling of the offence in the heart, this hoarding of the injury in the mind betray, but that, though you have professedly forgiven the wrong, you have secretly embalmed its memory! Is this like God? Will you in this spirit repair to the mercy seat, and ask God to forgive you *as* you forgive others? No; you dare not. All the while that your mind broods over the wrong done you by a fellow-sinner, you are harbouring "hatred, malice, and all uncharitableness;" and with this leaven of evil fomenting in your heart, with this fretting leprosy of sin tainting your prayers in the closet, at the domestic altar, and in the public sanctuary, you daily pray, "Forgive us our trespasses *as we forgive them that trespass against us."* Oh, be like God—generous and magnanimous—forgiving and forgetting. Such is the teaching, and such was the example of Him whose disciple you profess to be. *"I say unto you, Love your enemies, bless them that curse you, do good to them that hate you, and pray for them that despitefully use you, and persecute you; that ye may be the children of your Father which is in heaven."*

With regard to the debts themselves, the schedule is an *extended* one—for if offences must needs come, "in *many things* we offend all." To what extent we are to include the *worldly debt* which a brother may honestly have incurred at our hands, must be left to God and the conscience. At the same time, if the obligation presses upon my brother, and he, through no fault of his own, is unable to meet it, and the thought of its existence and of his own powerlessness to cancel it occasions him misery and distress, shall not the love of God, shall not our obligation to Him who became our Surety constrain us to say, "The pecuniary debt my fellow-servant owes me, and which to him is a running sore, shall be buried in oblivion. My Father has freely and fully forgiven me *all* my debts; I as freely and fully forgive my brother this." God grant that in this matter these terrible words may never vibrate on our ear—*O thou wicked servant, I forgave thee all that great debt, because thou desiredst me; shouldest thou not then have had compassion on thy fellow-servant, even as I had pity on thee?* Look at this question in the tender light of the cross; look at it in the solemn light of eternity—and then *act!*

But the debts more specially referred to by our Lord are those moral offences, injuries, and wrongs inflicted by man upon man, by brother against brother, which prevail in our present but imperfectly-sanctified state; and which God wisely and graciously overrules for the exercise of that grace of forgiveness which, both in its letter and in its spirit, the Divine Father enjoins and the Divine Saviour illustrated. Oh what pain, what deep, lasting injury, may be inflicted by an unkind word, an unkind look, an unkind action; by a wrong judgment, a misinterpretation, an unjust suspicion, a malicious and false report; by violated confidence, by evil-speaking, idle gossip, and harsh insinuation— how much may spring out of all this affecting the peace, reputation, and usefulness of a child of God! What a field for the exercise of forgiveness, that Christian act of which it has been remarked, "It requireth more grace to forgive an injury than it doth to suffer martyrdom."* A man requires less grace to endure the hardest toil, to carry the heaviest cross, and to submit to the severest suffering, than to hold out his hand to an offending brother and say, "I freely and fully forgive." The greatest display of grace in God is in the pardon of sin; the greatest exercise of grace in man

---

* James Harrington Evans.

is to forgive and forget an injury. But this grace Jesus can and is engaged to give.

But nothing more strongly invalidates the fact of our own forgiveness of God than an unforgiving spirit towards man. Upon no scriptural warrant whatever can we put in the claim of filial relation to God, no valid evidence can we adduce that we are partakers of divine grace while under the influence of a want of forgiveness. We may imagine we are pardoned, may speak of our spiritual raptures, and boast of our Christian experience; we may frequent the Lord's table, and respond loudly to the Lord's Prayer, but all the while we are woefully cajoled by Satan, are fatally deceived by our own hearts, and are passing to eternity with a lie in our right hand. We have asked of God in solemn prayer to be forgiven *as we forgive*. What if He should take us at our word?— "Thou wicked and unmerciful servant, *I will!*" might justly be His indignant and withering reply.

No Christian precept did our Lord enforce with greater minuteness and solemnity than that of *forgiveness* of our enemies. Thus He speaks concerning this duty—*"If ye forgive men their trespasses, your Heavenly Father will also forgive you; but if ye forgive not men their trespasses, neither will your Father forgive your trespasses." "Forgive, and ye shall be forgiven."* Equally explicit is His instruction respecting the *frequency* of our forgiveness. Peter, recognising the duty, inquires, *"Lord, how oft shall my brother sin against me, and I forgive him? till seven times?"* This was the utmost limit of the disciple! But Jesus, putting a definite for an indefinite number, *"saith unto him, I say not unto thee until seven times, but until SEVENTY TIMES SEVEN."* Such are the forgivenesses of our God! *"Let the wicked forsake his way, and the unrighteous man his thoughts: and let him return unto the Lord, and he will have mercy upon him; and to our God, for he will abundantly* [margin, *multiply*] *pardon."* How often, my reader, has your God forgiven you? Suppose He had dealt with you as you in your heart have dealt with your brother, or, perchance, in reality are dealing with him now—limiting His forgiveness of sin to the seven offences—perhaps to the *one!* Where and what would you now be? But, countless as the sands that belt the ocean have your sins against God been! And yet, the ocean of His love has again and again tided over them all, and still it flows, day by day, hour by hour, moment by moment. Where your sins have multiplied, exceeded and abounded, His rich, free pardoning grace has much more abounded. Oh, if your Lord should deal with you as you now may be dealing with a fellow-servant—and why may He not?—you would be cast into prison, and by no means come out until you had paid the uttermost farthing.

Closely connected, too, is the overcoming of enmity and the exercise of forgiveness *with our worship.* We cannot worship God with a clean and true heart, with an approving conscience, or with a service acceptable to Him while an unforgiving spirit towards an offending brother is rankling within us. How pointed and impressive the injunction of Christ. *"Leave thou thy gifts before* [not *upon*] *the altar, and go thy way; first be reconciled to thy brother, and then come and offer thy gift."* With what freedom or hope of response can we penetrate within the Holy of Holies and commune with that God whose sweet, delightsome property is mercifully to forgive, while there is a secret reserve in our hearts of ill will and unforgiveness towards an offending brother? Can you honestly comply with the exhortation, *"Ye people, pour out your heart before Him,"* while some deeply-shaded cloister of that heart you cannot pour out before God—you dare not place in the light of His countenance? How solemn are the words, *"If I regard iniquity in my heart, the Lord will not hear me."* But be honest! Look at the matter, however distasteful and painful it may be, fairly, fully in the face. Has any relation, Christian brother or sister, offended, injured, wounded you? Have you been evil spoken of? Has unkind suspicion rested upon you? Have you been unjustly suspected, wrongfully accused, coldly slighted, cruelly slandered and spoken against? Are there any with whom you are not upon good and friendly terms? Do you meet in society, pass each other in the street, worship in the same sanctuary, and approach the same sacred table of the Lord's Supper without friendly recognition, or Christian intercourse whatever? In a word, associating, worshipping, and even assembling at the Holy Communion, as total strangers? Yea, what is infinitely more offensive to God, meeting as bitter and irreconciled *enemies!* What a scandal to Christianity! what a dishonour to Christ! what a tainting spot upon your feast of charity! what a lamentable spectacle to the eyes of the world!

And must this painful state of things exist? Is there no kind and skilful hand that will seek to cauterise and heal the fretting wound? Perhaps the offer of mediation is made. Some mutual friend undertakes the holy yet self-denying office. But you decline! Your injury, resentment, and pride are too deep, persistent, and unbending even to listen to the proposal; or, if the attempt is made, the concessions you demand are too imperious and humiliating, and so all effort to effect a reconciliation and restore peace falls to the ground, and you are left to a judicial spirit of revenge, malice and unforgiveness accompanying you to the grave and upward to the judgment-seat.

But this lamentable state of things need not and must not continue. In His Name who, when we were sinners, loved us; who, when we were enemies, died for us; who, when we were rebels, overcame our evil by His grace, truth, and love—I beseech you, ere the sun shall go down upon your wrath, seek out the brother or the sister whom you have offended, or who has offended you, and hold out your hand of reconciliation. <u>If he is in the wrong wait not for his acknowledgment—God did not wait for you!—but make the first advance; and if that advance is repelled, make it again and yet again, for in so doing you shall heap coals of fire on his head which may melt down his proud, unrelenting spirit into contrition, forgiveness, and love.</u> Or if *you* are in the wrong, go at once and honestly and frankly acknowledge the wrong, and seek the forgiveness and reconciliation of the brother you have injured. Having done this— then bend together, the offended and the offender, before the mercy-seat, and together pray—*"Father, forgive* us *our trespasses, as we forgive them that trespass against us."* Happy reconciliation! Blissful moment! How many a heart thrills with joy, how many a home is radiant as with a new-created sun at the touching spectacle. The alienation of years is reconciled. The congealed affection of long dreary winters of discontent is melted. Misunderstandings are explained, differences are adjusted, acknowledgments are interchanged; relatives long estranged, families long divided, friends long alienated meet once more beneath the same roof; within the same sanctuary, and around the same sacramental table, and joy pulsates through every heart, and music, like a whisper from the celestial choir, breathes from every soul. Methinks I see the white-haired sire, the venerable mother, the aged minister who had long prayed for the arrival of this hour, clasp the hands in thanksgiving, and exclaim, "Now, Lord, lettest thou thy servant depart in peace, for mine eyes have seen thy salvation!" Reader, it may be in your power to create a scene like this! By the pardoning mercy of God towards you, by the redeeming love of Him who died for you, by the dove-like peace of Him who dwells in you, by your hope of forgiveness at the last great day, I beseech you, I implore you, yea, in the name of Christ I command you, to lose not a moment in securing its accomplishment. The blessing of the peace-maker will then light upon you, and a faint reflection of the joy that brightened the Saviour's heart when He reconciled us to God will brighten yours, and gild the clouds that cast their shadows upon your homeward path. But God the Holy Spirit, the Author of peace and lover of concord, shall speak—"LET ALL BITTERNESS, AND WRATH, AND ANGER, AND CLAMOUR, AND EVIL-SPEAKING, BE PUT AWAY FROM YOU, WITH ALL MALICE: AND BE YE KIND ONE TO ANOTHER, TENDER HEARTED, FORGIVING ONE ANOTHER, EVEN AS GOD FOR CHRIST'S SAKE HATH FORGIVEN YOU." Whensoever any may have sought to injure your fair name, to lower your influence, to impair your usefulness—wilfully, wickedly, slanderously—imitate Jesus, and render not evil for evil, and when reviled revile not again. Revenge not yourself, but commit the matter to God, and by a silent spirit and a holy life *live down the imputation.* Your *good* may be evil spoken of, and your *evil* may be magnified and exaggerated— nevertheless, by a meek and quiet spirit, by a consistent walk, and by well-doing, you may put to silence the strife of lying tongues and the ignorance of foolish men, and thus glorify your Father who is in heaven.

"Should envious tongues some malice frame,
　To soil and tarnish your good name,
　Grow not dishearten'd, 'twas the lot
　Of Christ, and saints exempt are not.
　Rail not in answer, but be calm,
　For silence yields a rapid balm.
　　　Live it down!

"Far better thus, yourself alone
　To suffer, than with friend bemoan
　The trouble that is all your own.
　　　Live it down!

"What though men evil call your good,
　So Christ Himself was misunderstood—
　Was nail'd upon a cross of wood;
　And now shall you for lesser pain
　Your inmost soul for ever stain,
　By rendering evil back again?
　　　Live it down!

"Oh! if you hope to be *forgiven,*
　Love your foes, the bitterest even,
　And love to you shall flow from heaven.
　And when shall come the poison'd lie,
　Swift from the bow of calumny,
　If you would turn it harmless by,
　And make the venom'd falsehood die,
　　　Live it down!"

"Dearly beloved, avenge not yourselves, but rather give place unto wrath: for it is written, Vengeance is mine, I will repay, saith the Lord. Therefore if thine enemy hunger, feed him; if he thirst, give him drink: for in so doing thou shalt heap coals of fire on his head. Be not overcome of evil, but overcome evil with good."

CHAPTER X.

THE WATCHFUL SPIRIT OF
THE LORD'S PRAYER.

"Lead us not into temptation."—Matt. vi. 13

HIS solemn petition—perhaps the most solemn one of the whole prayer—would appear a natural and impressive sequence of the preceding one for *forgiveness*. In the contemplation of that petition, the mind was necessarily led into a deep and grave consideration of sin in its various forms, and of the confession of sin in its minute detail, and of the forgiveness of sin in its daily renewal. Passing from that theme, it would seem as if the next utterance of the wakeful, tremulous heart would be, "Lord, lead me not into temptation. If such is sin; if such the sore penitence to which its commission leads, and such the humiliating acknowledgment in which it results, and such the costly pardon—the price of blood—which its guilt demands, Lord, keep me, fence me, surround me; that, having been washed every whit clean, I may tread no path, be placed in no position whereby I may be exposed to the power of temptations which I cannot evade, whose strength I cannot resist, and thus *relapse* from my high and holy walk with Thee. Thou hast given me absolution from sin, but no *indulgence* to sin. I would be as free from the tyranny as from the condemnation of sin, and would find my most precious, powerful, and persuasive motive to seek after the

attainment of holiness in Thy full, and free, and most loving
forgiveness; Having washed my feet, how shall I defile them!"

The present scene of the Christian is a scene of *temptation*. One
is almost led to inquire, Where has it not been? Even in the
paradisiacal age of the world and history of the Church it was so.
Who would have thought of temptation lurking in the leafy bowers,
and of the serpent's trail along the sylvan walks of Eden? And yet
thus it was. Strange to say, that dark deluge of evil which for
centuries has rolled its angry billows over the earth, bearing
myriads on its bosom to the ocean of a forfeited and awful eternity,
had its rise in a yet unsinning paradise. Behold our primal parents!
Stately trees of righteousness, beauteous plants of paradise! Yet
the enemy came in like a flood, and swept them before its powerful
and resistless force. Thus there never has been a scene of our
humanity, or an era in the history of the world, in which the,
Church of God has been exempt from temptation.

But much more is this the case *now*. How should it, in the
nature of things, be otherwise? Man is a fallen being. He is, by
nature, one unmitigated mass of sin, there dwelling in the flesh
no good thing. The world, with all its landscape beauty, its
mountain grandeur, its Alpine sublimity, its countless forms of
loveliness, is a sin-tainted, curse-blighted world. More than this,
it is Satan's empire,—where he holds his seat, rules, and reigns
by God's permission, over myriads of the human race, until Christ
shall come to overthrow his sovereignty, and will make all things
new. Such is the solemn truth which underlies the whole remedial
scheme of the gospel of the blessed God. But do our legislators,
our philosophers, our educationists, and even some of the ministers
of religion, clearly see, fully recognise, and broadly enunciate these
facts—that man is totally fallen, and the world wholly corrupt?
Nay, to a great degree, the legislation, and the education, and the
preaching of the day is a solemn ignoring of these truths. But not
so those who are enlightened by the truth and the Spirit of God.
The wonder to them is, not that man is so sinful, but that, by the
grace of God, he should become so holy. Not that the world is so
evil, but that, by the restraints of God's power, it should be so good.

Such is the scene through which the believer passes to heaven. His road homewards is across the enemy's country; his path to glory winds its way through a world lying in the wicked one. Is it any marvel that the present state of the Christian should be of universal and incessant temptation? But let us particularise.

The word "temptation" sometimes signifies *trial*. God's people are a tempted or a tried people. Temptation is that process by which the Christian is tested—his religion, his principles, his hope, are brought to the proof. It is in this sense we first regard the process to which the believer is subjected, more immediately by God Himself. In Gen. xxii. 1, we read, "God did TEMPT Abraham." In the Epistle to the Hebrews, xi. 17, we find the significance of the word, "By faith Abraham, when he was TRIED." And again, "Blessed is the man that endureth TEMPTATION, for when he is TRIED," (Jas. i. 12.) Now, in this important sense, God may be said to *tempt* or to *try* His people. He sometimes, as in the case of Job, unchains, as it were, the enemy for a little while, permitting him to come in like a flood, to worry and annoy the believer. And, again, God may permit inbred corruptions to have a measured and momentary power over the believer, and then *sin* seems, for the time, to be in the ascendant. Once more, God may allow His child to pass through a great fight of affliction, for "the Lord *trieth* the righteous," and by this process subject him to great and sore temptation. But all this springs from the depths of His infinite wisdom and love.

Two objects He thus seeks to accomplish. The first is the unfolding of His own character in the eyes of His people. God remembers that, even at best, how limited is our knowledge of Him; but how much smaller the measurement that is not gauged by the test of trial. We know Him revealedly in His Word; we know Him symbolically by His providence; but it is in the school of His direct and personal dealings with us, and of our direct and personal dealings with Him, that His character is the most experimentally unfolded, His perfections are the most distinctly made known, and His glory passes before our eye. To this end God *tries* us. "Show me now Thy way, *that I may know Thee.*" Thus, in all our temptations and trials, we trace His wisdom in ordaining, His sovereignty in permitting, His power in controlling, His faithfulness in directing, and His love in soothing us. And Jesus, the tried Stone, becomes better known, and more intensely endeared, in one fiery temptation, in one sore trial, than, perhaps, in all the passing events of our history combined. The second object God would compass is, our personal benefit. Our personal religion advances in the same ratio with our spiritual and experimental acquaintance with God in Christ Jesus. By the process of temptation or trial to which He subjects us, we know ourselves better, are more deeply instructed in the knowledge of the word, are emptied, humbled, proved; are taught our own weakness, learn wherein our great strength lies, and that, upheld only by the power of God, we are kept from falling and are preserved unto His kingdom and glory. By this process, too, the work of moral purification advances, the alloy is consumed, the vile is eliminated from the precious, and the believer emerges from the season of temptation tried, purified, and made white. *"Take away the dross from the silver, and there shall come forth a vessel for the finer."* Placed in the furnace, it may be, in the mass, shapeless and uncomely, such the wondrous transformation, it comes forth a vessel divinely moulded, symmetrically formed, exquisitely pencilled—a vessel of honour fit for the Master's use. Thus are we to interpret God's more immediate hand in the temptations or trials of His saints. But there are other sources of temptation to which the saints are exposed.

There are the temptations that arise *from the power of Satan.* It is marvellous what opposite and what false views men entertain of the devil. There are ill-informed and timid religionists who almost deify him, by ascribing to him the attributes of omniscience and omnipresence which belong alone to God. Then there are those who, in this Sadducean age, go far to deny his very existence, or who, if admitting that there is a devil, denude him of his power and wrest from him his sovereignty. Oh, it is a solemn thing to trifle with the Evil One, either by exalting his attributes, or by ignoring his existence. But he is the great tempter and accuser of the brethren. Our first parents fell like stately cedars before his arm, and we, the offspring of a fallen sire, who, like the tinder, are ready to ignite with every spark that is struck, are not exempt from his fiery darts. Nay more, if our merciful High Priest was in all points tempted like as we—yet without sin—from this very source, who are we to expect exemption from his assaults? Be not, then, dismayed at the sceptical doubts he insinuates, at the bold blasphemies he suggests, at the profane and impure thoughts he engenders, or at any mode by which he assails the foundation of your faith, and tempts you to give up Christ and cast away your confidence. There is not a moment that he is not plotting your downfall, but there is not a moment that Christ is not upholding you on earth and interceding for you in heaven.

Then there is the believer's temptation from *the world*. We must pass through it, for there is no escape. It is the empire of the Evil One, and it is the empire of evil. It is essentially and emphatically an evil world, all its works evil, and nothing but evil. The ungodliness of the world is appalling. Whether we view it in its savage or its civilised state, in its refined or its gross forms of society, *"we know that the whole world lieth in wickedness,"* or, in the wicked one. Thus from every quarter is the world a snare and a temptation to the holy. Awed by its frowns we may be dissuaded from taking up Christ's cross, seduced by its smiles we may he persuaded to lay it down. Our very circumstances in life may expose us to peculiar temptation. Affluence may ensnare us into wasteful extravagance and worldly living; poverty may tempt us to depart from strict uprightness and integrity; a moderate position may tempt us to better ourselves by wild and ruinous speculation. And then there is the *worldliness* of the world—how powerful and ever-present a snare is this to the child of God. *"Demas hath forsaken me, having loved this present world,"* is the sad record of many a religious professor once standing so high, but now swept away and no more walking with Jesus, by the resistless current of the world's gaieties, the world's enterprises, and even the world's religion.

But what a scene of temptation is there *within the Christian*. It is here—perhaps a foe, a spy, or a traitor within the citadel—his greatest danger lies. From this there is no escape. *"The sin that dwelleth in us"* is that lurking spy, the wicked heart throbbing within our breast, *"deceitful above all things, and desperately wicked,"* is that concealed traitor. From this, I reiterate, there is no escape. Go where we may, plunge we into the pathless desert, escape we to the mountain solitudes, hide we in the caves of the earth, buried in a monastery, imprisoned in a nunnery, immured in a hermit's cell, still the traitor lurks within, prepared, at any moment, to open the gate and admit the besieging foe. In the eloquent words of a writer already quoted, "In no scene of earth, in no condition, are we exempt from the incursions of temptation. If we flee to the desert, and brook not the sight of our fellow-creatures' face, we bear thither the fiend within; we cannot build out or bar out the indwelling devil. The gratings of the monastery cannot exclude the wings of the fallen seraph, nor solitude sanctify the unregenerate heart. In the garden or the grove, the palace or the hermitage, the crowded city or the howling wilderness, sin tracks us and self haunts us. If the poor are tempted to envy and dishonesty; the rich, as Agur testified, are equally endangered by pride and luxury. If the man of ten talents is puffed up with self-confidence and arrogant impiety, the man of one talent is prone to bury slothfully the portion entrusted to him in the earth, and then to quarrel with its Holy Giver. The great adversary has in every scene his snares, and varies his baits for every age and variety of condition and character. Each man and child of us has his easily-besetting sin. The rash and the cautious, the young and the old, the rude and the educated, the visitant of the sanctuary and the open neglecter of it, the profane and the devout, the lover of solitude and the lover of society—all have their snares. Satan can misquote Scripture and misinterpret providence, and preach presumption or despair, heresy or superstition, or infidelity, as he finds best. He can assume the sage, the sophist, or the buffoon, the canonist or the statesman at will. He spares not spiritual greatness. Paul was buffeted. The most eminent of God's saints, of the Old Testament and the New, Noah, Abraham, David, Hezekiah, and the apostles, have suffered by him. He spares not the season of highest spiritual profiting. Ere you rise from your knees, his suggestions crowd the devout heart. Ere the sanctuary is quitted, his emissaries, as birds of the air, glean away the scattered seeds of truth from the memory. When our Lord Himself had been, at His baptism, proved from heaven as the Son of God, He was led away by the Spirit in the wilderness *to be tempted.* And how often does some fiery dart glance on the Christian's armour, just after some season of richest communion with his God. Descend from the mount of revelation with Moses, and at its foot is an idolatrous camp dancing around a golden calf. Come down with entranced apostles from the Mount of Transfiguration; and the world whom there you encounter, are a grief to the Holy One by their unbelieving cavils. As John Newton pithily said: It is the man bringing his dividend from the bank door who has most cause to dread the pilferer's hand. Yes, temptation spared not Christ HIMSELF. Mother and brethren tempted our Lord, when the one would prescribe to Him the season and scene of putting forth His veiled godhead at the marriage-feast of Cana of Galilee; and when the other would have hurried the hour of His going up to the temple at Jerusalem. Disciples tempted Him when they cried, God forbid, to His predictions of His mediatorial sufferings, and quarrelled about the division of seats in His kingdom. The multitude tempted Him when they would be received as the disciples, not of His truth, but of His loaves, and were eager to force upon the Antagonist of all carnalism in religion a carnal crown, and a carnal throne, and a carnal policy. The lawyer and the Pharisees tempted Him with questions as to the tribute-money for Caesar, and as to the weightiest matters of the law, and as to the sanctity of the Sabbath and the temple; and the Sadducee continued the work on another side with cavils as to the resurrection and the law of divorce. Satan buffeted Him at the introduction of His public ministry; and, as we gather from the prophetic Psalms, at the close of Christ's earthly course renewed his assaults by the most ferocious onset, when *'the bulls of Bashan and the dogs'* of hell bellowed and howled against the meek and Atoning Lamb. Describing His own career, and bidding farewell to His little flock, He called them those who *'had continued with Him in His temptations;'* as if all the pathway which they had trodden at His side had led through a field strewn with snares and pitfalls at every step. And besides all these, the temptations which Scripture has expressly indicated, how constant and severe must have been the pressure of temptation, not explicitly described by the New Testament, against which His human nature must have been necessarily called to struggle in controlling the exhibition at times of the indwelling Godhead. "Had *we* been vested with Divine Sovereignty and Lordship over twelve legions of angels, could our human endurance have brooked, like His, the injustice and cowardice of Roman praetors and the insolence of Jewish kinglings, whose faces a glance of His Divine eye could have mouldered into ashes? Had *we* His omniscience, could we have locked it down and kept it under restraint from exposing in open day the hidden enormities of the hypocritical foes that confronted and pursued Him along all His meek and beneficent way? Had *we* the resources of the wide universe at our command, could we have brooked the crown of thorns, the sceptre of reed, the society of malefactors, and the cross, with all its agony and all its ignominy?"* O Thou spiritual Joseph of Thy Church! the archers did sorely grieve Thee, and from every quiver and with every bow did shoot at Thee, that Thou mightest in all points be tempted like thy brethren, and teach them how to meet and endure temptation. Every arrow that pierces us left its point and its venom in Thee; and falls at our feet quenched and harmless. Yet we fly to Thee in this time of our temptation, for sympathy and succour, and ask that every "fiery dart" may impel us closer beneath Thy sheltering wing, that we may know Thee more, and love Thee better, and learn of Thee to succour them that are tempted.

Turn we now to the petition itself, "Lead us not into temptation." Two remarks seem necessary to its clearer understanding. The first is, that entire exemption of the believer from temptation would be entire exemption from some of the greatest *blessings* of his life. This, therefore, cannot be included in the prayer. Had Abraham been exempted from the trial of offering up his son Isaac, there would have been wanting that illustrious exhibition of his faith, which in all future ages has been, and to all future ages will be, the instruction and comfort of the faithful. Had Hezekiah been

---

* Rev. William R. Williams, D.D., New York.

exempt from the temptation of display when he paraded his treasures and his wealth before the ambassadors of Babylon, what a loss had been that record of his spiritual history! Had Peter been exempt from the temptation to deny his Lord, it would seem as if the Bible had been incomplete without that wondrous page which records the Saviour's anticipatory intercession on behalf of His devil-tempted disciple: *"Satan hath desired to have thee, that he might sift thee as wheat; but I have prayed for thee; that thy faith fail not."* Had Paul been exempt from the *"thorn in the flesh, the messenger of Satan to buffet him,"* what a loss to the Church of Christ had been the marvellous declaration which that temptation of the apostle elicited from the Saviour, *"My grace is sufficient for thee, for my strength is made perfect in weakness."* And, most of all, had our blessed Lord been exempt from the temptation in the wilderness—His forty days and forty nights' conflict with Satan— what chapter of the Bible could have supplied that precious truth— *"We have not an High Priest which cannot be touched with the feeling of our infirmities; but was in all points tempted like as we are, yet without sin?"* And were we, beloved, entirely excluded from this same fiery ordeal of temptation, what a dead-letter, what a sealed book, would much of God's own Word be in our experience. We cannot, therefore, suppose that this petition is a prayer for exemption from what all the saints of God, and the Son of God Himself, have more or less passed through. This would be, as I have remarked, to exempt us from some of the deepest instruction and holiest blessings of our spiritual history.

Our second remark is that, we are not to infer from the petition that God can *solicit* men to evil. This seems to require no argument; and yet the Holy Spirit has met the idea: *"Let no man say when he is tempted, I am tempted of God; for God cannot be tempted with evil, neither tempteth he any man."* And yet the dark, the malignant thought, *has* found a lodgment in many a guilty breast—"If God had not placed me in this position, I had not fallen into this sin." No! is the solemn and indignant reply—but every man is tempted when he is drawn away of his own lust, and enticed. *"Now, when lust hath conceived, it bringeth forth sin; and sin, when it is finished, bringeth forth death."* Oh it is a solemn thing—an act of daring temerity, fearfully augmenting our guilt—to charge God with the responsibility of our sin! What is this but to make Him the Author of sin?

But the petition is a prayer that God would, by His providence, keep His child out of the way of temptation. "<u>My Father, consign me to no place in which I may be tempted to sin against Thee, to dishonour the Name of Jesus, to grieve the Holy Spirit, and to bring discredit upon my Christian profession</u>." We can suppose a young believer just entering upon public life, bending before the mercy-seat, and sending up this petition to Heaven, "My Father, I am about to detach myself from the hallowed restraints of the parental roof, from the guardianship of those who, from infancy and childhood, have watched over me with an eye of love that has never slumbered or wearied, be Thou the Guide of my youth, and suffer me to embark upon no career of life which will expose me to peculiar and overpowering temptations. I am deficient in experience, limited in wisdom, feeble in strength, pliable and irresolute, soon and easily led astray. My Father, lead me not into temptation. Let me not dwell in Potiphar's house, nor pitch my tent towards Sodom, nor flee into Zoar, nor sit with the servants in the palace of the high priest, nor listen to any price for the betrayal of my Lord. Suffer me not to be tempted above that I am able to bear. My Father, lead me not into temptation. The prayer of Thy servant Jabez would I make my own: 'Oh that thou wouldest bless me indeed, and enlarge my coast, and that Thine hand might be with me, *and that Thou wouldest keep me from evil, that it may not grieve me!'* Oh, what a solemn, wise, and holy prayer is this! Is it yours, my young reader? Is it the exponent of the thoughts, and feelings, and desires now rising within your soul? Then God, even your Father in heaven, will answer it, as He did the prayer of Jabez, and, by His providence, so dispose of you as that you shall not be exposed to the temptation you thus so holily and earnestly deprecate; or, if exposed, will sustain you under it.

It is a prayer, too, that God would either weaken the power, or remove entirely all existing temptation. The temptation is a formidable one. It assails you, perhaps, in the most vulnerable and least-defended part of your nature. It presents itself in its most fascinating and irresistible form. You are conscious of its power. It is just the thing which your imagination has often pictured, and which your heart has often craved. It holds you like a charmed bird within its serpent-like spell, and you feel but little inclination, still less power, to break it and escape. And yet, alive to your danger, trembling and lowly, you bend before the Mercy-Seat, and lift up your prayer—"My Father, I am a weak, helpless child, safe only as I am out of the way of temptation, or sheltered beneath Thy outspread wing. Thou knowest my present assault, and how impotent I am to resist it. Weaken its force, or give me grace to overcome it, or remove it entirely from my path. Lead me not into temptation."

It is a petition, too, that God would not withdraw His restraining check from the believer. It is said of Hezekiah, that *"God left him to his own heart."* How often, for the moment, has this been the sad history of some of the most eminent saints—as eminent for the greatness of their sin as for the greatness of their grace. Lot, dwelling in Zoar—David, walking upon the roof of his house—Solomon, in his years of mellowed experience and wisdom—Peter, sitting among the servants of the high priest's court—Cranmer signing an abjuration of his faith—were all left to know what was in their heart, and a host more of illustrious saints, whose histories present a solemn comment upon the apostolic exhortation, *"Let him that thinketh he standeth take heed lest he fall."* But each and all were the subjects of *restoring* grace, emerging from the fiery ordeal through which they passed, sadder but wiser and holier men. When, then, you pray, "Lead me not into temptation," you ask of God to withdraw not those divine restraints, to remove not those salutary checks by which, as in the case of David, you may be kept from falling into a snare. *"I kept thee,"* says God, *"from sinning against me."* So may God keep us!

And does not this petition involve a prayer to be preserved from the great tempter? Not only preservation from the evil that is in the world, but preservation from the EVIL ONE of the world, should be our daily prayer. With the galling consciousness of having lost his prey, with all the fiendish malignity of a foiled foe, with his ancient inveterate hate of the Christ of God, Satan traverses the earth bent upon the momentary discomfiture of the saint. It is not with the dead but the living soul he more especially has to do. The dead, well he knows, are floating silently and surely down with the stream that sweeps them on to the dread gulf whither they are borne. Marvel not, then, that you should be a selected object of his assault, distinguished, I had almost said, by the especial envy and malignity of his attack. These very fiery darts hurled so fiercely at your soul, these strong temptations by which your faith, integrity, and hope are assailed, but evidence the life of God within you. Suppose you for a moment that he would waste his ammunition upon a spiritually dead sinner? that he would suggest to a victim, still chained and pinioned by his resistless power, the imaginary crime of having committed the sin against the Holy Ghost? that his transgressions were too many and his guilt of too deep a hue to come within the scope and power of divine forgiveness? Would he, the Evil One, place his mouth to the ear of a soul dead in trespasses and in sins, and with the softest whisper breathe into it those blasphemous thoughts, those infidel doubts, those sinful suggestions, those promptings to presumption and despair, of which Bunyan and Cowper and Newton were once the victims, and of which a cloud of witnesses in God's Church still are? No; it is only the lambs he frightens, the sheep he worries, the children of God whose downfall he plots. Let us, then, in our daily prayer, "Lead us not into temptation," include yet this needed petition, "and keep me from the power of the tempter." You approach One who has been tempted by this self-same foe, than whom none in the Church of the tempted could enter so intelligently and feelingly into your case.

> "O Thou! the sinner's only Friend,
>   On Thee alone my hopes depend,
>   That Thou wilt guard me to the end,
>   My Saviour!

"I do not weep that joys are fled,
Or those so fondly loved are dead;
For greater griefs my tears are shed,
   My Saviour!

"The Accuser seems so constant near,
And almost drives me to despair,
That ne'er again Thy voice I'll hear,
   My Saviour!

"He taunts me with my sins, dear Lord,
And tempts me sore to doubt Thy word,
That not for me was shed Thy blood,
   My Saviour!

"Oh, come, Thou Holy, Heavenly Dove,
Fill my lone heart with Thy pure love,
And let me rise to joys above,
   My Saviour!

"Then shall I walk in peace with God,
Nor fear to tread the thorny road,
But kiss the hand that bears the rod,
   My Saviour."*

Some practical and solemn conclusions naturally flow from the important subject of the present chapter. While praying not to be led into temptation, we should be watchful against voluntarily running into it. There is such a thing as *tempting the tempter.* Although we can be in no position entirely exempt from his assaults, we yet may incautiously and needlessly expose ourselves to some powerful onslaught of the foe. Thus it was with Peter. Where should he have been when his Divine Master was under arrest? Side by side with Him at the bar of the high priest. *"But Peter stood at the door without."* He had already paved the path of his downfall by *"following Christ afar of."* And when he stood and warmed himself with the servants and officers of the court—the congregated enemies of his Lord—it is not surprising that before a very facile assault—a little maid charging him with the crime of being Christ's disciple—

---

* E. F. Clibborn, Brooklyn. N.Y.

he fell as a star from its orbit. What a beacon light for us! If we
needlessly go into the world, if we sinfully sit among the foes of the
Redeemer, and associate with the scoffers at religion—if we cross
the boundary of the Church and the world and fraternise with the
assailants of the truth, the contemners of revelation, the avowed
foes of the Bible—if we are found in association with the Antichrist
of Rationalism, or the Antichrist of Ritualism, or the Antichrist of
Formalism, thus presumptuously venturing within the enemies'
lines, what marvel if we find ourselves looked upon as deserters by
the loyal, or are arrested as prisoners of war by the enemy! While,
then, praying not to be led into temptation, we have need to be upon
our watch-tower, lest we be surprised by the besieger at the gate.
"Sin lieth at the door" ready to spring in the moment it is
incautiously unlocked or too widely opened.

Mark the *unselfishness* of the petition, *"Lead us not into
temptation."* If I am a true child of God, I am to embrace in my
intercession each member of the brotherhood exposed, like myself,
to temptation. I am to regard the holiness and happiness of my
brother, as second only to my own. Nay, seeing that by our
incorporation into the same body of Christ, we are members one
of another, his preservation from temptation, his upholding in
temptation, his deliverance out of temptation, should be a matter
of as deep concern to me as my own. Seeing that, perhaps, in
consequence of his talents, his popularity, his elevated and
responsible position, he is a more conspicuous target for the
Archer—standing, it may be, as upon a lofty pinnacle of the
temple—how fervent and earnest should be my prayerful
intercession in his behalf. To this end ought we to send up our
petition for missionaries and ministers, for pastors and evangelists,
for directors, secretaries, and treasurers to whose fidelity are
entrusted the momentous and precious interests of Christ's truth
and kingdom. Is there not a grave defect in our practical religion
touching this matter? Is there not too little consideration of the
responsibility of these servants of our Lord, too little sympathy
with their dangers and their trials, and too little intercessory
prayer for their divine upholding, begirt and assailed as they are

by many peculiar and strong temptations? If Moses needed, and Paul craved, and Christ leant upon the prayers and the sympathy of the saints, how much more these our brethren!

And in *whose Name* is this petition, as, indeed, the whole prayer, to be offered but the Name of Him who taught it—Himself the Tempted One. There is not a view of the subject of this chapter so instructive and soothing as the life of temptation to which our Lord Himself was exposed. I say the life of temptation, for from the moment that His feet touched the horizon of our planet, to the moment that He sprang from earth into heaven, His whole course was one continuous battle with temptation, in some of its many forms, and from some of its countless sources. His mother tempted Him on the occasion of His first miracle at Cana to a precipitate unveiling of His deity. His brethren tempted him on the one hand to anticipate His sufferings, while His disciples on the other hand tempted Him to forego them altogether. The excited populace would have forced upon Him a crown, while the subtle lawyer would have entrapped Him into an act of disloyalty to Caesar. The ritualistic Pharisee tempted Him touching the weightier matters of the law, while the infidel Sadducee assailed Him with cavils at the mystery of the resurrection. To this must be added the incessant and fierce buffetings of Satan, from the period that, baffled in the encounter, "he left Him *for a season*" in the wilderness, until his last onslaught in Gethsemane and his final defeat on the cross. Thou crowned and adorable Victor! all these temptations endured in Thy person were for me, that Thou mightest be *"touched with the feeling of my infirmities, and be in all points tempted like as I am, and yet without sin."* Tempted believer! to the sympathy and the succour, to the grace and protection of this tempted Saviour resort.

> "He knows what sore temptations mean,
> For He has felt the same."

You will not find in the whole Church of God, even among those who have most fiercely struggled with the arch-tempter, one who can so clearly understand you, so tenderly sympathise with you, and so effectually shield you as Jesus. He taught you the petition, *"Lead us not into temptation."* He counsels you to watch and pray lest you enter into temptation. He anticipates your temptation by intercession, that your faith should not fail. And when the temptation actually comes, He infolds you within the robe of His sympathy, and encircles you with the shield of His might, for *"in that He Himself hath suffered, being tempted, He is able to succour them that are tempted."*

If such the fiery ordeal, and such the difficult salvation of the righteous, who are "scarcely saved," how fearful, how fatal your condition who still are entangled within the coils of the serpent, led captive by him at his will! Unregenerated by God's Spirit, unconverted by His grace, your whole life is one scene, one series, one act of temptation. Error tempts you, and you fall. Ritualism tempts you, and you yield. The world tempts you, and you are seduced. Wealth tempts you, and you are ensnared. Sin tempts you, and you comply. But what will the end of these things be? Oh, too fearful to contemplate, too terrific to describe. An ETERNAL HELL! For ever with the tempter! Reaping the wages of sin, and receiving the due and the just reward of your unrighteous deeds. "Who among us shall dwell with the devouring fire? who among us shall dwell with ever lasting burnings?" All, *all* who have denied the truth, who have hated God, who have neglected salvation; who have rejected the Saviour, and who have lived and died the followers of the world, the objects of concupiscence, the servants of sin, and the vassals of Satan,—there, *these* are as fuel seasoning for the last and the unquenchable fire. But yet there is hope! You are within its region and its grasp. Repent, and be converted! The Ark is still open, the life-boat floats at your side, the City of Refuge is within your reach, a loving, beseeching Saviour invites you to the asylum of His wounds, to hide you there from the WRATH THAT IS TO COME.

CHAPTER XI.

THE DEVOTIONAL SPIRIT OF
THE LORD'S PRAYER.

"But deliver us from evil."—MATT. vi. 13.

THE spirit of the Lord's Prayer is essentially and pre-eminently _devout._ It is the soul and essence of true prayer. Were this more solemnly and profoundly felt, there would be less cold neglect of the prayer on the one hand, and less superstitious idolatry of it on the other. Its _graceless_ use by some individuals may evaporate, so to speak, its volatile power, as to leave nothing but the dry residuum of a lifeless form, as offensive to the spiritual nature of God, as it is deadening to the spiritual religion of the worshipper. Nevertheless, those who _pray_ this prayer, who find it an appropriate and living embodiment of the heart's utterances, are deeply conscious of its high, devotional, and spirit-elevating character; to such it is, as I have remarked, the soul and essence of prayer. It should be remembered that the words of this Prayer flowed from His lips in whom the Spirit dwelt without measure; that they were taught us by Him who, as the Divine Mediator between God and the soul, undertook both to present and answer our petitions; that they embody the great verities of our faith, and express the deepest need of the living soul,—who can question, then, the _devotional spirit_ of the Prayer, or, what should be the devout state of mind of him who breathes it?

But, perhaps, the truth most dear to the devout heart illustrated by these words is—*the preciousness and power of prayer*. The mention of this privilege can never be too frequent, nor can either its importance be too exaggerated, or its enforcement be too earnest. The prayer of faith is a power with God—we might almost say, the only power that man has with Heaven. It is this simple yet mighty weapon in the hands of the weakest saint, the obscurest believer, which—we write it reverently—overcometh God. Thus did the angel of the covenant address the holy wrestler—*"Thy name shall be called no more Jacob, but Israel: for as a prince hast thou power with God and with men, and host prevailed."* In thus yielding to the power of prayer, Jehovah yields to Himself. It is His own power in the soul that overcomes Him. Prayer is the breathing of the Spirit, it is the life of God in men, it is the divine nature in communion with the human. "Prayer, like Jonathan's car, returns not empty. Never was faithful prayer lost at sea. No merchant trades with such certainty as the *praying* saint. Some prayers, indeed, have a longer voyage than others; but then they return with the richer lading at last." Oh, the power with Jehovah of simple, childlike, believing prayer! That single word "Father!" lisped by a child, or uttered by a stammerer, exceeds the eloquence of the most persuasive oratory. It leaps into heaven, and draws back its richest treasures. *"My prayer returned into my own bosom."* Man in audience with God is the sublimest moral spectacle on earth. Angelic students bending from their thrones gaze with holy awe upon, and gather deep instruction from, the hallowed scene. The believing hand, touching thus the divine electric wire, in a moment each petition, want, and sorrow is laid upon the heart of God. No two friends dwelling at the most remote distance from each other are so instantaneously and closely brought into mental contact by this highway of thought, as the believing soul is into the divine presence by prayer. In the twinkling of an eye the believer is in possession of the ear and heart of God. So *simple* too is prayer. We but ask, and we receive. We but seek, and we find. We but knock, and it is opened to us. We present the name of Jesus, plead the blood of Jesus, enlist the advocacy of Jesus, and our suit is granted. Thus are we taught that it is not the *gift* of prayer that prevails with God, but the *grace* of prayer. Man may applaud the beauty of the one, but God yields to the power of the other. As Bunyan pithily puts it, "It is better to have a heart without words, than words without a heart." And since it is to the heart alone that God looks, let not your want of words, your stammering speech, your defective eloquence, discourage you from pouring out your soul before Him. Nor let your heart, because it is cold, and sinful, and sad, deter you from prayer. You *must* give yourself to prayer, be your temporal condition, your spiritual frame what it may. None can help you but God. None can intercede for you but His Son. None can sympathise with you but Jesus. Then arise and approach the Mercy-seat. The blood of atonement is upon it. The God of all grace and comfort, the God of peace and of hope, holds His court, and waits to accept and answer prayer. Hesitate, then, not to enter, since the blood of Jesus admits you within the holiest?

The burden of the prayer we are considering is deliverance from evil. In its widest application, but less articulated utterance, it is the voice of humanity, the cry of the race. Conscious of the incubus of the curse, and of the working of evil, yet with no intelligent idea or spiritual perception of the cause, men everywhere cry, "Who will show us any good?" in other words, who will deliver us from all evil? And what is the cause—the one, primal, unrepealed cause—of all the evil beneath which our common nature is bowed, and from which it sighs to be delivered? What but the sinfulness of man, the original and universal corruption, of our race. And yet, how is this truth diluted, controverted, denied—not merely by moral reformers, by earnest educationists, and by political economists, but even by men religious in creed, and teachers of religion by profession, who scoff at and reject as wild and visionary the doctrine of man's original and total depravity. But, the whole structure of the Bible, the entire scheme of Redemption, the cross of Calvary standing in its own solitary grandeur, the regenerating work of the Holy Ghost in the hearts of thousands, demonstrate the great fact that, man has sinned, and that in consequence, "human life is but one long conflict with suffering apprehended, or one prolonged contact with suffering endured." But let us regard this petition as the prayer of the penitent and devout Christian, "Deliver us from evil." From what evil, my reader?

You pray to be delivered *from the evil of—SIN*. This is the greatest evil. Emancipated from this, you are disenthralled from all evil, for it is the prolific parent of all. It is your heaviest burden, your bitterest grief. The liberty wherewith Christ makes His people free is the only liberty that can free from this galling chain. But from whence this cry?—from the knowledge of the plague of your own heart. And from whence this knowledge?—from the teaching of God's Holy Spirit. Knowing their existence, conscious of their inbeing within your heart, you long to be delivered from the evil passions, the carnal lusts, the worldly affections, the idolatrous attachments, the sordid cares that enchain and fetter you, and to float into a higher and holier region, as upon the snowy wing of an unfallen angel; or upon the yet loftier wing of the spirits of just men made perfect, who, in virtue of the blood of Christ and the robing of His righteousness, soar higher and approach nearer the throne of God than the loftiest angel in heaven. There is a *present* deliverance from the evil of sin in the experience of every believer. Christ has delivered us from the guilt, the tyranny, and the condemnation of sin. Oh, what a real, present, and glorious deliverance is this! *"Christ hath delivered us from the curse of the law?" "He hath put away sin by the sacrifice of Himself." "The blood of Jesus Christ CLEANSETH us from all sin."* These marvellous declarations clearly indicate a *present* deliverance from the evil of sin, so far as relates to its guilt and dominion. The believing conviction of this enters essentially into our growing sanctity of life, and our consequent peace and joy. And yet the spirit sighs for *more*. So long as sin exists within us, though its guilt be cleansed and its sceptre is broken, we cannot rest. So long as one foot of territory is occupied by the foe—so long as a single "Canaanite" yet dwells in the land, we cannot, we dare not, lay down our arms—we must fight to the hilt, and fight to the last. Thus we cry, "Deliver us from the evil of sin. Lord, subdue its power, cleanse its guilt, weaken its assault, and let not any iniquity have dominion over me." Is this the breathing of your heart, my reader? Rejoice, then, that the "Spirit of holiness" has His temple within you. Nought but a moral ill savour exhales from a nature totally unregenerate and corrupt: its taste may be refined, its conceptions poetical, its thoughts intellectual, nevertheless, these are but the flowers which wreath and garnish the gangrene corpse. The sweet fragrance of holiness, the heavenly perfume of righteousness, can only breathe from a holy and a heavenly nature implanted in the soul by God the Holy Spirit. Art thou mournfully conscious or indwelling sin? Do you loathe it, battle with it, and pant for the annihilation of the last link that binds you to corruption? Do you hunger and thirst for righteousness, sigh for purity, long for holiness? Oh, the sweet spices which filled the sacred temple with their cloud of fragrance, never emitted so rich perfume as that which breathes from your soul, wafted up to heaven in sighs and prayers for conformity to the divine holiness! What evidence more assuring of your being a partaker of the divine nature than this?

Again, you pray to be delivered *from the evil of the world.* With this the intercessory prayer of Jesus is in the closest sympathy. *"I pray not that Thou shouldest take them out of the world, but that Thou shouldest keep them from the evil."* Our Christianity is not to exile us from the world. The religion of Jesus is not that of the hermit. Asceticism is not an element of the gospel of Christ. Christ did not ask of the Father our translation to the kingdom of glory immediately upon our calling into the kingdom of grace. The rule of the gospel is this—*"Let every man abide in the same calling wherein he is called."* This apostolic rule may admit of some qualification, without in the least degree contravening its authority or questioning its wisdom. For example, the grace of God may convert an individual pursuing an occupation—as in the case of the eminent John Newton, when engaged in the traffic of slaves— essentially irreligious and immorally wrong. The immediate abandonment of such a calling admits of not a moment's hesitation. How many a man of God, too, is now an earnest and useful preacher of the gospel of peace, at whose side once dangled the sword of war! How many an able and faithful minister of Christ is now pleading in the pulpit powerfully for God, who once pleaded eloquently at the bar for man,—the advocate, perhaps, of a cause in direct and painfully excruciating antagonism to his judgment, conscience, and feelings! These men may, therefore, relinquish their position, not because either the military or legal profession— once adorned with the names of Colonel Gardiner and Judge Hale—is essentially or necessarily incompatible with a Christian profession and with Christian usefulness; but simply because they felt that divine grace had developed in them powers and had conferred upon them gifts pointing to a more genial as to a more extended sphere of service for God. But, a man is to abide in his rank, or wealth, or occupation, provided he can as well glorify God. His Christianity does not teach, nor his Christian profession require, that he should lay down his rank, remove from his social position, relinquish his wealth, and *level* himself to a grade other than that in which the providence of God placed and in which the grace of God found him. In all these things he is to *live to God.* If his rank gives him influence, if his affluence provides him with means, if his talents arm him with power, if his social or ecclesiastical position opens to him an extended and important sphere of usefulness, let him remain what and where he is, writing "HOLINESS TO THE LORD" upon all.

But for what did our Lord pray on behalf of His people? He prayed that, keeping His people for a while in the world, as the school of their grace and the scene of their conflict, God would preserve them *from its evil.* All is evil here! He who made, and sustains, and governs the world, has pronounced both it and its works to be evil—their nature evil. Sin has disorganised and tainted everything that was primevally good, perfect, and pure. Nature is less lovely, because it is accursed; the air is less vital, because it is tainted; the springs are less healthful, because they are poisoned; the flowers are less fragrant, because they are blighted. Every object in nature teaches that man is fallen, that sin reigns, and that, because of sin, the curse has smitten and blighted all. But it was *moral evil* our Lord more especially deprecated in the name of His people. He did not pray that they might be exempt from the afflictions and trials, from the reproaches and persecutions, or even the temptations of the world—but from the moral evil that is in it—the corruption that is in the world through lust, its religion and its friendship, its ungodly principles and its sinful practices. Knowing the danger they were in, and their inability to keep themselves, ere He quitted the world in the midst of whose fires He was about to leave them, He bears them in the arms of His intercession, and lays them upon the bosom of God. *"Keep them from the evil."* Oh, then, be it our daily prayer—its employments, its pleasures, its gaieties, its friendships—nothing that is holy, nothing that is in sympathy with the life of God in our souls, nothing that can aid our growth in holiness, and speed us on our heaven-bound way. Quite the contrary. The more we have to do with this evil world, the more we seek to please it, to conciliate it by concession, to win it by compromise, to serve it by sacrifice, the more deeply shall we be sadly conscious of its evil, and its taint, and its sting. Pass through the world as a stranger, having as little to do with it as possible. From its malice and its slanders you cannot expect to be exempt. It will attempt to do you all the injury in its power. It is evil,—and it will *speak* only evil. It is evil,—and it will *imagine* only evil. It is evil,—and it will *invent* only evil. It is evil,—and it will do only evil. The holier you live, the more distinguished a mark will you be for the venom of the world. Jesus was perfectly holy, yet never was one so traduced and maligned, so slandered, wounded, and ill-treated by the world as He? *"If any man will live godly in Christ Jesus, he shall suffer persecution."* But heed it not. Fear the world's smiles rather than its frowns; its caresses than its revilings; its eulogy than its slander; its commendation than its condemnation. Let us aim to live holily, to walk humbly with God, and to deal justly and kindly with men, and we may confidently leave our personal and dearest interests in the Lord's hands. Ever bear in mind one great end of Christ's death was, our death to the world. *"Who gave Himself for our sins, that He might deliver us from this present evil world."* How great the evil, since to rescue us from its power, it demanded an expedient so great, a sacrifice so costly and precious! Thus in the light of the cross we learn what an evil world this is, that nothing less than the sacrifice of God's beloved Son could weaken its power or emancipate us from its thraldom. When invited to go into the world, when tempted to imitate the world, when falsely accused by the world, turn and look at Jesus, and in the holy, tender, solemn light of that august scene—Jesus upon the cross—commune with your own heart, interrogate your conscience, and inquire if your appearance at the theatre, the opera, the oratorio,—if your presence in the ball-room, at the card-table, or the race-course,—if your perusal of works of unholy fiction or of religious error, are in harmony with the sacred and solemn profession you have made of discipleship of Him whose Church and religion, whose gospel and followers are not of this world, but who *"gave Himself for our sins, THAT HE MIGHT DELIVER US FROM THIS PRESENT EVIL world,"* that we should be a *"holy nation, a peculiar people, a royal priesthood."* Thus, our hearts sequestered in Gethsemane, and our souls in frequent communion at the cross, we shall be crucified to the world and the world to us. This is the victory that overcometh the world, even the faith that deals with the *unseen,* walks with the invisible God, loves an unseen Saviour, and takes frequent excursions into the eternal world, returning, as the believing spies from Canaan, laden with its precious fruit. It is this fellowship with unearthly and eternal realities that enables us to live *above* the world, and to live *down* the world, alike unseduced by its blandishments and its smiles, as indifferent to its judgment and its frowns.

You ask to be delivered *from evil men.* There are few wiser or more needed petitions than this. Evil men are agents in the hands of the Evil One of accomplishing his evil designs. Our Lord would not commit Himself to the hands of men, *"because He knew what was in man."* David prayed, *"Deliver me, O Lord, from the evil man."* And the Apostles ask the prayers of the Thessalonians that they might be *"delivered from unreasonable and wicked men."* On another occasion Paul warns the saints to *"beware of men."* And in the same words Jesus uttered precisely the same caution, *"Beware of men."* How divinely inspired the desire of the royal penitent, *"Let us fall into the hands of the Lord; for His mercies are great: and let me not fall into the hand of man!"* The knowledge of what the fallen creature is in its worst estate, and of what the renewed creature is in its best, will, in all circumstances prompt the wise and holy desire that we may rather be at God's disposal than at man's. We cannot, indeed, be indifferent to the divine instruction, the spiritual refreshment, the holy consolation, the soothing sympathy we have derived through a human channel; nevertheless, it is infinitely better to lie in the hands of a correcting God, than to repose upon the bosom of a caressing saint. The *frowns* of our heavenly Father have more of *love* in them than the *smiles* of His most loving child. Again, we repeat, We thank God for all that He has made the saints to us; and yet who will say that his expectations have ever been fully realised? Who has not, in some instances, found their love fickle, their promises capricious, their opinions often harsh, and their judgment always fallible? But this is, perhaps, more our fault than theirs. We have expected too much from the creature, more than any creature could possibly give, or we ourselves possessed. We reposed a while beneath our pleasant gourd, and in a night it perished. We nursed our bosom-flower, and in an hour it died. We leant upon the strong and beautiful staff, and in a moment it broke. We came to the crystal stream that had so oft refreshed us, and, lo! it was dried! Alas, we drained of all its sweets the sponge of creature good, and it became at last aridity itself! But it is more from the *evil* that is in the *ungodly* that we should pray to be kept. If our Lord shrank from committing Himself into their hands, what greater need have we to pray with David, *"Deliver me, O Lord ,from the evil man: preserve me from the violent man; which imagine mischiefs in their hearts. Keep me, O Lord, from the hands of the wicked!"* Oh to be kept— divinely kept—from the wickedness, the maliciousness, the deceitfulness, the depths of concealed evil dwelling in the ungodly! Pray that you may not fall into their power. *"Alexander the coppersmith did me much harm,"* was the lamentation of an inspired apostle. Thus yet more earnestly may we pray to be delivered from the evil of *false religionists,* of deceived and deceiving Christian professors. More are they to be dreaded, avoided, and prayed against than even the openly profane and ungodly. Religious hypocrisy is a far more potent element of evil, is a more baneful and noxious weed in society, than the avowed irreligion, the undisguised worldliness, the unblushing impiety of those who make no pretensions to godliness, and who, if they are unholy and profane, possess at least this merit, that they are *sincere.* Less to be dreaded and shunned are they than the honeyed religious deceiver, and the varnished Christ-professing hypocrite! What a wise and holy request of the apostles, *"Brethren, pray for us, . . . that we may be delivered from unreasonable and wicked men: for all men have not faith!"* Let this be our daily prayer for ourselves, for the saints, and especially for Christ's ministers.

We have already, in the preceding pages, referred to the temptations of the Evil One. We may be pardoned for again returning to the subject in connexion with the present petition, seeing how much *satanic power* has to do with the saints of God, and yet how imperfectly the subject is understood. Satan is the prince of this world, and the sworn and eternal foe of Christ and of the Church. Wounded, and writhing in the anguish of his mortal bruise, he is yet, until Christ shall come, the reigning sovereign of a fallen world, against whose plots we have need to be watchful, and from whose power we must pray to be delivered. He is everywhere, without being omnipresent—knows every being, without possessing omniscience—is potent, without omnipotence. As one of the reformers quaintly remarked, he is a diligent prelate, always at work in his diocese; a sovereign, ruling vigilantly his kingdom; a foe, whose malice never sleeps; a roaring lion, going about seeking whom he may devour. Let us, then, pray to be delivered from this Evil One, *"lest Satan should get an advantage of us, for we are not ignorant of his devices."* It is essential to our foiling of this our great adversary that we should not be so. It is the want of a more intelligent acquaintance with his mode of warfare that often leads to our momentary defeat. One of his favourite devices, we too often forget, is, to select as the object of his toils the most gracious and useful saints. He is too crafty a pirate, as Bishop Cowper remarks, to attack an empty vessel, but seeks to waylay those vessels chiefly which are richly laden. "When the coat of a saint is cleanest, the devil is most anxious to roll him in the mire." It is a remarkable fact in the history of Christ that the two most eventful periods of His life—His baptism, which commenced His public life, and His passion, which closed it—were those in which He encountered the fiercest assaults of the devil. From this circumstance we are instructed to seek a large measure of grace when called to occupy some more prominent part in the Christian Church; and to be, with the prophet, whole nights in our watch-tower when engaged in some eminent service for God. If he wounded Peter, and buffeted Paul, and shot at our Lord, let those to whom, by the sufferance of their brethren, some distinguished and important mission in the interests of God and of truth is confided, take heed lest through a like assault, but unfortified by a like grace, they fall. The secret of our safety in so elevated and perilous a position is, in *looking up,* keeping the eye single and fixed upon God, and the heart, tremulous and anxious, reposing upon Christ.

But even the obscure position, the shaded path of a child of God, is no exemption from the shafts of Satan. He will find out the Lord's "hidden one;" and shoot at them privily. One of his most common weapons is, the suggestion that their sins are so many and so great as to exceed the pardoning mercy of God in Christ Jesus. The quiver of Satan is full of arrows of this temper. But this base insinuation proves its origin. To represent a believer's sins before conversion, and his relapses in grace after conversion, as too great for the restoring grace of the covenant, the atoning blood of Jesus, the subduing power of the Spirit, is the most daring fiction ever perpetrated by the "father of lies." But are you assailed, my reader, by this fiery dart? Are you filled with dismay at the greatness, the number, and the aggravation of your sins? and are you tempted to limit the provision God has made for their present and full remission? Oh, weigh this vile suggestion of the enemy, endorsed, perhaps, by your own cruel unbelief; with that precious and magnificent declaration of God's Word, which, to the latest hour of time, will be as fresh and potent as when it first flowed from the pen of inspiration, "THE BLOOD OF JESUS CHRIST HIS SON CLEANSETH US FROM ALL SIN," and you will quench the dart and put to flight the foe.

There is no divine truth before which Satan more trembles, or the believing hold of which more effectually neutralises every doubt and stifles every fear arising from conscious guilt, as the ATONING BLOOD. The moment faith apprehends the blood, we are brought into peace with God, the tempest ceases, and there is a great calm. Guilt-bowed, sin-distressed soul! this blood fully meets your case. Take hold of it by faith, for it is yours. I emphatically and confidently repeat—*yours*. The Holy Spirit's gracious work in your soul is the divine warrant for believing that this blood was shed for *you*. All whose sins the Son bore, the Father draws, the Spirit convinces, and the blood cleanses. Receive, then, the comfort and peace a believing apprehension of Christ's blood will give you. Why hesitate? If this blood has satisfied divine justice, it may well satisfy your conscience. If Jehovah is well pleased with it, surely you may be. If God has accepted it, why should there be any hesitation or demur on your part? And remember how closely connected is this blood with a fruitful profession of Christ. If this blood is at the *root* of your religion, you will be *"like a tree planted by the rivers of water, that bringeth forth his fruit in his season."* Daily sprinkled upon your conscience, constantly moistening the root of your Christian profession, your obedience to God will be unreserved, your service for Christ will be perfect freedom, your endurance of the cross, whatever its shape, will be meek and cheerful, your carriage under your Father's discipline will be quiet and submissive, your converse with man will be holy, and your walk with God will be humble. If this blood be daily apprehended by faith, you will be as perfectly conscious of safety as the Israelite when the blood of the paschal lamb was upon his door, and as Rahab when the scarlet line floated from her window. Oh for more exalted views of atoning blood! Is it not a humbling reflection that, with all our religious profession, we know so little of that blood in which our dearest, holiest interests are involved—that blood that ought to make our daily life a bright sunbeam and a pleasant psalm? And should it not be a cause of deep shame to us as ministers of Christ that, with all our preaching, we have presented so imperfectly, have lifted up so obscurely, have unfolded with such timid, almost criminal, reserve the ATONEMENT of the Son of God? And yet, what is our ministry without it, but a sounding brass, or a tinkling cymbal?

Such is the holy and much-needed petition Jesus has taught us to present. Let it be our daily prayer. Oh, to what evil may *one day* expose us!—the evil of our own hearts—the evil in the hearts of others—the evil attaching to our professional and business life—the evil, in a word, that lies in ambush along every path we tread. Who can deliver us but He who is acquainted with all our ways, who knows our down-sitting and our uprising, and our thoughts and dangers afar off. "Lord! Thou hast been my deliverer times without number. When my feet had almost gone, when the clouds were lowering, and the sky was wintry, and the winds moaned like a funereal knell, when trouble was near, and evil threatened, then Thou hast delivered! And I will testify to Thy faithfulness, and sing of Thy love, and extol Thy power, that others may take heart and learn to put their trust in Thee the Great Deliverer!"

But our final and full deliverance speeds on. The day of our death will be the day of our life: the day that binds our limbs with his icy fetters will be our perfect *freedom* from all evil. Then we who have often cried, *"Who shall deliver me from this body of death?"* will, by death, be delivered from the last fetter of sin, and the last vestige of corruption, and the last shade of sorrow. Shrink not, then, O Christian, from dying! If, "in the midst of life we are in death," enclosed in Jesus, in the midst of death we are in life! Let the solemn summons come when or where it may, absent from the body, in a moment we shall be present with the Lord. And when the Lord comes in personal majesty and glory to raise and glorify His saints, then we who sleep in Jesus, *"waiting for the adoption, to wit, the redemption of the body,"* shall spring into perfect liberty, exclaiming, "O grave! where is thy victory?"

"Absent from flesh! O blissful thought!
　　What unknown joys this moment brings!
Freed from the mischief sin has brought,
　　From pains, and fears, and all their springs.

"Absent from flesh! illustrious day!
　　Surprising scene! triumphant stroke
That rends the prison of my clay;
　　And I can feel my fetters broke.

"Absent from flesh! then rise, my soul,
　　Where feet nor wings could never climb,
Beyond the heaven, where planets roll;
　　Measuring the cares and joys of time."

"THE LORD IS FAITHFUL, WHO SHALL STABLISH YOU, AND KEEP YOU FROM ALL EVIL. THE LORD SHALL DELIVER ME FROM EVERY EVIL WORK, AND WILL PRESERVE ME UNTO HIS HEAVENLY KINGDOM: TO WHOM BE GLORY FOR EVER AND EVER. Amen."

CHAPTER XII.

THE ADORING SPIRIT OF THE LORD'S PRAYER.

"For thine is the kingdom, and the power, and the glory,
for ever and ever. Amen."—MATT. vi. 13.

HAT a truly sublime and appropriate close of this marvellous prayer! It ends, as it began, with GOD. It begins with His parental, and ends with His regal relation. It opens by teaching us to love Him as a Father, it closes by teaching us to adore Him as a King. Leighton remarks that prayer moves as in a circle, always conducting us back to the point from whence we set out—"the GLORY of that God to whom we pray, and who is the God that heareth prayer." We may with equal fitness illustrate prayer by the magnificent bow which appeared in the apocalyptic vision of St John round about the throne. One end of this divine and resplendent arch—the bow of prayer—rests upon the earth, where in childlike love we cry, "Abba, Father" then, vaulting into the skies, it spans the throne of the Eternal, and, descending again to earth, meets once more at the spot where the suppliant breathings of the child are exchanged for the adoring homage of the subject—*"Thine is the kingdom, and the power, and the glory!"* Within this sacred arc is embraced the personal history of each child of God. Blended with its sacred tints is every petition of the believing soul, from the first sob of penitential grief—*"God be merciful to me a sinner"*—to the last

note of joyous triumph—*"Victory through our Lord Jesus Christ!"*
Believer in Jesus! live as under this divine crescent. Go where
you may, it encircles you. From the lowest depth of your soul's
need it springs into heaven, sweeps past the lowering clouds,
touches the golden altar where Christ our High Priest appears in
the presence of God for us, and returns freighted with blessing.
No prayer of faith, wafted to heaven in the name of Jesus, shall
fail of a response. Let your believing eye rest where God's
complaisant eye reposes, upon *the bow of prayer.* The rays of the
Sun of Righteousness reflected through the tears of a humble, sin-
burdened suppliant, will paint this symbol upon the cloudiest sky,
filling the heart with hope that when God beholds it, He will
answer, forgive, and bless.

It may be proper in the outset to remark, lest we should be
thought indifferent to the fact, that a few Greek copies do not
contain this last clause of the Lord's Prayer, and that some critics
have noticed its omission by St Luke. We see no just reason,
however, to question its integrity. Found as it is in the Syriac copy,
the most ancient version of the New Testament—standing as it
does in close harmony with the very first petition of the prayer—
and maintaining a strict analogy with the whole tenor of God's
Word, we feel no difficulty in accepting it as genuine. Then, with
regard to its omission by the evangelist Luke, as Dr Williams very
forcibly puts it, our Lord was often wont, in recording the same
thing, to avoid an exact repetition of Himself, and frequently, in
reproducing a parable or a saying, presented it in a somewhat
disjointed or fragmentary form. And, in addition to this, when He
communicated the prayer to St Matthew, His audience was chiefly
composed of an indiscriminate mass of hearers, many of whom
were totally ignorant of divine truth, while others were armed with
prejudice and hostility both to Him and His mission. On the other
hand, when reiterating the same formulary in the hearing of St
Luke, He was more immediately surrounded by His *disciples,* who
would, by their subsequent teaching on the mediatorial work of
Jesus, be able to supply any apparent vacuity or break in the
prayer. On these grounds, then, and on others which it may not

be necessary to mention, we give an unhesitating and unqualified assent to the accuracy of the passage, accepting it as a genuine clause of the prayer. Let us now briefly examine its teaching.

"Thine is the kingdom." To whom could these words be properly addressed, but to Jehovah? All other kings are but mimics of Him, and all other kingdoms but shadows of His. They exist and reign by God's will, and as instruments for the accomplishment of His purpose—the setting up of His kingdom of righteousness and truth in the earth. And when earthly monarchs vaunt themselves of their power, and give not God the glory, He knows how to abase them. What a solemn illustration of this is presented in the history of Nebuchadnezzar, king of Babylon! Listen to the narrative:—*"At the end of twelve months he walked in the palace of the kingdom of Babylon. The king spake, and said, Is not this great Babylon, that I have built for the house of the kingdom by the might of my power, and for the honour of my majesty? While the word was in the king's mouth, there fell a voice from heaven, saying, O king Nebuchadnezzar, to thee it is spoken: The kingdom is departed from thee."* (Dan. iv. 29-31.) But oh, unutterably blessed the truth God taught him by the overthrow and humiliation to which he was subjected—just the truth this page seeks to unfold. *"At the end of the days I Nebuchadnezzar lifted up mine eyes unto heaven, and mine understanding returned unto me, and I blessed the Most High, and I praised and honoured Him that liveth for ever, whose dominion is an everlasting dominion, and His kingdom is from generation to generation."* Seven years of mental aberration, of deposition from his kingdom, and of herding with the beasts of the field, were needed to abase the pride of this haughty and vainglorious monarch, and to teach him that the sovereignties of the earth belonged to God, who putteth down one and raiseth up another; and to discipline and fit him for re-establishment in his kingdom more firmly and amid more glory and power than ever. Is God dealing in a similar way, my reader, with you? Lifted up by your position, and boastful of your gifts and achievements, you have not given God the glory. He has, perhaps, drawn a momentary cloud-shade over your mental powers, or has incapacitated you

physically for the trust confided to your hands, and, like the deposed monarch, He has removed you from place and power into a school to you the most humiliating and painful. But, be still, and know that He is God. A bright light shines in this dark cloud. God's thoughts towards you are thoughts of peace, and not of evil. Humble yourself under His mighty hand, and He will exalt you in due time. Yield not to despondency, still less to distrust and despair. God will not forsake you, nor Christ cease to pray that your mind be preserved, and that your tried and sifted faith may not fail. All these emptyings and ploughings are but to prepare you for larger blessings and greater fruitfulness. Thus was it with the king of Babylon, and thus will it be with you. *"At the same time my reason returned unto me; and for the glory of my kingdom, mine honour and brightness returned unto me; and my counsellors and my lords sought unto me; and I was established in my kingdom, and excellent majesty was added unto me. Now I Nebuchadnezzar praise and extol and honour the King of heaven, all whose works are truth, and his ways judgment: and those that walk in pride he is able to abase."* Cheer up, then, thou afflicted saint of God! happier days and brighter scenes await you.

"Thine is the kingdom" of *Nature. "The earth is the Lord's, and the fulness thereof."* This beautiful world, beautiful in its very ruin, belongs to God, and is the theatre upon which Christ is carrying forward His designs with regard to the salvation and gathering together of His redeemed Church. The Christian mind delights to recognise this magnificent and important world as belonging to God. He created it, ordained its laws, appointed its seasons, sustains its existence, and supplies its sources of fertility. He rides upon the wind, flashes the lightning, rolls the thunder, controls the storm, and makes the clouds His chariot. "Thine, O Lord, is this beautiful kingdom and its government; seed-time and harvest, summer and winter, the drought and the deluge, the heat and the cold come at Thy command, and are Thy servants doing Thy will, and accomplishing Thy purpose. All nature illustrates Thy power, exhibits Thy goodness, evidences Thy wisdom, reflects Thy beauty, is fragrant with Thy breath, and shows forth Thy glory. Oh, give me grace to see Thee in every flower that blooms, in every star that shines; in the golden beams of the sun, in the silver rays of the moon, and in the gentle gale that wafts to us the fragrance of a thousand sweets. Through all the varieties, beauties, and grandeur of this Thy creation, may my heart ascend in adoring love to Thee, the wonderful, the bountiful Creator of all."

"Thine is the kingdom" of *Providence*. This world is not a kingdom without a throne, a throne without a sovereign, or a sovereign without a sceptre. By no blind accident are the affairs of this planet governed. God is in the history of the world,—its past, its present, and its yet unshapen future. The statesman and the politician may not recognise this fact; but it is so. And did the Christian mind more distinctly see it, how much more instructive would history be; what new light would the passing events of each day throw upon the inspired page. The Bible and history are closely linked. The Bible foretells history, predicts its events, and shapes its outline. History accumulates its evidence around the Bible, affirms its divinity, fulfils its predictions, and authenticates its truth. No Christian should study either past or present history but with God's Word in his hands. This is the chart, this the map, this the lamp by which he shall be able, spiritually and intelligently, to study God's providential government of the world in connexion with the increase and final destiny of His Church. God preserves and governs the world for the Church. For her sake the world exists and is ruled, the "pearl of great price" is quarried in the world; and having purchased the field for the sake of the pearl, Christ is carrying on its government, working His own mine, with a view to the gathering together unto Himself a people *"afore prepared unto glory."* Thine, then, O Lord, is this kingdom of providence. Thy hand is moving and controlling all events and circumstances, national and social, public and private; giving birth, and shape, and tint to those phenomena in the history of nations, and to those affairs in the history of individuals, which to human ken are often enshrouded in mystery so awful and profound. Let this view of God's providential reign hush all murmurings at our lot, making us content with such things as we have, assured that

He will never leave us nor forsake us. Let it bow our soul in meek submission to His sovereign will, in view of those painful and inexplicable events which sometimes cast the darkest shade upon our sunniest landscape, and dash from our lips their sweetest cup of joy. Let it incite our gratitude for the blessings loaned us so long, though now removed, and for the blessings which still remain to soothe, and gladden, and cheer us onward. Let it strengthen our faith, in the Divine assurance that our daily bread shall be given us, our path shielded amid engirdling evil, and our soul, guided by His counsel and kept by His power, eventually and safely conducted home to glory. Yes, Lord, the kingdom of providence is Thine, and I would see Thy hand, and trace Thy wisdom, and taste Thy goodness in all the shaping and tinting of my whole history. I would deal alone with Thee in all the lights and shadows of my daily life. Those lights and shadows are of Thy pencilling, O Lord. If joy thrills my heart, it is of Thy inspiration; if sorrow breaks it, it is of Thy sending. Teach me that I have, in all things, to do only with Thee. Preserve me from seeking to please man at the expense of Thy glory. Pleasing the creature never entered, Jesus, into Thy life. And yet Thy whole life was labour, and suffering, and love for man—seeking not Thine own glory, and pleasing not Thyself but the Father who sent Thee.

"Thine is the kingdom" of *grace.* This is Christ's highest kingdom in the world; and for the setting up and completion of this kingdom, both the kingdom of nature and of providence exist and are subservient. This kingdom, as we have shown in a preceding part of our work, is both internal and external. There is the kingdom of grace in the soul of the believer—"the kingdom of God is *within you*"—and there is the kingdom of grace in the world, *"the Church of God, which is the pillar and ground of the truth."* This kingdom is the Lord's. It is His kingdom of *grace:* He is the *King* of grace; His reign is the *reign* of grace; His people are the *subjects* of grace; His throne is the *throne* of grace; and the benedictions which He so lavishly and so freely bestows, are the *blessings* of grace. Thus, *"by grace are ye saved."* Precious truth! the chimes of heaven fall not more sweetly on the ear of the glorified saints than do these words—"Saved by grace,"—on the ear of a sinner taught by the Spirit his vileness, poverty, and helplessness. Not by human works, not by self-doing, not by creature merit, but by God's sovereign, unpurchased, unmerited, most free grace, is the sinner saved. This is the truth that empties, humbles, and abases the soul in the dust. We enter, for the most part, this kingdom of grace through the *"north* gate," with a deep conviction of sin, and dreadful apprehension of wrath. But we are led out by the *"south* gate" into the pleasant garden of God's free, forgiving love, to pluck the fruit of peace, and joy, and hope, and to recline upon the sunny slopes and by the side of the quiet waters of that River that makes glad the Church of God. Let nothing, then, dare deter or interdict your coming to Christ. Come with an empty hand, come with a dry vessel, come with filthy rags; come just as you are—for your salvation is the *gift of free grace.* There is not a round in the ladder that lifts you from earth to heaven,—from the first, down in your dark dungeon, to the highest, bathed in the sunshine of glory,—but is of *grace.* And as you mount higher and higher, your song will grow sweeter and louder—"Grace, GRACE, GRACE !" Be not afraid of *little* grace. It is not the quantity, but the *reality* of grace, that sanctifies and saves. As Rutherford says, "Christ soweth His living seed, and He will not lose it. If He have the guiding of my stock and state, it shall not miscarry. Our split works, losses, deadness, coldness, wretchedness, are the ground where our good Husbandman laboureth." Nor let us be dismayed if indwelling grace is sometimes, through indwelling sin, much dimmed, impaired, and obscured. As the fruits we receive from a southern clime partake not of the freshness, and the sweetness, and the fragrance of their original perfection, so our graces during this present life must necessarily be defective, and will remain so until we reach that heaven of glory from whence they came, and where they grow; and then we shall eat of the tree of life bending over on either side of the river—our grace full, our graces perfect, and the anthem of grace floating in the sweetest music from the soul.

If then, this kingdom of grace is the Lord's, recognise His right to rule and reign singly and supremely in your soul. He may dislodge the idols that divide, and overthrow the rivals that usurp His possession and sovereignty. The kingdom is Christ's—let Christ reign alone. Rebel not against the mode He adopts to preserve you entirely for Himself. Murmur not at His dealings. Repine not under His dispensations. You are Christ's—Christ is your King—your soul is His empire—your heart is His throne— you are His subject: *"From all your filthiness, and from all your idols, will I cleanse you."* This sometimes is done by the spirit of fire and of burning. Nevertheless, if He did not love you, were not His gracious kingdom within you, He would not take the pains He does to cast out from it everything that would taint its purity, shade its lustre, and impede its growth. "Lord, the kingdom within my soul is Thine own; Thine let my heart be, Thine my obedience, Thine my service; Thine my life—all, *all* Thine own."

But this adoring acknowledgment of God's regal glory includes a yet future and yet wider kingdom. "Thine is the kingdom" of *glory.* This kingdom yet to be set up, while it will include the kingdom of nature, of providence, and of grace, will yet be a kingdom distinct from, and independent of, them all. It will be the exponent, the consummation, the crown of each. It will include all the beauties of the first; it will explain all the mysteries of the second; and it will perfect all the glory of the third. This is the kingdom of which the prophet Daniel thus writes: *"And in the days of these kings,* [the ten kings or kingdoms into which the Roman empire is divided, symbolised by the ten tribes,] *shall the God of heaven set up a kingdom, which shall never be destroyed; and the kingdom shall not be left to other people,* [as the Babylonian monarchy was to the Medes, and as the Persian monarchy was to the Greeks, and the Grecian monarchy was to the Romans, it shall he left to the saints of the Most High;] *but it shall break in pieces and consume all these kingdoms, and it shall stand for ever."* Again: *"And the kingdom and dominion, and the greatness of the kingdom under the whole heaven, shall be given to the people of the saints of the Most High, whose kingdom is an everlasting kingdom, and all dominions shall serve and obey him,"* (Dan. ii. 44; vii. 27.) To this end we pray, *"Thy kingdom come."* And what will be the sign and the period of its coming? The apostle Paul tells us in 2 Tim. iv. 1, *"I charge thee therefore before God, and the Lord Jesus, who shall judge the quick and the dead at His appearing and His kingdom."* Thus it is clear that the SECOND ADVENT OF CHRIST, and the COMING of HIS KINGDOM OF GLORY, harmonise as to character, and synchronise as to time, and will, in fact, be identical and contemporaneous. The Lord Jesus Christ will come as the KING OF GLORY, and then will transpire those august events already referred to in a preceding chapter of this work,—the overthrow of Antichrist, the resurrection of the saints, the ingathering of the Jews, and the final and most blessed of all, the creation of a new heaven and a new earth—the fit and eternal dwelling place of the now gathered and glorified Church. Then will ascend from a multitude which no man can number, and with a shout such as never reverberated through the universe before, the glorious TE DEUM of the Church— "THINE IS THE KINGDOM!"

"And the power." God is a Great King, and His power is commensurate with His greatness. It is infinite, *"Twice have I heard this, that power belongeth unto God."* All the power of the creature is derived. He receives it from God, He holds it by permission of God, and employs it under the restraint of God. Power is an essential perfection of His being. The power of an earthly sovereign is lodged in his subjects. He may have power to command, but he has no power to enforce obedience. His power to exact compliance with his will rests with the affections and the loyalty of his people. But God possesses a power essentially His own. He has power not only to make laws, but to exact compliance; not only to issue commands, but to enforce obedience. *"Thy people shall be willing"*—willing to love, willing to do, willing to come,— *"in the day of Thy power."* His is the power of *conversion.* His power breaks the chain, dislodges the enmity, and erects the kingdom of grace within the soul. His power guards and carries forward the work thus begun. His power keeps the feet of His saints, preserves them from falling, and brings them unto His heavenly kingdom. *"Thine is the power."* All this power, saint of God, is on your side. All power on earth and in heaven belongs to our Immanuel. There is no foe from whom He cannot defend you; not a difficulty from which He cannot deliver you; not a want from which He cannot relieve you; not a sin which He cannot subdue in you; not a good which be cannot bestow upon you. Thine is the power! All power is essentially and mediatorially Christ's. Is any thing, then, too hard for Him? *"Thou hast given Him* POWER *over all flesh, that He should give eternal life to as many as Thou hast given Him."* This power, O believer, is pledged to bring you safely to glory. No one shall wrest you from its grasp, none shall ever pluck you from Christ's hands. *"All* POWER *on earth and in heaven is mine."* Come, O thou timid dove, and shelter beneath the wing of Jesus' power. Come, thou weak believer, and learn that He perfects His strength in weakness. Come, thou child of God who hast no might, and learn that to such He increaseth strength. Thine, O Lord, is the power! In Thee have I righteousness and strength. Thine is the power to dethrone every form of Antichrist, to remove out of the way every impediment to the progress of Thy kingdom and the triumph of Thy truth. Thine the power to overthrow error, to foil Satan, to crush Thy foes, to defend Thy gospel, and to conduct Thy Church to a final and triumphant victory over all her enemies.

This is one of the greatest and most sanctifying lessons in our education for heaven—the *power of God.* And this lesson is only learnt in connexion with yet another—our own utter *weakness.* We become experimentally acquainted with both at one and the same time, in one and the same school of temptation, trial, suffering, and service. Oh, it is a grand thing to know when we are weak! All secret declensions of soul, all outward backslidings from God, may be traced to an ignorance of this. If he thought his bow weak, would the archer trust to it? If he thought his boat fragile, would the mariner go to sea in it? If he thought his foundation insecure, would the architect build upon it? Trace David's, and Solomon's, and Peter's fall to its cause, and you will find that it was overrated strength, unconscious weakness—a forsaking of God's power, and a reliance upon their own fancied strength. But is our weakness a disadvantage to us? By no means; it is all in our favour. Should it discourage us? Not at all; it should cheer and animate. When the vessel is exhausted, it will receive more of the ocean. When we have come to the extreme of our weakness, we approximate the nearest to Almighty power. God's power is never exercised but in alliance with man's weakness. Thus the apostle could reason, paradoxical though it may be—*"When I am weak, then am I strong."* God sometimes withholds assisting strength, that He may exhibit supporting strength in upholding weak grace. He allows the believer, as it were, to go to the end of his tether ere He comes to his rescue. His strength shall be perfected in weakness. Thus, oh how strong the almightiness of weakness! When I am weak, then am I strong— strong as David when he slew the lion, destroyed the bear, laid the vaunting Goliath in the dust. "It may be thou art a poor, trembling soul, thy faith weak, and thy assaults from Satan strong; thy corruption great, and thy strength little; so that, in thy opinion, they rather gain ground on thy grace, than gain ground to it; yea, now and then thou art apt to dread that thou shalt one day be cast as a wreck on the devil's shore. And yet to this day thy grace lives. Thou art still longing, panting, desiring, wishing, and groaning after God. Is it not worth while to turn and see this strange sight? A broken ship, with masts and hull rent and torn through a tempestuous sea—not tempestuous only, but thick-set with armadas of sins, afflictions, doubts, and temptations, brought safely into God's harbour. To see a poor rush candle in the face of the boisterous winds, and liable to the frequent dashes of quenching waves, yet not blown out! In a word, to see a weak stripling in grace held up in God's arms until all enemies are under His feet. This is the Lord's doing, and it is marvellous in our eyes."* Thus does our conscious weakness serve us well. It weans us from self; it endears to us Christ; it allies us with God; and it schools us experimentally in the knowledge of that blessed doxology, *"Thine is the power!"* Thine the power, Lord, by reason of which Thy poor, bruised reed is not broken, Thy faint, smoking flax is not quenched, Thy feeble, trembling child is enabled to hold on His way through many sharp trials of faith, and many sore thrusts of Satan, and many sad sins and failures, and many

---

* Gurnall.

infirmities, tribulations, and sufferings—*"faint, yet pursuing,"* with the certainty of arriving in glory at last. Wilt Thou plead against me with Thy great power? No: but Thou wilt put strength in me.*
Thy power is all on my side. It is pledged to perfect itself in my weakness; in waiting upon Thee, to renew my strength; out of weakness, to make me strong; to keep me through faith unto salvation, and to present me faultless before the presence of Thy glory with exceeding joy. Thine, Lord, is all this power.

Thine is *the glory."* Power and glory are essential properties of God. They are attributes of earthly sovereigns; but are divine and infinite perfections of Jehovah. He is "clothed with *majesty and strength."* The great end of all that God does, is His own glory. All things, and all events, terminate in Himself. *"He hath made all things for Himself,"*—that is, all things were created by Him and for *Him,* and all shall contribute to His supreme and endless praise. It has ever been the confederate effort of Satan and fallen man to thwart God in this His purpose; in other words, to rob Him of His glory. By impeaching His veracity and questioning His goodness, Satan accomplished the fall of our first parents in a yet unsinned Eden. The moment the Divine glory was invaded and shrouded, the creature was seduced from his love and allegiance to God. Since that fatal moment—fatal, indeed, to the eternal happiness of myriads of the race—it has been man's wont, having learnt his lesson from an apostate sire, to rob God of the glory justly due to His great and holy Name from every part of His vast empire, The Pantheist robs Him of His glory in nature by deifying it. The Atheist robs Him of the glory of His being by a denial of His providence. The Rationalist robs Him of the glory of His revelation by the homage of reason. The Ritualist robs Him of the glory of His worship by superstitious ceremonial. The Sacramentalist robs Him of the glory of His sacrifice by mystic grace. Such is the fearful sacrilege of which fallen man is guilty, than which we can conceive of no crime of greater magnitude, or one which more strongly evidences man's deep depravity and total

---

* Job xxiii. 6.

alienation from God. Are we giving God the glory that belongs to Him? Are we ascribing to Him the supreme, undivided glory of our talents, and usefulness, of our wealth, rank, and influence? Do we ascribe the glory of our salvation to His electing love, His sovereign mercy, His free grace? And is our daily life as a sweet cloud of incense, ever ascending to the honour and praise of Him who, in the exercise of His unmerited mercy and discriminating love, has called us out of darkness into His marvellous light? Can we honestly say, "For me to live is Christ?" Oh, give Christ the glory, all the glory, the unrestrained, the most free, willing ascription of glory, for all that He is, and for all that He has done. Thine, O Son of God, is the glory! To Thy everlasting love, to Thy precious blood, to Thy justifying righteousness, to the power that holds me up moment by moment, and to Thy grace, pledged to preserve me unto Thy heavenly kingdom, I ascribe the praise, honour, and glory most justly Thine. Oh, give God in Christ the glory! Take not one note from the anthem of His praise, separate not one beam from the sun of His renown—lay all at His feet, exclaiming, "THOU ART WORTHY!"

But richer far will be the glory that will accrue to God from the salvation of His Church. The "many crowns" which deck the Saviour's brow when He appears the second time, will pale before the splendour of the diadem of Redemption. Redemption will be the crown of crowns. This was the master-work of Deity. In it He embarked His whole resources, His entire being. To take out of this fallen world a people for His praise; to redeem them by the sacrifice of His Son; to regenerate them by His Spirit, and to preserve them by His grace, and finally to bring them to glory, the wonder and admiration of principalities and powers, will constitute a source of glory, honour, and prise, lasting as His throne, endless as His being. The redeemed and glorified Church will be the grand Censer of the restored world, from which will ascend a cloud of adoration, praise, and glory, encircling the throne, and filling the universe through eternity. Oh, we have but the faintest conception of the glory that will arise to the Triune Jehovah from the scenes of Bethlehem, and Gethsemane, and Calvary, and the new tomb in the garden, in which was never man laid, save the God-man, the Resurrection and the Life. Thus will redemption, from first to last, fill heaven with glory, and replenish eternity with song. His, too, will then be the glory of that UNIVERSAL KINGDOM of whose dominion, and government, and honour there shall be no end. All empires shall then resign their sovereignties into His hands, and all kings shall lay down their crowns at His feet, and all sceptres shall be broken before Him, and God in Christ shall be all in all.

> "Our song employs all nations, and all cry,
> 'Worthy the Lamb! for He was slain for us;'
> The dwellers in the vales and on the rock;
> Shout to each other, and the mountain tops
> From distant mountains catch the flying joy;
> Till, nation after nation, taught the strain,
> Earth rolls the rapturous hosannas round."

Could this work more gracefully close than with the words which, in his spiritual exposition of the Lord's Prayer, Archbishop Leighton, of seraphic piety, has woven into impressive petitions which every devout reader of these pages will make his own:— "Good reason we should desire earnestly the sanctifying of Thy name, and the coming of Thy kingdom, and obedience to Thy will, seeing these are so peculiarly due to thee, namely, *kingdom, and power, and glory,* And seeing Thou art so great and rich a King, may we not crave with confidence at Thy hands all needful good things to be bestowed on us, and that all evil may be averted from us; that we may find Thee gracious to us, both in giving and forgiving; and as in forgiving us the guiltiness of sin, so, in freeing us from the power of sin, and preserving us from the power of our spiritual enemies that would draw us into sin? We are under Thy royal protection, we are Thy subjects, yea, Thy children. Thou art our King and Father, so that Thy honour is engaged for our defence. Whatsoever sum our debts amount to, they are not too great for such a King to forgive; they cannot rise above Thy royal goodness; and whatsoever be our enemies, all their force is not above Thy sceptre: though they be strong, too strong for us, yet Thou art much too strong for them; for *power* is Thine. And this we know, that all the good Thou dost us will bring back glory to Thy name; and it is that we most desire, and that which is Thy due; the *glory is Thine.*" "For ever." Significant and solemn words! "FOR EVER!" We are born to live for ever. Immortality is our birthright. Sin has forfeited, but grace restores its endless bliss. Blissful word to you who through grace believe in Jesus, who are looking for the coming of the Lord, and anticipate the privileges and the glories of the New Jerusalem. *"So shall you EVER be with the Lord."* But what, O sinner, will be *your* "for ever?" What, O thou unconverted man and woman, will be your endless future? Alas, dying as you live, yours will be a "for ever" of woe! The fires of Tophet—*for ever!* The gnawings of the worm—*for ever!* The shrieks of agony and the groans of despair—*for ever!* 'The society of demons and the companionship of the condemned—*for ever!* The wrath of God— *for ever and ever!* No cessation of being, no eternal sleep, no annihilation of existence will be the condition of those who die in their sins, die unconverted, die out of Christ. What a boon would annihilation be to such! But it is not theirs. You recoil from death now—you will seek it *then!* You fence, you foil, you keep at bay the "last enemy" now. Then you will beseech and implore him to come—but he comes not. "And in those days shall men seek death and shall not find it; and shall desire to die, and death shall flee from them." Heaven and hell are alike eternal. "These shall go away into everlasting punishment; but the righteous into life eternal." Reader! what will your "for ever" be?—a for ever of hell, or a for ever of heaven! There yet is hope! *"Christ died for the ungodly." "It is a faithful saying, and worthy* of *acceptation, that Christ Jesus came into the world to save sinners."* He receives all, and casts out none who come to Him. His *mission* authorises Him to save sinners. His *work* engages Him to save sinners. His *love* constrains Him to save sinners. His *power* enables Him to save sinners. His *grace* pledges Him to save freely and to the uttermost all who come unto God by Him. Lose not a moment in coming to Christ. Come away from your sins, from your self-righteousness, from your ritualism, from your formalism, from your infidelity, from your worldliness, from your carnality, from your empty profession, your soul-deception, your false hope, from the foundation of sand upon which your solemn and interminable *future* of happiness is built. From all this erelong you will "go away"—but whither? Escape from it now, and hie you to Jesus the City of Refuge, the Hiding Place from the wind, the Covert from the storm, the Saviour from the wrath that is to come, lest your lamentation through eternity should be—*"I am not saved!—* NOT SAVED—NOT SAVED!"

"Whither can a sinner flee?
Who, oh who, will rescue me?
Dreading my deserved sentence,
Weeping tears of deep repentance!
Yawning grave! I fear to die,
Such burdens on my conscience lie,

"Hark! I hear the Saviour say,
'I can take thy guilt away;
I have bled that men might live,
Full salvation I can give!
I will help thee, soul distrest,
Come unto Me—I'll give thee rest!'

"Almighty Lord! I know Thy voice,
In Thee believing I rejoice,
My Prophet, Priest, and King!
Now I can sing of joys on high;
O grave, where is thy victory?
O death, where is thy sting?"

"AMEN." Thus closes a Prayer which for its simplicity and sublimity, its SPIRIT and comprehensiveness, is unequalled. The word "Amen" is of Hebrew origin. It was of frequent use among the Jews, and was afterwards imported into the Christian Church and engrafted on its more simple and spiritual worship. It signifies that which is itself true, which the mind accepts in faith, and for which the heart expresses its ardent desire, assured hope, and firm belief that all shall be fulfilled. To all the revealed doctrines, to all the holy precepts, to all the precious promises, to all the animating hopes, to all the devout petitions, and to the doxology of praise, thanksgiving, and glory contained in this sublime Prayer, taught us by the Lord, let us breathe our believing, solemn, and lasting—"AMEN!" "BLESSING, AND HONOUR, AND GLORY, AND POWER BE UNTO HIM THAT SITTETH UPON THE THRONE, AND UNTO THE LAMB FOR EVER AND EVER. AND THE FOUR BEASTS (living creatures) SAID, AMEN. AND THE FOUR AND TWENTY ELDERS FELL DOWN AND WORSHIPPED HIM THAT LIVETH FOR EVER AND EVER."

"Abba Father! high in glory
Is Thine everlasting seat,
Where ten thousand hallelujahs
Wake their music at thy feet;
Let Thy pilgrim sons and daughters
Catch the echo—and repeat.

"While we sojourn still in Mesech
On the barren mountain side,
Let 'Thy kingdom come' within us,
Sit Thou at the helm and guide,
Till by every tongue and people
JESUS shall be glorified.

"Shouldst Thou lay Thy hand upon us,
Bringing clouds across our sun,
And our 'pleasant' household 'pictures'
Fade in darkness—one by one;
Take the dove into Thy bosom
There to weep—'Thy will be done.'

"Day by day vouchsafe to scatter
Manna on the desert floor,
'Give us food convenient for us,'
From Thy never-failing store,
And with Christ, the bread of heaven,
Satisfy us evermore.

"Lord, 'with Thee there is forgiveness,'
Mercy nestles 'neath Thy wing,
Drop the precious 'balm of Gilead'
On our burning bosom-sting,
Send us forth to show our brother
Mercy is a pleasant thing.

"From the byways of temptation
Keep us, Saviour, lest we stray,
Oh, preserve us from the evil
Ever lurking round our way.
Let our path grow clearer, brighter,
Till it end in 'perfect day.'

"Hallelujah! power and glory
And dominion be to Thee!
Even here we strike the key-note
Of our song of Jubilee,
'UNTO HIM WHO LOVED AND WASH'D US'
BE THE PRAISE ETERNALLY!"*

---

* Ellen H. Willis.